INTERIM SITE

The Pied Pipers of Rock 'n' Roll

Radio Deejays of the 50s and 60s

LONGSTREET PRESS

Published by
LONGSTREET PRESS, INC.
2150 Newmarket Parkway
Suite 102
Marietta, Georgia 30067

Text copyright © 1989 by Wes Smith

Photo page 173 courtesy of Cleveland, Ohio, Plain Dealer. *All other photos courtesy of the* Chicago Tribune *photo library.*

Printed in the United States of America

1st printing, 1989

Library of Congress Catalog Number 89-084531

ISBN 0-929264-69-X

This book was printed by Berryville Graphics, Berryville, Virginia through Anderson, Barton & Dalby, Inc. The text type was set in Century Expanded by Typo-Repro Service, Inc., Atlanta, Georgia. Design by Paulette Livers Lambert. Jacket photo of author by George Thompson.

To my wife Sarah, our rock-'n'-roll son Andrew and the baby we await as this book goes to press. I love you.

And in memory of Rick Baker.

ONE

Booze, Broads, and Bribes

iami Beach, Florida, was looking fine in May of '59. Shaped like a drain basin in the downspout of the continent, Florida always did seem like a good place to trickle down to when you were on the lam from the law, the ex-wife, or just the creeping heebie-jeebies of life. And if you happened to be a Moon Dog, Hound Dog, Daddy-O, Dr. Jive, Poppa Stoppa, or Woo-Woo rock-'n'-roll radio disc jockey at that painful point in time, it would not have been unusual for all of the above to apply.

Elvis, after all, was in the hunka-hunka U.S. Army. Drafted, many suspected, because some Senator's daughter had made too much of a fuss over his lower lip and pokin' hip. Little Richard had packed up his piano and his purse and headed for Bible college, and Jerry Lee Lewis had just married his great-gawdamighty thirteen-year-old second cousin and caused an international incident when he introduced the blushing baby bride at the start of a tour in England.

In February, Buddy Holly, Ritchie Valens, and J. P. "Jape" Richardson, a former Texas deejay also known as the Big Bopper, went down in a plane crash in the upper reaches of Iowa. Waylon Jennings, another Texas deejay-turned-rocker, later to turn outlaw country star, had given up his seat on the plane to Richardson. Waylon went back to KLLL in Lubbock after the plane went down and, like rock-'n'-rollers and deejays across the country, was still having crash nightmares.

Rock-'n'-roll pioneer Sam Phillips, a former radio announcer turned independent record producer at Sun in Memphis, where Elvis and Jerry Lee got their starts, was telling everyone in the spring of 1959 that rock-'n'-roll was turning soft. At the same time he was out messing around with a string of "no-rock" radio stations staffed with all-female deejay crews, called "femcees." Femcees?

Sam was right, though. Rock-'n'-roll was getting softer than Fabian's baby cheeks. You couldn't find a hard-butt Chuck Berry or Fats Domino on the radio dial because of all the Pepsodent pop stuff that was being hyped on Dick Clark's *American Bandstand* show. All those beardless wonders like Frankie Avalon, Paul Anka, Bobby Darin, and Alvin and the rest of the Chipmunks were turning rock-'n'-roll into white teenage nursery rhymes.

And then there was the Curse of the Top-Forty Format. Some of the biggest radio station chains around the country were ordering their deejays to play only the top forty hit records on their shows. The same forty songs over and over and over again. It was like working in a damn factory. Rock-'n'-roll radio brought to you by Henry "Model T" Ford and the Assembly Line. It was taking most of the fun and nearly all of the muscle out of the job. Deejays at the top-forty factories didn't get to play what they wanted anymore, and thus they couldn't help out the small record company promo men who took them out to dinner, bought them a round of golf, paid for a new backyard pool, or left a bag of maryjane in the glove

Pepsodent pop turned rock-'n'-roll into white teenage nursery rhymes, according to some (from left, an unidentified announcer, Dick Clark, Fabian, Neil Sedaka, Freddie Cannon, Bobby Rydell)

compartment of the car. This top-forty stuff was really cramping the lifestyle to which deejays had become accustomed.

More threatening were the virtue vigilantes out there who saw rock-'n'-roll and the deejays who played it as threats to every image America held dear in the 1950s. Inflation, the communist threat within, the Korean War, the atomic bomb, and racial discrimination were heavy issues in those days, but the country preferred to view itself as it was reflected in its shiny new mirror: television. The wild gyrations of teens dancing to that heavy beat, particularly white teens under the manipulations of black musicians, ran up hard against the well-controlled lily-white world portrayed on *Father Knows Best, Ozzie and Harriet,* and *Leave It to Beaver.* When pop singer Nat King Cole, an extremely mellow and unthreatening figure, dared to add a darker tint to the television screen with his own show, no advertisers — the ultimate investors in the American image — would sponsor it.

These were borderline paranoid times when every man with a shovel was digging a bomb shelter out back and his children were awakened by nightmares about fending the neighbors away with shotguns when the Big One dropped. Rock-'n'-roll and the disc jockeys who championed its wildest and blackest forms were perceived as the same sort of insidious threat as "The Bomb," commie-loving actors and authors, Red spies in government, civil rights leaders, mobsters, and inflationary dollars. In 1959, author Vance Packard, who had already yanked the bedcovers off the sneak-thief advertising industry in his investigative report *Hidden Persuaders*, told a Senate subcommittee on communications that rock-'n'-roll deejays were poisoning the defenseless minds of young people with "cheap" music.

There was also talk around Congress that once an investigation into reports of cheating on television quiz shows was completed, the legislators might go after radio disc jockeys who were suspected of taking so-called "payola" from record company promotion men. There was nothing new about it — forms of the practice dated back to vaudeville and the dawning days of radio — nor was it illegal, as long as it showed up on the income tax report. At least, that's what everyone thought. A favorite line of the times that played upon the paranoia of the deejays was attributed to a record promo man who told a big deejay, "Play my record, or I'll send you money." Powerful hit-making deejay Bill Randle of Cleveland reported that someone had attempted to blackmail him by threatening to report him as a payola-taker. Another jock, Phil Lind of Chicago, asked for police protection, claiming he had received telephone threats after airing an interview with a small record producer who claimed it cost him $22,000 to get a record played in Chicago.

The deejays were not just paranoid, there really was someone out there trying to get them. The big rock-'n'-roll jocks, the guys who played the hottest stuff on big-buck stations, had always taken a certain amount of flak from church leaders and do-gooders, but suddenly there was more than just loose talk going around. The Catholic Youth Organization's newspaper, *Contacts*, told its readers in the summer of 1958 to "smash the records you possess which present a pagan culture and a pagan concept of life. . . . Resist the pressures created by the money-mad record hucksters and the popularity-hungry disc jockeys." In Boston, the Reverend John P. Carroll told the Teachers Institute of the Archdiocese that "Rock-and-roll inflames and excites youth like the jungle tom-toms readying warriors for battle." The reference to "jungle tom-toms" was not out of the same book as "Love thy neighbor as thyself." Everybody knew who beat the jungle tom-toms. The jungle bunnies. The coons. The niggers. Racism wore a thin veil in these times, occasionally even a clerical collar.

The musical threat came primarily from blacks, and that made bigots nervous. In the early days a few of the deejays

White parents feared rock-'n'-roll partly because of its black roots

heard catcalls of "nigger lover." Some were treated to cross-burnings outside their radio stations or homes. It was only rock-'n'-roll, but some people didn't like it.

In the happy days that came immediately after World War II, the country had been too war-weary and generally too busy to start tearing at its own hair again over internal racial problems. Some genuine strides toward lessening racial discrimination had been made. In the early and mid-fifties, the rock-'n'-roll deejays could shrug off taunts and threats from the paranoid fringes. Their music was not only popular; it also sold advertising. But by the late fifties, things turned uglier and uglier. In 1958, just four years after *Billboard* magazine had proclaimed the rock-'n'-roll deejay the "undisputed king of local radio programming," several of the top personality jocks in the country were shot down, shoved out, and shackled. The highest profile radio disc jockey in the country was Alan Freed, the deejay who popularized the term "rock-'n'-roll" as a way to sell black music to white teenagers. Freed was fired from his job at WINS in New York in 1958 after trouble at one of his concerts in Boston. The trouble—muggings and fights—may have had little or nothing to do with Freed himself, but his position had long been tenuous as far as the maintainers of law and order were concerned. The rock-'n'-roll deejay already had an FBI file that rivaled those of suspected Red spies.

Freed came to New York in 1954 after rocking the bobby sox off Cleveland teens with his rowdy *Moon Dog Rock-'n'-Roll Party,* and his concert promotions drew huge audiences of both white and black teenagers. He led radio station WINS in Manhattan from the basement to the top of the ratings in a few months, but his outspoken advocacy of black music—he refused to play the more acceptable white "covers" of black tunes by Pat Boone and others—aroused the suspicions of the Klan, the Catholic Church, and J. Edgar Hoover, to name a few, who didn't like the beat or the way teens were dancing to it. Freed became a primary focus for their fears that the country was going to hell in a transistor radio.

Repeated news photos of white teenage girls dancing with black teenage boys or white teens in adulatory poses around black performers at Freed's concerts increased the racial tension. Because Freed was popularizing music and musicians traditionally relegated to the far reaches of the radio dial and the back bins of record stores, the entrenched powers of the music business were also alarmed. The American Society of Composers, Authors, and Publishers was the established music-licensing organization that oversaw royalty payments to those who created music, at least to those whites who created music. ASCAP had traditionally excluded black, Hispanic, and hillbilly performers. Its protectionist officials complained loudly that the only way this awful rock-'n'-roll could be getting so much attention was if someone was being paid royally to play it.

Freed managed to dance outside the clutches of these opposing forces for about four-and-a-half years of celebrityhood in New York, but when violence erupted outside the concert in Boston, a town with a low boiling point when it came to mixing the races, he came home to a termination notice at WINS in May of 1958. He had gotten too hot. Within a few days of his downfall, a poll by Teen-Age Survey, Inc., named a new radio king in Manhattan: William B. Williams, who ran number one with college students, number one with housewives, and tied with another deejay, Peter Tripp, in popularity with teenage girls. William B. was more at home with the Andersons, the Nelsons, and the Cleavers. Alan Freed was the enemy within.

Another unruly deejay on the East Coast was brought down a peg about the same time that Freed's microphone was unplugged at WINS. George "Hound Dog" Lorenz, a disc jockey in Buffalo and Niagara Falls, had been the first deejay to "rock the pot" by adjusting the volume controls to the beat, the first jock to talk over an instrumental so the music never stopped, and the deejay who first delivered rock-'n'-roll to Canada. Lorenz did not draw Freed's national publicity, but he was just as big a pioneer and had just as many battles with management over his right to play whatever he wanted. He finally quit in 1958 because management wouldn't let him pick his own records anymore. He moved on to a little station in Connecticut and obscurity.

Bob Horn in Philadelphia, another rock-'n'-roll radio pioneer was run right out of the business, out of town, and into bankruptcy. He had gone from doing the Esslinger Beer show, *Bob Horn's Bandstand*, as top jock at WFIL radio to hosting his own television music-and-interview show in 1952. Called *Bandstand*, it was one of dozens of local-broadcast teen dance shows around the country, but it would become the big daddy of them all. Horn played rhythm-and-blues and rock-'n'-roll records for the teens and let them rate the songs. The show was a big hit in Philadelphia, but then Bob got himself arrested for drunk driving. He was fired, and the ambitious, clean-cut kid who was his backup, radio deejay Dick Clark, took over. Later, Horn was charged with the statutory rape of a fourteen-year-old girl — he was found not guilty — and along came a second drunk driving charge. In April of 1958, he was working for a little station in McLendon, Texas, when the IRS tracked him down and nailed him for failing to report $392,000 in income. That was enough to take him out of radio forever.

These were the deejays with big-money jobs, guys who brought in hundreds of thousands of dollars in advertising and promotional fees to their stations. If these pioneers were getting run out of their jobs, it didn't look good for the rest of the record jocks around the country. In what may have been an omen for the rock-'n'-roll deejays of the day, the only decent hit on the airwaves as they were packing up their swimming suits and party jackets for the second annual deejay convention in Miami Beach was a Drifters' tune, "There Goes My Baby."

Another bad omen: the convention was being sponsored by the Storz radio station chain. Todd Storz was the inventor of top-forty radio. He came up with this brilliant strategy while listening to the same songs being played over and over again by the discerning clientele in some beer joint. He figured, correctly as it turned out, that radio listeners would tune in to the station that played their favorite hits more than any other station. In dictating to deejays what they could play, the top-forty format cut off the power source for the personality disc jockeys and, many believe, led to the dilution of the power of rock-'n'-roll.

The chill climate around rock-'n'-roll radio in the early months of 1959 made Miami Beach all the more appealing. This convention had to be better than the last one, the first deejay get-together, in Kansas City, Missouri. Only about nine hundred deejays and assorted radio and record types had come out in the cold, sleet, and snow, and from the deejays' viewpoint there was entirely too much talk about "community public service" and the responsibilities of "air personalities." What was this, General Electric?

Mitch Miller, an old-school executive at Columbia Records, added to the icy atmosphere of the Kansas City convention when he vented his disgust over rock-'n'-roll and the deejays who played it for their teenage listeners. He said, "You carefully built yourselves into the monarchs of radio and then you went and abdicated your programming to the corner record shop, to the eight- to fourteen-year-olds, to the pre-shave crowd that makes up 12 percent of the country's population and 0 percent of its buying power. You used to play music because you liked it; it was part of the personality of your show. Now you play it for Sam, Joy, Flo, Sal, Mickey, and Joyce loves Shorty and will he please meet you after three at the sweetshop, second booth from the rear."

There were others singing along with cranky Mitch at the Kansas City convention, but the deejays felt they didn't have to listen. At that point in 1958, they felt nothing could knock them out of the broadcast box. The record jocks had been riding increasingly higher and higher on rock-'n'-roll and the adulation of baby-boom teenagers since about 1951, when "Moon Dog" Freed, a long-time classical music lover, figured out that teens were tuning out Mommy and Daddy's Bing Crosby and Dinah Shore and turning on to rhythm-and-blues by Riley "B. B." King and other performers black and bodacious.

Freed hosted *The Moon Dog Rock-'n'-Roll Show* on WJW, a powerful fifty-thousand-watt station that rode the nighttime ozone skip across Ohio and into Pennsylvania. It was like nothing else on radio. Other stations had played the music before, particularly WLAC radio in Nashville, where the legendary trio of Gene Nobles, John R. Richbourg, and Hoss Allen began playing black music for hundreds of thousands of listeners as early as 1946. Deejays Zenas Sears in Atlanta and Hunter Hancock in Los Angeles and dozens of deejays, black and white, male and female, at small stations around the country had also played the music for their listeners long before Freed caught on. But they hadn't played it quite the way the Moon Dog played it.

A microphone to Freed was like blood to a werewolf. It set him to baying at the moon and flailing with his fists on the Cleveland municipal telephone directory. Teenagers loved it. And he was playing his music for more and more white kids. For them, this back-alley boogie and blues seemed to come up from dark and secret places where no adults dared journey. The word spread, and before long radio stations around the country were following Freed, who had, in fact, followed the less flamboyant Nashville deejays in playing that kind of dirty-fingernail-and-sweaty-collar music, heavy-petting music.

Freed had a younger audience than most radio announcers, as they were known in the early going. It was also bigger in number. The unleashed lust of hundreds of thousands of soldiers home from the war had predictable results. And in the postwar prosperity of the fifties, when wages increased 130 percent from the thirties (though inflation cut the increase in buying power to 35 percent), those baby-boom teenage children were allowed to stay in school rather than contributing their labors to the family business or the war effort after high school. They had more time and more disposable income on their hands than any previous generation had. Their parents, who had endured hardship during the war years, were prone to spoil them once there was extra cash in the house. There was a sense that everyone deserved a break. It was time to shake off the war-time blues and to shake and rattle and roll a bit.

One survey in the late 1950s claimed that teenage girls spent $432 million on party food alone in one year, one hell of a lot of Saltines. These middle-class, early baby-boom kids liked to party, they liked to dance, and they listened to the radio. They had their own language, their own clothes, and, for the first time, their own music.

In the previous decade, teens had listened to the same music as their parents: big bands and crooners. Sinatra sent them swooning at first, but as he moved to more adult songs, the young went scrounging around in record stores for something different. In their group grope for an identity that was not hand-me-down from their parents, the fifties' teens were more open to exploring different cultures. They sampled record store bins that had previously gone unheeded and discovered the music of another group whose identity was emerging: Negroes.

This music had followed southern blacks and whites as they migrated north for industrial jobs that opened up during and after World War I. Migration from the South slowed somewhat during the Depression, then picked up and held strong again. In 1944, *Time* magazine estimated that since the beginning of the decade fifty thousand black people had left Mississippi for the North, where they settled in neighborhoods occupied by earlier arrivals: poor southern whites and immigrant Europeans. World War II had thrown together white and black draftees; poor hillbillies and poor blacks discovered they had poverty and music in common, particularly the working man's Sunday salvation, gospel music. Even when you're broke and lost in the city, you can still sing and you can still dance, they discovered.

The resulting cultural blend produced a more urban, livelier musical sound. The new music crept out of the shanty-towns of New Orleans, Memphis, Macon, and Muscle Shoals to melting-pot points in Chicago, Detroit, Cleveland, Atlanta, Philadelphia, Houston, Austin, and Los Angeles. Rhythm-and-blues acts on the South's "Chitlin Circuit" followed their audience farther and farther north, and their success lured many of their

Baby-boom teens started dancing anywhere and everywhere

gospel-singing brethren out of the churches and onto the road as performers, too. Soul came from shanty taverns and from the churches where gospel "shout" singers like Sister Rosetta Tharpe rocked religiously. The first to perform "This Train," among other gospel classics, with her soulful singing and bluesy guitar style, she has been claimed as an inspiration by performers as diverse as Jerry Lee Lewis, Sleepy LaBeef, Carl Perkins, and Johnny Cash. Acts such as Antoine "Fats" Domino, John Lee Hooker, and Little Richard Penniman found audiences in places where blacks had rarely ventured before, and their gospel-blues inspired music began to cross-pollinate with the popular "rockabilly" sounds of white performers such as Hank Snow, Tennessee Ernie Ford, and Lefty Frizell.

Although whites had long been supporters of black musicians such as Count Basie and Duke Ellington and had flocked to the Cotton Club in Harlem (where blacks performed for a whites-only crowd), rhythm-and-blues was a different beast. It was "ghetto" music, loud and lewd. The performers sang black and sang proud. They weren't black men singing essentially white music. Before *Billboard* magazine and the record companies called their music rhythm-and-blues, it was called "sepia" music, a euphemism for the earlier labels "race" music and "Negro" music. "Race music" had been used by record companies to segregate black music, but at the end of World War II, in which Americans defeated a "racist" government, that foreboding term was dropped in favor of "rhythm-and-blues." The new name may have sounded better, but it was still a code phrase to separate music for whites from music for blacks. Ironically, the term "rock-'n'-roll," which Freed popularized to lessen racial implications, had other negative connotations.

Since the 1920s, when blues singers like Trixie Smith, who sang "My Man Rocks Me (with a Steady Roll)" wailed about their urgent need "to rock" or "to roll" and "to rock and roll," it had been clear they weren't talking about gymnastics. It was churning, burning lust they were shouting about. The dirty deed. The love connection. So much for cleaning up the act. Often the lyrics of Negro or race music played by the deejays were loaded with sexual innuendo; sometimes it was more in-your-face bawdiness than mere innuendo (as in the case of many Chuck Berry hits, including "My Ding-A-Ling"). Such explicitness was all the better to feed raging teen hormones. Rock historian Charlie Gillette noted in his *The Sound of the City* that the original version of "Shake, Rattle, and Roll," as written by Charles Calhoun and performed by Joe Turner in 1954, had a chorus in which the singer rolled his eyes and gritted his teeth as he went "way down underneath." When white singer Bill mystery all the more appealing. The emotions of both sides were aroused by the same obvious fact: this music was coming from the black side of town.

The origins and content of the music played by Freed and other deejays scared the hell out of those unenlightened parents who saw the black man as a physical, sexual, moral threat. Although record companies offered rhythm-and-blues and rock-'n'-roll for the sole purpose of making money, the format also had the side effect of exposing middle- and upper-class whites to the black culture, often for the first time. Occasionally, the two worlds even touched. When teen masses filled the streets of Brooklyn on Washington's Birthday in 1957 with screaming and dancing outside an Alan Freed concert, befuddled adults went searching for explanations to this behavior. Fainting at a Frank Sinatra concert was one thing, but over a black man? This must be hysteria. Luckily, there was a convention of shrinks in town at the same time. On February 23, 1957, the ever-earnest *New York Times* called the doctors and put the kids on the couch.

Psychologists queried by the *Times* said that the rock-'n'-roll craze seemed to have its roots in "rhythmic behavior patterns" dating back to the Middle Ages. One shrink described the Paramount frenzy as "spontaneous lunacy." The *Times* quoted a 1949 study that found that as many as 20 percent of children rock and roll as a natural instinct in their beds, but another study found the new music and dance craze similar to the disease St. Vitus's Dance, also known as chorea major, a mass, dance-like, whirling dervish frenzy that struck Germany and then the rest of Europe in the fourteenth century. Victims would start dancing and then be unable to stop. The Italians attributed the behavior to the bite of the tarantula, and called it "Tarantism."

The same study said this sort of contagious dance fever occurred in the Children's Crusades and in the fable of the Pied Piper of Hamelin, according to Dr. Joost Meerlo, whose study was cited by the *New York Times* reporter. The fever occurred in the Children's Crusades and in the fable of the Pied Piper of Hamelin, according to Dr. Joost Meerlo, whose study was cited by the *New York Times* reporter. The juke box rhythms inspired the young people to throw themselves into "prehistoric rhythmic trances," the good doctor said, until their dancing progressed beyond accepted forms of cultural expression.

This sort of dance demonstrated the "violent mayhem" long repressed elsewhere in the world, the psychiatrist asserted. Dr. Meerlo also saw political implications in that such rhythmical sounds and motions could be used to induce mass ecstasy by leaders such as Hitler and Mussolini to sway the masses in political rallies. "The call repeats itself into the infinite and liberates the mind of all reasonable inhibitions." Under such conditions, he said, "As in drug addiction, a thousand years of civilization fall away in a moment."

In a note of consolation, the expert assured the *Times* and its readers that this contagion of dance furies would pass, as had the Charleston and other momentary lapses of public inhibition. He concluded, however, that rock-'n'-roll was a sign of "depersonalization of the individual, of ecstatic veneration, of mental decline and passivity."

He warned that if these of rhythmic narcosis were not stopped, civilization could fall in the "midst of pandemic funeral dances."

While adults furrowed their brows and postulated scientific-wise, their hysterical hepcats and kittens were yanking the rug up from the rumpus room floor and doing the mad St. Vitus to the unholy shrieks of Little Richard, a he-she-devil if ever there was one. The whites called it black music because they didn't know any better. The churchgoing blacks were just as fearful. In the meantime, Bud and Wally and Kitten and Candy were buying records in black record stores and going to black nightclubs to listen and dance among blacks. Things happened.

When parents and church leaders and politicians reacted in horror to photographs of their young white darlings hip-to-hip in black clubs with the wild dancing darkies, the little darlings turned on their own. It was teenage rebellion. Things were getting worrisome, and to make matters even more alarming for parents who preferred their children mix only with their own, the U.S. Supreme Court ruled, in May of 1954, that public schools had to be racially integrated.

Rock-'n'-roll in the fifties caused some of the first cracks and fissures of what later became known as the "Generation Gap." Teenagers, whose numbers had swelled in the postwar baby boom, grew possessive and protective of their music when it was attacked by "the establishment" that saw it, with some accuracy, as a corrupting influence. Then again, in the fifties, nearly everything was suspected of being corrupt or corrupting. The flourishing comic book industry was investigated for subversive motives, and in 1956 the Internal Revenue Service conducted an investigation of (waiter, the check!) tipping malfeasance. Hans Paul, headwaiter at the Waldorf-Astoria Hotel in Manhattan, was indicted on charges of not reporting tips averaging $500,000 to one million dollars a year. He was fined seventy-five hundred dollars and locked up, without room service, for four months.

In this suspicious time of McCarthyism, black lists, and red-baiting, people were quick to choose up sides and point fingers. It was not a big leap, then, for at least a portion of those white teenagers who defended black rhythm-and-blues to later side with the blacks when they decided not to ride in the back of the bus, eat outside the restaurant's back door, or go to the niggertown school.

Dick Clark was criticized for favoring white performers on his television show, but he brought out not only the cuddly Chubby Checker (actually former chicken-plucker Ernest Evans, whose nickname was assigned by Clark's wife, Bobbie), but also more potentially malevolent black artists, including Chuck Berry and James Brown. The dancing teenagers on *American Bandstand* were integrated one year into the show's network run, very slowly and carefully because network affiliate stations were staunchly conservative. Clark sweated out the first show that featured a black couple dancing among the whites, but, to his surprise, he says, "There was not one call or letter protesting it." Today, he views rock-'n'-roll as "the most subtle form of integration that ever existed."

The racists didn't miss the subtlety. Fresh KKK material showed up every morning, stuck on the front windows and parking meters outside Stan's Record Shop in Shreveport, Louisiana, when owner Stan Lewis began advertising rhythm-and-blues and gospel record packages on radio station KWKH in 1949. The executive secretary of the Alabama White Citizens Council got right to the point in the early fifties: "The obscenity and vulgarity of the rock-'n'-roll music is obviously a means by which the white man and his children can be driven to the level with the nigger. It is obviously Negro music." That distinguished fraternal organization made headlines again in April of 1956 when its director was one of six men arrested after they stormed into a concert in Birmingham, all lathered up about "bop and Negro music" and knocked a black performer off his piano stool and dragged him down from the stage. They were proceeding to kick the hell out of him when police intervened. The offending singer was once again the mellow and completely unthreatening crooner Nat King Cole.

When critics in the churches and news media disdained rock-'n'-roll as "jungle music," the allusion was hardly subtle. It was just short of calling it "monkey music." More artful critics put it down as "primitive" music, but the racist implications were the same. In 1956, *Time* quoted a *Denver Post* editorial writer on the subject of rock-'n'-roll: "This hooby-dooby, de-addy boom, scoobledy gobbledy dump—is trash."

That same year, in December, a black woman was arrested and fined ten dollars for refusing to give up her seat on a bus to a white person. A few months later, the U.S. Supreme Court ruled that segregation on public buses was unconstitutional. In February, the University of Alabama was ordered to allow Autherine J. Lucy, its first black student, to attend classes. Three days into integration there, she was attacked by people throwing rocks and eggs and later suspended for her

Dick Clark introduced many blacks, including Chubby Checker, to his TV audience

own safety. The courts ordered the university to let her back in, but officials refused. A year later, Governor Orval E. Faubus of Arkansas ordered the National Guard to prevent nine black students from entering Central High School, an all-white school in Little Rock. Segregationists tried to privatize public schools to keep blacks out. The guardsmen were removed by court order, but the resulting violence moved President Eisenhower to federalize the Guard and send in U.S. paratroopers to restore order.

In August of 1957, Senator Strom Thurmond of South Carolina set a filibuster record by speaking for twenty-four hours and twenty-seven minutes. His topic? The danger of civil rights legislation. As Kent State University professors Robert D. West and Edmund P. Kaminski point out in their paper "Radio, Rock-'n'-Roll, and the Civil Rights Movement," the movement was building, and the sides for and against had pretty much been predetermined according to those who favored the black-based sounds of rhythm-and-blues and rock-'n'-roll and those who saw such music as an insidious threat to law and order and the country-club dinner dance.

This music was often played on late-night radio, when teens were grappling on lovers' lanes or home in bed wishing they were grappling on lovers' lanes. This huge population of teenagers may have been the first television generation in one sense, but Davy Crockett's coonskin caps, *Leave It to Beaver*, and *Bonanza* were not the only hot trends of the era. With the invention of the transistor radio by Texas Instruments in 1953, radio staged a comeback. Suddenly, it was portable. You could do other things while listening to the radio. You could listen to it in the car, and you could sneak it under your pillow at night, a practice so pervasive that Hoss Allen, as well as other deejays around the country, started an "Under the Covers Club."

Between 1953 and 1956, 3.1 million portable radios were being sold each year. That figure quadrupled by 1965. And radio announcers across the country were suddenly wailing and ranting at teen listeners from New York to Chicago to Los Angeles and all stops in between. This was music from the dark side of town, and the deejays brought it into the light. They seduced the sons and daughters of the middle class and helped create a teenage subculture. They planted seeds of rebellion.

Rock-'n'-roll became a symbol of teen churlishness, particularly with the release in 1955 of one of the first films about teenage angst and juvenile delinquency (which many adults associated with rock-'n'-roll): *The Blackboard Jungle*. The movie's theme song, actually chosen at the last minute, was Bill Haley's "Rock Around the Clock," and because of the movie it became the first rock-'n'-roll tune to reach number one on the charts.

From that point on, to be a rock-'n'-roller was to be a rebel. The role models were provided by another pair of films: *The Wild One*, with Marlon Brando, and *Rebel Without a Cause*, featuring James Dean. Elvis put their acts to music, with a few pelvic thrusts thrown in for good measure. If Elvis was regarded by rock-'n'-roll fans as the harmonic convergence of their music and mankind, those who hated and feared rock were mortified by this greasy southern cat (he used Negro hair dressing, Royal Crown Pomade) from the wrong side of town. The sound that came out of Elvis, half-hillbilly, half-black menace, was transforming the music business.

This rocking white man's version of the black man's rhythm-and-blues — the highbrows called it "aural miscegenation" — was taking over radio and by 1953 selling fifteen million dollars in records annually. To some, Elvis was the dark emperor who transformed teens into boorish, sex-maniac madmen and madwomen. He was reviled and written off by critics as a "hootchy-kootchy" carnival act, "Pelvis Presley." Ed Sullivan, legal guardian of Topo Gigo, said such a demented act would never appear on his star-maker show, *Talk of the Town*. But after Sullivan's wily rival television host Steve Allen brought Elvis on and whipped Mr. "Talk of the Town" into a mutter, Sullivan thought again. It cost him fifty thousand dollars for three appearances to lure what *Billboard*, for some odd reason, decided to describe as "the most controversial act since Liberace."

Of course, anything this successful had to be threatening to someone, and the new sound continued to develop enemies. The racy lyrics, pounding beat, and subversive effect on impressionable teens provoked a backlash from parents and pulpits, and even the less hip radio jocks. One bunch of righteous deejays on the East Coast formed a group to combat the "smut and racial derogation" of rhythm-and-blues. Boston, which harbored many racial problems, banned the records, and deejays there offered a strange antidote to the rhythm-and-blues pox — mambo music. The sheriff of Long Beach, California, put out unwanted posters for "spicey" records. Even WDIA in Memphis, home of Rufus Thomas and B. B. King (although it was owned by whites at the time), banned "Honey Love" and similarly suggestive titles — among them "Toy Bell," known more notoriously as "My Ding-a-ling." This rocking-and-rolling music was rattling the world; loose morality meant things were getting out of hand. Why, there was even a new magazine in Chicago with bare-breasted women sprawled across its foldout page. (The articles were excellent, however.)

If rock-'n'-roll was jungle tom-toms, and, as Marshall McLuhan said, radio served as the "tribal drum," then the deejays were the drum-beaters. Until the early 1950s, deejays were known as "announcers," and making announcements was about all they did. They introduced the music and read commercials. Until the late 1940s musicians playing live in the studio provided most music heard over radio, but when television crimped radio's budgets, station management quickly discovered that it was cheaper to have a single deejay play recorded music than to pay an entire orchestra. There were political battles to be fought. The musician's union went down kicking and screaming in a fight over the right of radio stations to play recorded rather than live music.

By the end of the forties, however, record buyers and retailers were hailing the announcers as the best thing for record promotion since the discovery that even good girls would do "bad" things under the influence of the right music and gauzy moonlight. Disc jockeys found themselves with considerable power, and they immediately let it go to their heads by becoming "personalities."

Although few of them were allowed on the air, black radio announcers were more colorful and personality-oriented than their white counterparts. Mellow fellow Arthur "Red" Godfrey, whose personable radio manner was an inspiration to scores of future rock-'n'-roll deejays, was considered one of the more innovative white announcers of his time, primarily because he relaxed on the radio. The black announcers were performers, often straight from the minstrel show stage, whose antics were as entertaining as the music they played. Rufus "Bear Cat" Thomas of WDIA in Memphis, for example, was a former minstrel show comedian and singer, who would also become a pioneering rhythm-and-blues and soul performer.

The first white "personality" deejays to reach large audiences modeled themselves after black announcers, in part because their audience in those early days was predominantly black. Black announcers, in turn, had generally adopted the speech patterns of the top orators in their communities, the preachers. Those early white deejays, particularly John R. Richbourg at WLAC in Nashville and Alan Freed at WJW in Cleveland, mimicked black speech to the point that listeners often could not tell if the deejays were white or black, which only made them more interesting to their mixed audiences.

A few white deejays came by their jive talk legitimately. Bill "Hoss" Allen at WLAC in Nashville, who now does "mature southern" voice-over work in commercials for clients such as McDonald's and Budweiser, grew up under the care of a black nanny, Anna Day, and with black playmates in Gallatin, Tennessee, which made a black speech pattern natural for him. His speech was further affected by a youthful inclination to run wild, so that many of the phrases that Allen used in his broadcasts at WLAC were borrowed from black culture, particularly from black pimps. Such terms became pervasive in radio in the fifties and sixties and are now generally regarded as acceptable conversational speech, suitable for the board room and Junior League luncheons.

On the streets of certain neighborhoods in Gallatin and nearby Nashville, if something was good, it was "tight like that." So if Hoss heard a good record or a good performance, he described it as "tight like that." Often when he used that sort of phrase, he would get mail or telephone calls from readers saying, "You gotta be black. White men don't talk like that." Another phrase that prompted that reaction was "git down time." Black pimps used that phrase to refer to the time of night when prostitutes took to the streets. Hoss often used it as an opening for his show: "It's git down time with Hoss Allen." One night a black man called to inquire about where Allen had heard the expression. When Allen asked the man what he did for a living, he replied, "I run some women myself."

White deejays also adopted the sort of hepcat nicknames used by black announcers, who were broadcasting under such fanciful appellations as the "Jet Pilot of Jive," "Fatman Smith," "Sweet Chariot Martih," "Dogface," "Lord Fauntleroy," "Satellite Papa," "Professor Bop," "Jockey Jack," and "Daddy-O Hot Rod." At the peak of the personality deejay era, radio station chains created a deejay personality, gave it a nickname, then used it like franchised hipness at each of their stations. So there were Dr. Jives, Doctor Daddy-Os and Poppa Stoppas broadcasting in different voices all over the country. There were more than a few Dizzy Lizzys out there, too. Women deejays were not as prominent as men in most markets, but they were out there, thanks in large part to the "femcee" efforts of Sam Phillips. His WHER in Memphis, a one-thousand-watt station, went on the air with Dottie Abbott doubling as assistant manager and deejay. With her was Marion Keisker, who may have been the first woman to swoon at an Elvis record when she worked for Phillips at Sun Records and convinced him that there was something to that truck driver from Tupelo.

Martha Jean "The Queen" Steinberg was among the first of the rhythm-and-blues women deejays. She started in the early 1950s at WDIA in Memphis, and she did it by boldly transforming what was supposed to be a homemakers' show into a "hot-cookin'" music fest. Other pioneering r&b women deejays were Zilla Mays, the "Dream Girl" at WAOK in Atlanta, and Vivian Greene at KTLN in Denver. In January 1954, *Billboard* writer June Bundy noted that women deejays were showing up throughout what had been a male-dominated business: "Everybody from a Miss America runner-up to a former child movie star is joining the ranks."

Television, which used women in commercials with great effectiveness, had spurred radio station management to alter its thinking, Bundy wrote. Miss Maryland of 1954-55, Phyllis Leftwich, was reigning at the turntable of WAYE in Baltimore, and child star Ann Gillis (who played Becky Thatcher to Jackie Cooper's Tom Sawyer) was broadcasting at KDKA in Pittsburgh. Musical comedy star Martha Wright had moved to WCBS radio in New York, while another singer, Ruby Mercer, had a show at WOR. Gloria Brown at WTAM was the first woman announcer in Cleveland. Fifteen-year-old Sheila Owens was broadcasting for WEIC in Charleston, Illinois; Patty Boyd was at WMAX in Grand Rapids, Michigan. And in Portland, Oregon, deejay Moon Mullins turned his show over to his twelve-year-old daughter, Dariel "Misty" Mullins, for a half-hour each night at KEX. Deejay Lee Vincent at WILK in Wilkes-Barre, Pennsylvania, was doing the same thing with his daughters, Juanita, twelve, and Candy, five.

Music was the strongest link between teens and their disc jockeys, but it was not the only link. The jocks served as their advocates, too, in a society that had not yet learned to bend and listen to its increasingly sophisticated young adults. Don Bell, deejay with KRNT and, later, KOIA in Des Moines, Iowa, petitioned state legislators for a Teen-Day celebration and parade and also lobbied for student rates at area movie theaters, swimming pools, and other places where teens, who were too old for children's discounts but too young to afford adult rates, hung out. Deejay Dave Dreis of KENT in Shreveport, Louisiana, followed suit and proposed student rates for teens in his city, as did other rock-'n'-roll deejays around the country.

Deejays also staged teen talent shows, teenage guest deejay hours, and record hops. The hops were sometimes targeted for protests by union musicians, who lost performance gigs to the recorded music. The unions were successful in halting many guest appearances by big stars if live music was not on the venue, but teens still flocked to the dances.

Deejays joined forces with jukebox music operators in Detroit in 1955 and 1956 to stage more than sixty teen-oriented talent and variety shows and record hops, drawing a total of more than 100,000 teens. Jocks at even the smallest stations, like Gene Newbern of KBRS in Springdale, Arkansas, invited

The record hop is only one indication of the breadth of deejay power

their young listeners into their studios for late night hops and followed them on the road in mobile units like the "Red Rover" of KMHT in Marshall, Texas. The Rover trekked to basketball and football games and the popular hot spots. Art LeBoe of KXLA in Los Angeles parked his Roving Deejay mobile unit at Scrivener's Drive-In, taking "oldies but goodies" requests and responding to teens' letters about their personal problems.

It is significant that many deejays of this era had nicknames like "Daddy" or "Uncle." Jocks such as Dick Biondi at Chicago's WLS provided male teen listeners with perhaps their only step-by-step instructions on shaving during commercials for Gillette razors. The disc jockeys, then, were to the airwaves what Holden Caulfield and *Catcher in the Rye* were to literature and Marlon Brando and James Dean were to the movies —

sources of identification for the stirring teenage rebellion of post-World War II.

The music of that rebellion emerged from black nightclubs and honky-tonks and into high-school hops and dance parties. By 1953, 25 percent of all radio stations surveyed by *Billboard* were programming some rhythm-and-blues, with an average of two-and-one-half hours a week. Pop music and even country were getting more airtime by far, but the birthing of rock-'n'-roll was imminent.

The larger record companies had long ignored the rhythm-and-blues corner of the market. Thus, little armies of independent record makers marched into the unguarded flanks. At first rhythm-and-blues was hard to find anywhere except on the few radio stations that played it. In the late forties and early fifties, there were six major record companies that dominated the industry: RCA, Columbia, Decca, Capitol, MGM, and Mercury. Between 1946 and 1952, 162 records sold more than one million copies each, and all but four of them were released by one of the six big guys. But small independent companies were moving in quickly.

The first of the indies, as they were known, were Sun Records in Memphis, King in Cincinnati, Peacock in Houston, Dot in Gallatin, Tennessee, Jubilee and Atlantic in New York, Imperial, Modern, and Specialty in Los Angeles, and, among the best, Chess in Chicago (where they dipped a microphone in the toilet bowl to get echo effects). In the late forties and early fifties, most indies got started by tapping into the black honky-tonks and after-hours blues bars on the wrong side of the tracks.

Chess began when Leonard Chess decided to record the black bluesmen who performed in his South Side tavern, The Macomba. Later, he would drive down into the Mississippi Delta, put a recorder down between rows in the cottonfields, and get a test tape right there at the source. The independent record men discovered a lucrative market among blacks for rhythm-and-blues, gospel, and even country music. As white teenagers became interested in the black music, the independents cashed in while the big record companies played catch up.

The major record companies stepped in to tap the market pioneered by the independents by hiring white, mainstream performers to "cover" the songs of the blacks, often cleaning up the sexual innuendo, or at least diluting it, in the process. At the same time, the companies were searching for white performers who could match the sexual appeal of the blacks, an effort to out-sex the black man at his own sensual game. "There were two kinds of white counterattack on the black invasion of white popular culture that was rock-'n'-roll," writes Greil Marcus in *Mystery Train*, considered to be one of the best treatises on rock-'n'-roll. "The attempt to soften black music or freeze it out, and the rockabilly lust to beat the black man at his own game."

One of the primary tactics in this counterattack was the "cover" song. If a rhythm-and-blues tune on a small label started moving up the record charts, the major record makers would move in, copy the arrangement note for note, and release it with the face of one of their white superstars on the promotional ads. Georgia Gibbs, a white singer, sounded exactly like the black Lillian Briggs when she covered her "I Want You to Be My Baby." But no way did Pat Boone render "Ain't That a Shame" with the same soulfulness that the original performer, Fats Domino, put into it. Fats's rendition inspired five cover versions, none of which climbed above number seventeen on the charts until the white bucks of Boone walked in, covered the song, and captured number one on the pop charts.

The implications of Little Richard's original version of "Tutti Fruitti" are quite different than those of the cover by the whiter-than-whitebread Boone. But Boone, who was among the most notorious and successful cover men, sold more records. Other cover artists included Ozzie and Harriet's boy Ricky Nelson, who took Fats Domino's "I'm Walkin'" into an entirely different neighborhood. A classic case of the cleaned-up cover was Georgia Gibbs's lily-scented "Dance with Me, Henry," which was the virginized version of "Work with Me, Annie," by Hank Ballard. His rendition definitely mixed work with pleasure.

Although the practice of "covering" songs came to have heavy racial implications for a time in the mid-fifties, it actually has a much longer history and was practiced by all artists of all colors with all forms of music. It would be unfair to say that rock-'n'-roll was nothing more than white theft of black music. The list of top-selling artists during the peak years of rock-'n'-roll is about as racially balanced as such a list at any time in the history of popular music. Chuck Berry, Fats Domino, Little Richard, and the Coasters were trading shots note for note with Bill Haley, Buddy Holly, Elvis, and Jerry Lee Lewis.

Many rock-'n'-roll scholars have noted, for example, that "Hound Dog" was written by the white team of Leiber and Stoller, a couple of Jewish boys from the East Coast, and given by them to Johnny Otis, a white rhythm-and-blues bandleader who often passed for black. Otis, in turn, claimed that he had written the song and gave it to blues singer Big Mama Thornton, who recorded it in a bluesy style. Then along came Elvis, the white hepcat, who shot "Hound Dog" full of rock-'n'-roll and made it a classic, only to have some claim that he had merely covered a "black" song. It has also been observed that Lieber and Stoller probably wrote their song based on some ancient cry or chant out of the Mississippi Delta. The complex evolution of rock-'n'-roll is full of examples of white and black musicians together crafting the music, which the crazed deejays then delivered to the public.

Without big marketing budgets like those of the larger record makers, the independents resorted to cunning. They promoted records by greasing the palms, capping the teeth, and sodding the yards of radio deejays. The record companies often enlisted the glad-hands of their recording stars in order to stroke the radio jocks for more play. Artists generally appeared without pay at concerts and events promoted by the deejays, just to increase their goodwill.

"Every deejay was important in his town. You didn't write off any market if you were promoting a record," says Jerry "Iceman" Butler, one of the original Impressions and later a solo singer and songwriter. "Whether it was Dizzy Lizzy or Genial Gene Potts in Charlotte, Butterball in Miami, King Coleman in Fort Lauderdale, or Al Benson in Chicago, they were all celebrities in their own towns," Butler says. He and other performers would take deejays to dinner, shoot dice with them, drink with them, introduce them to fast women, and generally try to get them on their side so that when it came time to play their records the deejays were glad to do it. "The success of most black performers was reliant on deejays to play their rhythm-and-blues records. If a big-time deejay played your records, you could reach the half-million mark in sales and then it was gravy," according to Butler. The deejays, of course, became addicted to gravy themselves.

Often, the cultivation of deejays came in the form of cash or decidedly material goods. This practice dated back to the earliest days of commercial music, when Tin Pan Alley songwriters "plugged" their tunes with record companies—in the early days of the payola scandal some called it "plugola." Record promo men at first took deejays out to lunch or dinner to curry their favor. But as more and more independent record companies sprang up and as the big companies entered a market they had previously neglected, the stakes were raised. *Billboard* tried not to snicker when it reported that one record company was taking several "New York models" on the road to promote a tune, and tales of artists providing sexual favors for jockeys were not unheard of. One Texas record industry man was known to toss one-hundred-dollar bills into deejays' wastebaskets. A record producer claimed his payola budget alone came to two thousand dollars a month.

Soon that dinner became a night on the town, and the night on the town became a weekend out of town, then, another notch up the payola ladder, a condominium in Miami Beach. Many, many deejays had their own Miami Beach pads, courtesy of the record companies (so many, in fact, that of the two thousand to twenty-five hundred people at the Miami Beach convention, only about 720 were registered at hotels). The most mercenary deejays—and there were more than a few—boasted of the perks they were able to pry out of the record companies: everything from the orthodontic scaffolding on their children's teeth to the sod on their lawns to the luxury cars in their garages.

Dot Records founder Randy Wood says the most outlandish payola request he ever received came from a Los Angeles deejay who telephoned to announce that he was about to get married and go off on his honeymoon and, he wondered, would Dot mind furnishing his house while he was gone? Dot did mind. The deejay, whom Wood declines to identify, came home to an empty nest.

The smarter and more ambitious deejays set up their own companies so that they could tap into the market legitimately. If the most powerful disc jockey in, say Philadelphia, happened to own a record-pressing plant, it sure wouldn't hurt for a record company to have a few hundred thousand copies of its new single made there, even if he said it wouldn't make any difference in his decision about whether to play the tune. This arrangement was no different than Chicago city contractors buying their insurance from the mayor's family business. It couldn't hurt.

Big-market deejays generally got what they asked for from record companies. By the time the second annual deejay convention opened in Miami Beach, if a big-market deejay had an itch, a dozen record promo men were there pronto to scratch it. If the itch happened to be in a sensitive area of the anatomy, the record companies were only too happy to provide women scratchers. By that time, there were hotels in New York and Miami that specialized in providing full-service accommodations for greedy, grubbing, horny deejays brought in from the hinterlands by the promo men.

Maybe it was the hard times and the need for an escape. Maybe it was just the lure of Miami Beach in May, as opposed to that of Kansas City in March. Whatever it was, the Miami conclave hosted by the Storz stations lured more than three times as many deejays and programming executives as the first one. Formally known as the Second Annual Radio Programming Seminar and Pop Music Deejay Convention, it lured more than twenty-five hundred back-slapping, glad-handing, payola-packing record company executives as well as a huge contingent of local and imported hookers, eager to lay for pay those who played for pay.

In the weeks leading up to the convention, it became obvious that this was not going to be another yawner dominated by front-office starched shirts. The airport took on the look of a hooker layover station. The mayor of Miami Beach, Robert King High, proclaimed the week of the convention "Disc Jockey Week" and claimed that their presence would add millions to the local economy. He noted that many of the radio stars had planned two-week vacations around the convention. And why not? It was to be staged at the swank Americana Hotel, and the record companies were planning an all-out assault that would make this a convention that would go down in junket history, although perhaps not the sort of history the record promoters had in mind.

To court and pamper the two thousand to twenty-five hundred deejays and radio execs and their entourages of coat holders and record promoters, the record companies unleashed a shower of stars on the convention. An All-Star Show lineup included Pat Boone, Vic Damone, the Diamonds, Peggy Lee, Patti Page, the Playmates, Jimmy Rodgers, George Shearing, and Andy Williams. (Just because the deejays played rock-'n'-roll didn't mean they wanted to listen to it on vacation.) The show, to be staged Saturday evening, the last official day of the convention, would be hosted by Martin Block of WABC radio in New York. Block was a pioneer radio announcer, having hosted one of the first record shows, although not a rock-'n'-roll program, on radio with his *Make Believe Ballroom* on WNEW in New York in the 1930s.

To make clear that no one was expected to retire early on the last night of the convention, the All-Star Show was to be followed by a one A.M. Old-Fashioned Breakfast Dance and Bar-B-Q, sponsored by Roulette Records and featuring the Count Basie Band. In fact, nearly every meal and reception, breakfast, lunch, dinner, snack, cocktail napkin, and ice cube dished out at the convention was sponsored by one record company or another. At least twenty record producers rented Lanai suites along the hotel's outdoor pool to entertain the radio personalities and bigwigs.

In several cases cocktail parties doubled as recording sessions at which albums were cut. Peggy Lee and the George Shearing Quintet were set to make a record at the seven-thirty P.M. Friday cocktail party hosted by Capitol Records — the first company to provide free records to deejays. Julie London and Chipmunk trainer David Seville hosted another recording cocktail session on Saturday.

The record companies planned to mine the massive assembly of top-ranked deejays from around the country for all it was worth, and to them it was worth its weight in gold records. In 1959, they hoped to see record sales of $450 million and about 20 percent, or $90 million, of that came from singles aimed at the teens and young adults who were buying 20 percent of all records sold. Although their power had been eroded somewhat by scandal and the encroachment of top-forty formats, deejays were still the primary link between the record companies and their market.

"Nobody has to buy a record, so all the excitement generated by disc jockeys, hit charts, and independent companies helps music," said George R. Marek, RCA Victor vice-president, in a *Time* magazine report on the convention. RCA Victor, which had as big a stake as any in the record business, came up with one of the more inspired, and transparent, convention ploys, even though its promotions people were well-schooled in greasing the palms of deejays. One RCA exec told *Time* that his company spent $300,000 a year stroking the platter spinners or, as he put it, cultivating their friendship. It was a proven method. When a nasal-voiced nineteen-year-old named Neil Sedaka cut "The Diary," RCA spent fifty thousand dollars on the full deejay manicure treatment. Four weeks later, thanks to the deejay hype, the record reached the top ten, and Sedaka was a star who would never go away.

In a futile attempt to instill a bit of humility in the disc jockey stars of the convention before their pockets were lined with gold and their bellies filled with the finest enticements, the president of the National Association of Broadcasting, Harold Fellows, offered a few friendly admonitions in his keynote address delivered at 9:05 A.M. Friday. His speech was cordially received by the few who were not still in bed with two hookers, on the fairway, or slurping down the day's first Bloody Mary on the beach.

It was a commendable effort on Fellows's behalf, but utterly in vain. With the benefit of wondrous hindsight, history will note that he told them so. Fellows said in his speech that the key problem in radio broadcasting was management control versus deejay control. He cautioned the disc jockeys about taking themselves too seriously as a "personality" or "name." "In the last analysis," he said, "you are none of these; you are that station and all of the people who made it possible for you to be on the air." Deejays, he said, had become "so intent upon projecting themselves as characters ... that they failed to remember that they [were] part of this overall and comprehensive effort that [comprised] a thing we call a 'broadcast station.'"

Somewhere among the troops of General Custer, there must have been one sensible soldier who warned, "Sir, that looks like one hellùva lot of Injuns to me. Maybe we should go back for a few hundred more infantry." Mr. Fellows and that soldier should be standing side by side in the Hall of Unheeded Heroes.

In Miami, the deejays were golden. "Without you, we're dead, boy," came the chorus from the promoters, who sometimes said other things when the deejays were out of range, according to *Time*'s account, things like "Some of these guys actually believe they're God."

If they did, and they did, this was their heaven. "It was the greatest party I have ever been to in my life," recalls former Cleveland deejay Joe Finan. "I have many regrets about those years, but that convention is one thing I am glad I did not miss. Whenever I start talking about what went on there, people get this look on their faces like they don't believe me. I arrived in town with a close friend who was a cop and another guy who was my manager. There was a yellow Cadillac convertible waiting. I was there ostensibly to give a speech on public service. I gave it, but I was so juiced and so hungover I don't even know what I said. But I will never forget the hookers down there. They flew them in from everywhere. I remember one famous rock-'n'-roll star's manager brought in a gorgeous girl from Amsterdam. My manager went into a room with her while I was talking to the star's manager, and my guy came out and said 'Hey, she can't speak English.' If you were one of the deejays from Indianapolis or Akron, you had to stand in line for the hookers, but if you were a major-market guy, they were knocking on your door."

RCA Victor greeted each deejay at the convention with a wad of one million dollars in play money to be used in a final-day auction of real goodies, including stereo equipment, a color television, five hundred dollars' worth of clothing, a trip for two to Europe, and the grand prize (or booby prize, depending on your automotive history), a Studebaker Lark. Deejays were instructed that they could increase their play money stash by gambling with it and by making frequent visits to the RCA Victor hospitality suite, where a fresh drink and a fresh five thousand dollars in play dough would be awarded for each visit.

One news account of the convention claimed that by the time the auction rolled around the prostitutes, not the deejays, held most of the play money, and they were the highest bidders for the big-ticket items. The headline in the *New York Daily News* a few months later would read, "Say Playola Gals Were Payola Pals on Deejay Carousel," and the *New York Post* would offer lurid accounts of the convention's "vice dolls." Another story had a New York hooker driving back to Manhattan from Florida in a new Cadillac convertible purchased from her earnings during the convention.

At least fifty record companies staged promotions at the convention. It was a veritable deejay feeding frenzy. ABC-Paramount footed the bill for all taxi rides taken by deejays. Columbia Records made tapes of deejays interviewing celebrities and gave them to the jocks to play on the air at home. There were free bus trips, sign-ups for free trips to Mexico, and, according to news accounts, a squad of local beach girls that was relieved "by company-strength detachments flown in from New York." The term "orgy" kept coming up in later recountings of convention activities, though it was difficult—but not impossible—to find a deejay who admitted taking part in one.

There were other give-aways as well. A Texas company gave away eight pairs of sunglasses with built-in transistor radios, a nifty little gift reportedly worth about five thousand dollars retail. The Lanai hospitality suites were the most visible outposts for payola, but there were others. The jocks trolled from suite to suite, their backs reddened not by the sun and eighty-degree heat, but by the hearty gauntlet of backslapping record-promotions boys. The booze flowed literally from faucets as Panama Records dispensed martinis and Manhattans from spigots.

Inside the hotel, there were long lines made up mostly of small-town deejays. Those walking past the line heard talk about megawatts and James Brown and stock options and station management pains-in-the-butt. Typical jock shoptalk. The business. But these lines were not sign-ups for trips to the zoo. They were waiting lines for even more hospitable suites equipped with prostitutes who provided sexual favors to the deejays on behalf of the record companies.

The small-time guys from Akron or Dubuque may have had to line up and wait their turn, but the big-time guys from hit-maker markets such as Cleveland, Detroit, Chicago, and the like got more personalized service. Cadillac convertibles were dispatched to pick them up at the Miami airport upon their arrival, and things got only better from that point.

Like to do a little boating? How about a side excursion to Cuba, where the new dictator, Fidel Castro, had not yet closed down the capitalist nightclubs. Several star deejays were invited on such a journey aboard a private yacht carrying a special cargo of booze and an all-female crew. About fifteen miles offshore, the crew—not a tattoo or hairy chest among 'em—dispensed with all clothing. The party moved full speed ahead. Nautical and nice.

A few select jocks didn't even have to bother with the boat. They were flown to Cuba in a plane chartered by a record company, and the fun didn't stop there. On the Havana night-club and brothel circuit, they were treated to a performance by "Super Hombre," a native equipped with a male member that might have served as an emergency mast on a mid-sized schooner. Thirty years after observing the Hombre in action, one deejay is still impressed. "I swear, it was as long as from here to Chicago," says Hoss Allen of WLAC in Nashville. "We saw him in action, but the poor guy was really tired. He had to do this about ten times a day for visitors." Allen, who, along with cohort deejays "John R." Richbourg and Gene Nobles, was considered a key player in the southern radio circuit, was also taken to a "club" with about twenty friendly Cuban women. This was supposed to be a fun trip, so he picked two of the "friends." "But one of them ran the other one off," he recalls. He spent an enchanted evening with the victorious young lady out behind the club, disturbed only by the occasional stirrings of Castro's soldiers nearby. At least there was no unfriendly fire.

Bill Lowery of Atlanta, Georgia, went to the convention as a former deejay. He had been one of the youngest in the country but had turned to independent record production by the time the second deejay convention was held. He was thirty-four and small-time but had already had two hits sell over a million copies: Gene Vincent's "Bee-Bop-A-Lula" and "Young Love," sung by Sonny James and later Tab Hunter.

So the fresh-faced southern boy was fair game as far as the deejays in Miami Beach were concerned. "It was pretty wild," he says in recalling the convention. "There were women running all over everywhere — about half the hookers in Miami, and they brought in some outsiders as well. It was just a pretty wild scene any way you looked at it. A lot of alcohol and a lot of women. And it was the first time I, as a publisher, had ever been approached for payola. We were standing in front of one of those suites, and a jockey, whom I won't name, said 'I been playing your songs for years, and I think it's about time I got paid.' I said I thought you sold advertising on radio and that's how you got paid. I didn't know we were supposed to pay you, too. I laughed and walked off. He didn't think it was too funny."

When the Miami Beach convention ended, the well-greased golden boys returned home not only to play the music, but also to face it. The four days of conspicuous corruption had not gone unnoticed by print reporters, most of whom had never seen Patti Page in the flesh, let alone been offered a couple hundred bucks to play her new single.

The headline in the *Miami Herald* on Sunday morning — "Booze, Broads and Bribes" — is enshrined in the minds of those deejays who attended because it signaled the end of their glory days. "That headline ruined it all," says Allen.

The deejays attempted to end-around the controversy they saw brewing by quickly forming the National Council of Deejays and planning a fall meeting in Chicago, where they intended to announce that they had sinned in the past but would never sin again. They would police themselves, they decided. But the Chicago newspapers followed the lead of those in Miami and broke the payola scandal story on the very day that the deejays—including Dick Clark of Philadelphia, Joe Finan of Cleveland, Murray Kauffman of New York, and Hoss Allen— were meeting. After reading the morning paper, they opened their meeting and, with a startling lack of conversation considering the participants, promptly adjourned it. "We never even tried after that," Allen says.

The deejay jig was up. The *Miami News* referred to the deejays disparagingly as "little tin gods" and reported that an unnamed record company promotion man said he paid out one million dollars a year in payola to jocks. *Time* called the event "The Big Payola," and *Newsweek* described it as "the flip side of paradise." "One of the most pampered trades in the U.S.—the disc jockeys—had come to town and Big Daddy, in the shape of U.S. record companies, was there to take care of them," *Time* said.

The name that generally came up in loose talk about payola in the radio business was that of Alan Freed. The chief suspect was worried. He spent a good deal of his time at the Miami Beach convention huddled in his room with friends, plotting his strategy to avoid prosecution. His wife, in the meantime, spent a good deal of her time trying to avoid Mitch Miller, who, she claimed, was forever making passes at her. Freed did take time out to throw his wife into a hotel swimming pool—perhaps to protect her from Miller's grasp—in a moment of convention revelry. He noted caustically to reporters at the fun-fest that what was called payola in his business was known as "lobbying" in Washington, D.C.

There was some truth in his remark. In most other businesses many of the alleged payola activities were taken for granted as perks of the job or marketing and "client development." But the deejays were especially vulnerable. Many considered them to be a corrupting influence on youth. They played the sometimes nasty, thumping music of blacks and encouraged the mixing of races at dances and concerts. They were anti-establishment, rebellious sorts who had gotten too powerful. It would be silly to consider that there was a government or establishment conspiracy to overthrow the deejays, but the signs of the times for the personality jocks pointed one way: out of town.

Throughout 1959, newspapers and broadcast news reports carried stories about the rigging of television quiz shows, particularly *The $64,000 Question*. An investigation revealed that contestants were coached and tipped off in advance with the right answers as the shows' producers endeavored to keep things interesting by maintaining control over who won and lost. The news media, which had helped magnify the celebrityhood of deejays in the sort of articles and personality profiles that would later feature the first astronauts, also tore into the money-grubbing deejays. The blood in the water did not go unnoticed by public officials facing an election year in which Democrat challenger Senator John F. Kennedy was going to put a lot of heat on the Republican candidate, Vice-President Richard Nixon. The paranoia of the fifties was still running strong, fueled by reports from Washington that the communists had infiltrated not only comic books but also the top ranks of U.S. clergy and the Council of Churches. These reports accompanied growing church involvement in the civil rights movement.

The quiz-show scandal whetted the public's appetite, and the foes of deejays pushed for the investigators to move next into their high-profile, controversial field. It was ripe for the picking. ASCAP, whose members earned royalties through the sale of records and sheet music they had written or published, called for a wider probe into corrupt broadcast practices. Its members still felt that radio's use of records, instead of live musicians, reduced royalties. Most of the rock-'n'-roll performers belonged to ASCAP's rival, BMI, while ASCAP was primarily the representative body of the older style pop and classical performers who had been shoved back on the playlists with the boom of rock-'n'-roll radio. Revenge was sweet.

Life magazine, the picture book of conservative America, decided to help investigators and the public understand the issue by publishing a "deejay slang glossary" for the payola game. A "dead president" referred to cash payoffs bearing the likeness of the aforementioned elected official. Other terms introduced into the lexicon included "schlockmeister," a deejay who was good at his graft.

Detroit deejay Ed McKenzie added his righteous testimony in a first-person account in the November 23, 1959, issue of *Life*. McKenzie, then forty-eight, explained that he had quit his sixty-thousand-dollar-a-year deejay job at WXYZ eight months earlier because he could no longer tolerate working under the strictures of "formula" radio with "its incessant commercials in bad taste, its subservience to ratings, and its pressures of payola."

In his rather holier-than-those-guys account, McKenzie said that he had never accepted payola "because I felt it was completely dishonest," but, he noted piously, small record companies had offered him one hundred dollars to give their records "one-week rides." Oh, he had accepted a one-hundred-dollar government bond in his name sent by a record man, but after he cashed it, he added twenty-five dollars of his own money and sent it on to Leader Dogs for the Blind. And he never played the guy's record, either.

The deejay said another record promotion man once offered to install a bar in the basement of his home. Another Detroit jockey moved into a new home after his property was landscaped with hundreds of dollars worth of evergreens and flowering shrubs and trees, McKenzie claimed. He then pointed his finger at his brethren. He charged that many disc jockeys were on the weekly payroll of five to ten record companies, which could mean a side income of twenty-five to fifty thousand dollars a year. McKenzie explained that if a big deejay in a key record-selling city such as Detroit, Chicago, Cleveland, or Pittsburgh was paid to play a record, it stood a good chance of hitting nationally because regional hits were noted in the trade publications — *Billboard, Cash Box, Variety* — where other deejays around the country would see the title and take a cue.

There were more intimate methods of making hits, too. McKenzie reported that record promo men were known to lavish gifts and attention on women who worked on local record charting services. He also said that local television deejays were often given 50 percent interest in songs to get them played.

McKenzie told how singer Johnnie Ray was "sliced up" by another Detroit deejay and a "New York song plugger and nightclub owner." They promoted his records in exchange for a share of his earnings, McKenzie charged, but Ray didn't pay them off when he made it big. So he was afraid to return to Detroit until he bought back the nightclub owner's share.

The saintly McKenzie said that most radio station managers were aware of payola practices but allowed them to go on because the money supplemented the low salaries paid to most deejays outside the huge market areas. For the jocks in small markets, payola was regarded in about the same way that tips were viewed by bellboys. It was salary supplement, understood by all parties. The big-market deejays saw themselves as businessmen capitalizing on wise investments in their chosen field. It was not unusual then, nor is it now, for newspapers to own stock, for example, in the paper mills that supplied them their newsprint, so why shouldn't a deejay own part of a record-producing company or even a performer who supplies him with product?

Robert E. Lee, head of the FCC, gave the deejays occasion to stop and ponder their futures in November of 1959 when he commented that if a deejay took payola, his station could lose its license. Some dunderhead news director at WMCA in New York had chimed in that payola constituted "commercial bribery," which carried a five-hundred-dollar fine and a year behind bars — which was only slightly worse than being sentenced to play the top-forty for the rest of your life.

For once, the deejays stopped talking long enough to let that message sink in. Then a few of them began chiming like church bells in the wind leading a tornado. A crackdown was coming, warned conservative deejays Bill Randle in Cleveland and Howard Miller in Chicago. Another Chicago deejay played a tape of a small label owner saying that if he paid off to every Chicago deejay with an extended palm, it would cost him twenty-two thousand dollars just to get a record rolling in the city of big moochers. After the tape was played, the deejay had to ask for police protection because of the threatening telephone calls he received. One of the biggest wolf-crier deejays was later discovered to be the recipient of a power boat, courtesy of a record company.

The instant headlines prompted by the payola scare attracted the attention of the Harris Subcommittee on Legislative Oversight in the U.S. House of Representatives. Congressmen had already tasted blood and the publicity a high-profile investigation could bring them in the game-show probe, which uncovered sensational evidence of rigging and kickbacks. A fishing expedition into radio deejays was launched with hints, never fulfilled, that newspaper reporters would be the next target.

Legislators said they wanted to find out if any of this loose talk about pay-for-play on radio was true. Payola had long been part of radio, but there was nothing illegal about it because the laws had yet to be written, unless, of course, a deejay neglected to note his take on his tax form. Nor was there any ban on the opportunistic business practices of deejays such as Alan Freed and Dick Clark, two prominent examples of the American entrepreneurial spirit, who owned shares of records, performers, record makers, anything they could get a piece of.

The payola scandal unfolded on three fronts. The Federal Trade Commission filed complaints against a number of record companies, charging them with unfair competition. Most of the companies simply filed consent agreements saying whatever it was that the FCC thought they were doing wrong, they'd stop it. Simple as that. In Manhattan, the district attorney called a grand jury to investigate whether bribery charges should be filed against deejays and/or the record companies. As the grand jury began to hear evidence, the big guns out of Congress began firing on the third, and most active, front.

On February 8, 1960, the U.S. House Subcommittee on Legislative Oversight, led by Representative Oren Harris of Arkansas, opened an investigation of payola in the record industry in general and the Miami Beach convention in particular even though payola itself was not specifically forbidden by law. In the first week of testimony, the deejays who were called sang like canaries, and radio stations around the country loaded up on birdshot. The first to be called were Joe Finan and Wesley Hopkins from Alan Freed's launching point, Cleveland. Finan, who now hosts a talk show in Akron, was in those days a hard-drinking, feckless youth, he says. He admitted to taking fifteen thousand dollars a year in consulting fees from record distributors on top of his forty-thousand-dollar annual salary. Hopkins, to whom Finan actually subcontracted payola, confessed to taking twelve thousand dollars in "listening fees." Harris sanctimoniously called them "pathetic young men."

Looking back, Finan agrees. "It was a detestable business, and I was part of it," he says from the vantage point of sixty-two years of age. Finan says he believes he was "fingered" by an angry record company owner who had offered him money to play a song that he owned the publishing rights to. But Finan, who had payola arrangements with several other companies, refused to take his money because he preferred the cover version of the song, "Love Me Forever," as performed by Edyie Gorme. The record man went to Finan's boss and told him that the deejay was demanding a payoff, Finan says. "Everybody knew who was taking money in the business. Most of the heavy jocks were taking. But then the House Oversight Committee decided this payola stuff was a glitzy piece of meat," Finan says. The record man also wrote to the committee about Finan.

The deejay was fired, and he now blames only himself. "I allowed myself to be seduced. I was whoring," he says. "I was taking money. I was taking favors. I was set up for the 'You're the greatest baby, stuff.' My wife tried to warn me about the record promo guys, but I didn't have the insight she had. She was right, and I was wrong."

The payola hearings marked open season on the personality deejay. Many of them were handed slips that said, in effect, "Don't let the door hit you on the ass on the way out." Station managers were desperate to avoid anything that might look like an invitation to the FCC investigators. Even if the managers believed the deejays had done nothing legally wrong or out of the ordinary, they were at the mercy of the FCC, which was monitoring how its license holders responded to the payola investigation. There was a whole lot of shakin' up goin' on throughout the radio business.

Deejays poured for the exits or were booted in that general direction. In Detroit, four top jocks fell victim to the paranoia: Dale Young, Tom Clay, Jack LeGoff, and Don McLeod. All either quit or were asked to resign. In Philadelphia, the popular Joe Niagara hastened his resignation, and in Boston WILD said "so long" to three deejays — Stan Richard, Bill Marlowe, and Joe Smith — in order to deemphasize the personality jock format.

In January of 1960, the House Subcommittee on Legislative Oversight began questioning radio and television deejays and assorted management types in executive sessions closed to the public. Representative Walter Rogers of Texas emerged from the first few days of closed hearings to tell reporters that some deejays were handed one hundred dollars just to listen to a record. But Rogers, father of six children, added that considering many of those records were rock-'n'-roll, the deejays "were underpaid." The chuckles died down when other governmental bodies with criminal statute books in hand went after deejays.

On Thursday, May 19, 1960, a grand jury in New York City indicted five New York radio disc jockeys — including

Freed — one program director, and two former record librarians — on charges that they had accepted payola. The eight were charged with taking illegal gratuities totaling $116,580 from twenty-three record companies over the previous two years in return for playing certain records on their programs.

Public sessions began in February with Dick Clark as the first witness. His financial dealings inspired one admiring investigator to rail about "Clarkola." A young Philadelphia deejay turned Hollywood host, Clark had become a master at investing in his business, but the payola investigators viewed his involvement in a somewhat darker light when they called the handsome, personable young man to appear. Clark owned stock in record companies whose artists he invited to appear on his show, and he also owned music publishing companies. He was involved in thirty-three companies in the music business by the late 1950s, including three record companies, a management firm, and a record-pressing plant.

His business relationship with singer Duane Eddy was particularly symbiotic. Clark was Eddy's manager; he owned publishing rights to all of his songs and a share of Jamie Records, on which Eddy recorded. Clark invested $125 in Jamie Records and later sold the stock for $12,025. Between 1958 and 1960, Eddy released eleven records, and Clark played them a total of 240 times on his television show. When ABC ordered Clark to sever his ties with outside interests in light of the payola hearings, he did so, claiming it cost him eight million dollars.

All of this did not bode well for the status of the once-revered radio rock-'n'-roll deejay. The folks at Storz radio stations announced just a few weeks after the Miami convention that they were having doubts about hosting any more deejay gatherings, and, if they did, the next convention would not be in New Orleans as originally planned, but in a less tempestuous town such as Indianapolis or perhaps Minneapolis.

Todd Storz, head of the station group, told *Billboard* that he believed record companies had spent more than

Clark testifies on alleged conflict of interest

$250,000 applying butter to deejay toast at the Miami Beach party. He said both the record companies and his station managers hoped to make the 1960 convention a "shirt-sleeve working session" with fewer temptations than Miami Beach where "there was too much swinging." But after thinking it over a bit, the Storz people decided not to sponsor a third convention at all.

By November, the deejays had long lost their Miami Beach tans, but they had not escaped the heat. The Harris subcommittee came out with a list of twenty-one types of payola under investigation, and deejays around the country were purged, pushed out, or panicked into quitting. Alan Freed, the king of rock-'n'-roll, top deejay on radio and television, hop promoter, and producer of three rock-'n'-roll movies (*Rock Around the Clock, Rock, Rock, Rock,* and *Don't Knock Rock*) was booted out on the street without ceremony in light of increasing reports that he and payola were not strangers.

It was not the best of times for rock-'n'-rollers. Freed had hardly bounced once when word came out that Chuck Berry had been charged with violating the Mann Act for allegedly transporting a fourteen-year-old across state lines for immoral purposes, and the men known as the Platters had been arrested in Cincinnati with four nineteen-year-old girls of varying skin colors. As much as their record company hated the irony, it was too late to stop the release of their new album, entitled *A Girl Is a Girl Is a Girl.*

The Harris subcommittee did not get around to the convention in its investigation until February of 1960. Before that part of the investigation began, Boston deejay David Maynard testified as the first disc jockey before the subcommittee and admitted he took six thousand dollars in gifts and cash but said it was given "in appreciation" for his promoting records at teenage hops and advising distributors of the records' potential. Maynard's coworker at wBz in Boston, Alan Dary, testified that he received about four thousand dollars from record distributors as Christmas gifts each year. He also listed a hi-fi set, liquor, and a $650 carpet as gifts from record promoters and advertisers. Former WBZ deejay Norman Prescott, who had moved to a New York station, invoked the Fifth until the committee agreed to hear his testimony behind closed doors. Then, Harris said, he proved to be a "very cooperative witness."

Boston deejay Arnold "Woo Woo" Ginsburg, who is now a station executive, told House investigators that he had been paid forty-four hundred dollars for "good will" by record distributors in the two previous years. Ginsburg, who had the distinction of having a sandwich named after him, "the Ginsburger," admitted to his bosses that he took payola, but they did not fire him "because he promised to be good," said Maxwell Richmond, president of Ginsburg's station WMEX. Richmond himself was said to have taken one hundred dollars a week for fourteen weeks to play the records of a Boston distributor.

All the serious hoopla did not escape the humor of deejays and others around the country. One Chicago jazz disc jockey, who used the Daddio Daylie moniker on WAAF and had always billed himself as the city's number one deejay, announced—after learning that the investigation would focus only on the "top deejays in each city"—that he would henceforth be known as the "number twenty-nine deejay" in Chicago. Four Norfolk, Virginia, deejays were fired after they demonstrated outside the station all day with placards saying "We want payola, too. $100,000 salaries have to go." They also played one record 320 times in one day to demonstrate that no matter how many times a deejay played a record, if it was bad, the public would not buy it. The name of the record was "Pahalackaka." It never became a hit in Norfolk or anywhere else.

And down in Crowley, Louisiana, a crazy Cajun deejay named Alden Sonnier mailed off a confession to the FCC detailing his payola intake. He noted that one listener had sent him a dozen homegrown grapefruit for playing "Le Sud de la Louisianne" one time. Other payola on his list included twenty-five yards of boudin rice sausage, thirty-five yards of smoked sausage, seven muscovy ducks, one pork shoulder roast, one pumpkin, several watermelons, half a case of open-kettle cane syrup, three messes of sweet potatoes, a half sack of fresh-dug peanuts, a live guinea hen, one dish of hogshead cheese, a pound of hog cracklings, a paper sack of kumquats, and a wild goose well-dressed. The Cajun-jay also noted that he had to get off his conscience a gift sent after he sneezed one night on the air. A local spinster sent him a bottle of homemade Mau-Mau cough syrup.

Comedian Bob Hope was ubiquitous even then, and he presented a television skit based on the payola probe on his NBC show. He portrayed a deejay on radio station KLIP, with Ernie Kovacs costarring as an investigative senator who discovered that Hope had tried to kill himself with a record needle. He couldn't tell if he was dead, however, because he kept spinning on the turntable.

By the time testimony on the convention began, the news reporters were geared up. Now they could put some sex in their headlines: "Demand Hotel Books In Sex, Payola Probe." The committee subpoenaed the books of the Americana and six other Miami hotels after determining that record companies had picked up tabs totaling $117,664 for liquor, food, and room expenses at the Americana.

At first, the committee couldn't find any deejays who would admit to having attended a frolic on the beach, prompting Harris to observe, "Where did the twenty-seven hundred who were there come from? I can't find any who went." Chicago disc jockey Stan Dale of WAIT was called to testify on the convention in February, and he made gleeful headlines with his reply when asked if the event hadn't been a bit wild. "But isn't every convention? As a matter of fact, the plumbers were down there at the same time we were, and theirs was even more raucous than ours," Dale told reporters for the *Chicago Tribune*.

An official of the Americana told House investigators that eighteen record companies paid $117,664.95 for the convention. A single party given by Roulette records of New York cost $15,415, including $8,850 for the bar bill; $4,205 for a barbecue;

and $2,360 for a breakfast. The Roulette tab prompted Representative John Moss of California to note that "I had heard that three Bs were descriptive of this convention, but they weren't 'bar, barbecue, and breakfast.' I saw headlines describing it as 'booze, broads, and bribes.'"

Edward E. Eicher, special services director for the Americana, appeared to identify records of the hotel that had been subpoenaed by the investigators. Eicher testified that hotel records showed that Capitol Records paid $19,812.71 for the convention. Dot spent $19,485.92; Roulette, $19,158.60; Mercury, $8,843.32 and Vee Jay, $1,481.31. The record companies also paid room expenses for some deejays, Eicher testified. Pat Boone and his wife and the former governor of Tennessee Frank G. Clement and his wife came down for the convention, and their tabs were picked up by Randy Wood of Dot. The former governor, it turned out, had come to speak at the convention.

Eicher said that the deejays and their associates consumed two thousand bottles of bourbon during an eight-hour Count Basie recording session that started at midnight and concluded with a breakfast of scrambled eggs and coffee. When asked why Roulette's bar bill was so much higher than its breakfast bill, Eicher replied that "Bourbon costs a little more than eggs."

Stan Richards, an unemployed deejay from Boston, testified that he was the guest of a record distributor at the convention. His hotel bill was $279.61 for three days. There was also a charge on his bill of $117.42 for a jacket, a shirt, and a pair of slacks. The Boston rep for United Artists picked up the tab. Richards admitted that he accepted $6,225 from two record distributors but refused to characterize it as payola. He said, "This seems to be the American way of life, which is a wonderful way of life. It's primarily built on romance: I'll do for you. What can you do for me?"

In the end, no deejays were packed off to prison, but the broad brush wielded by the investigators ruined the careers of dozens and dozens of radio disc jockeys. The best-known deejay, Alan Freed, would be the best-known casualty. He never recovered and died both broke and broken-hearted.

The rock-'n'-roll deejay would never be as powerful and as prominent as he had been in the mid-1950s, but by force of personality and electronic broadcasting he would remain an influence on the lives of America's teenagers, who responded increasingly to his voice even when they refused to hear the one coming from the head of their own dinner tables.

The rock-'n'-roll deejay would be heard. Although their power might diminish with rock-'n'-roll's lessening influence, deejays would continue to reach their young listeners late at night or during rush-hour drive-time even in highly splintered markets. Through the sixties they would play to an increasingly rebellious audience, helping them find their way through civil rights marches, peace demonstrations, and funerals of assassinated heroes. In the seventies they muddled through disco and into the eighties, which saw big-city jocks trying to assert themselves with outlandish gags that rivaled but hardly challenged those performed by their soulmates of the fifties. Shock radio would make headlines, but even that ground had been cleared and prepared by those who came before.

Although their numbers have diminished and only a few have any power in the record industry, radio deejays have proven to be adaptable creatures, ones who evolved with the times. Occasionally there has even emerged a throwback to the glory days, the wild and woolly days of the pied pipers of rock-'n'-roll: "Ya, dis is da Wolfman comin' atcha! Get nekkid! Awoooooooooooooooooo!"

TWO

Hittin'
and
Gittin'

*D*emons hovered in droves around the bountiful bouffunk hairdo of James Brown in 1985. The devils from the Internal Revenue Service were at him, at him, at him, claiming he owed them nine million in back taxes. Business and woman troubles had him lost and confused, and although he would deny it even if he woke up buck naked and painted pink, there were some serious drug problems as well. In four years' time, the demons would do him in, and Brown would be in prison looking at a six-year stretch. But his simmering personal turmoil was forgotten the minute a call came from Nashville telling him John R. was broke and dying and needed some help. "I'll be there," said James Brown.

On March 26, 1985, the troubled Godfather of Soul gave them one like they hadn't seen from him in a long, long time. And he did it where it had never been done before, at least not the way James Brown does it. He shook the shingles of the

Grand Ole Opry House in a hellacious from-the-heart thirty-minute set. Ernest Tubb had walked that same floor, but he had never done to it what James Brown did that night. He screwed his knees into the stage, stabbed into the hardwood with his shoulder blades, and leaped above it hanging-high-time in flying splits. But throughout it all he never strayed far from his spot in a remote corner at the rear of the massive Opry stage. He could hardly be seen by many of those in the crowd; some even resorted to standing on their seats. This wasn't like the "hardest working man in show business." James Brown has always prided himself on delivering the goods in his live performances, but on this night he had only secondary concerns about anyone other than the frail, pallid man sitting in a wheelchair in a special roped-off section of the stage.

The Grand Ole Opry House was not such a strange place for James Brown to be, and a far corner of the stage was not a poor spot for him to be working if you understood exactly what that cancer-stricken white man in the wheelchair had meant to this black music legend. "He's been a father to me and also he's been a brother to me," Brown told *Nashville Banner* reporter Michael McCall backstage. "He didn't have to say he needed me to come. He just had to say he wanted me to come. I'm here. And I'm here because I love him. He gave me the chance to do the things I wanted to do."

Thirty years earlier, in the fall of 1955, James Brown was living in Macon, Georgia. He had only recently been released from the Alto Reform School, where he had spent three-and-a-half years for separating cars from their parts without permission. In reform school, he had earned the nickname "Music Box," and he actually sang his way to an early release on a sentence that had called for eight to sixteen years. Back on the streets, he began singing first gospel and then rhythm-and-blues with a group known as the Famous Flames.

They were strong on the white fraternity, juke joint, and black nightclub "chitlin'" circuits in the Southeast. Their act, though popular, was merely a sideshow to Macon's main event of the time, hot hometown boy Little Richard, whose manager was also handling the Flames. James Brown, who could do a mean imitation of Little Richard, occasionally filled in for him on appearances he couldn't make. Often, the audience didn't know the difference. During a break from the road, the Famous Flames went into the recording studio of Macon's radio station WIBB to cut a demo of a song that had been a big hit in their show. Called "Please, Please, Please," the song's lyrics were little more than the title pleaded over and over again.

The power of the song was the way lead singer James Brown sobbed the word with increasing intensity. Politeness had never been expressed with such raw pain. The rest of the Flames wrapped Brown's plaintive cries in a gentle gospel harmony that rose to a rousing climax. They cut the demo on a single microphone and shipped their first recording off to the world.

Macon deejay Hamp Swain played a copy of the demo on his WIBB *Night Ride* rhythm-and-blues show. Swain's show was aimed at the blacks who packed local clubs for his talent shows and sock hops, but he had a large "secret" audience of white teens, too. Other copies of "Please, Please, Please" were sent off to small record companies in Houston, Chicago, and Atlanta. Former tavern keeper Leonard Chess of Chicago's aggressive Chess Records had just turned down a demo from a white Memphis hillbilly named Elvis, but he liked what he heard when "Please, Please, Please" was played for him in January of 1956. He booked a flight to Atlanta to talk with the Famous Flames, but he was delayed by bad weather. About the same time that Chess heard the demo, another small but tenacious record producer, Syd Nathan of King and its subsidiary Federal, based in Cincinnati, learned of it from his rep in Atlanta, Ralph Bass. Wanting to beat out his rival Chess, Nathan dispatched Bass to sign the group without having heard the song.

The two record companies raced to get a contract to the Famous Flames. Bass won, but when Nathan actually heard the demo record Bass had only told him about, he fired his field man. The song was "a piece of shit," Nathan said, and this James Brown sounded like a stoned soul zombie. Even with that less than enthusiastic appraisal from the front office, the Federal Records representative in Nashville dropped off "Please, Please, Please" with WLAC deejay Gene Nobles in February of 1956.

By day, WLAC was a mild-mannered CBS network affiliate station programming affable Arthur Godfrey, Eddy Arnold, Ma Perkins, and *The Guiding Light.* Come late evening, however, long after Amos 'n' Andy, Gene Autry, and *My Little Margie* had gone nightie-night, WLAC dropped the country-bumpkin coveralls and put on its flying cape, sending out soulful rhythm-and-blues on a fifty-thousand-watt signal that went, in the words of Little Richard Penniman, "WOMP-BOMP-A-LOO-MOMP-ALOP-BOMP-BOMP," off into the ionosphere: out of the South, down Michigan Avenue in Chicago, up into Canada, west into the Rockies, and, on a good, clean BOMP, into Greenland, Iceland, and even Australia. The station regularly received mail from eighteen states and, yes, ships at sea in the Mediterranean.

Gene Nobles, a former carnival bingo-barker from Hot Springs, Arkansas, had been at WLAC since 1943 and was the first deejay there — and perhaps in the country — consistently to play black rhythm-and-blues for a large, racially mixed audience. Given to risque humor and sarcastic assaults on his studio engineer, his listeners, and his employers, Nobles was named "favorite disc jockey" by both Arkansas A&M and Mississippi State colleges.

Unlike most deejays of the rock-'n'-roll era who leaned heavily on listeners' telephone calls, the irascible Nobles, who never went into the studio without a bottle in hand, yanked the plug on his studio phone. When the rare call came through (perhaps because Nobles had just hung up on his bookie), the deejay addressed all males as "jerks" and all females as "fillies." They loved it. They also dug his music. Nobles knew his audience, and he established a formula that would be copied and claimed as original by disc jockeys all over the country. He made millions for the owners of his station even as the owners expressed contempt for the type of music he played. In partnership with his sponsor, Randy's Record Shop of Gallatin, Tennessee, Nobles set the pace for deejays everywhere with his selection of rhythm-and-blues records.

Nobles was familiar with James Brown and the Famous Flames. They had come to him once before with a gospel tune, to which he hadn't even listened. He did listen to "Please, Please, Please," took it off the turntable, and tossed it into his discard box. Syd Nathan was not alone in his low esteem for the tune. But Nobles was not the only record-slinger at WLAC. Several weeks later, utility deejay Bill "Hoss" Allen, who also worked in sales and production, was filling in for Nobles, who had taken off on one of his frequent visits to the pony track. Allen, a Vanderbilt graduate with a huge appetite for both black music and white lightning, rummaged throughout Nobles's rejects, as was his habit, searching for something interesting to play. Because he was not a full-time deejay at the time, Allen did not receive the daily deluge of demos and dubs that arrived for the regular disc jockeys. In those days, WLAC received records as fast as record companies could get a demo to them. A high percentage of the discs they played were nothing more than dubs, the first raw recording of a song.

Record companies dispatched these rough versions to the deejays for a quick test. If a song didn't get a good reaction, the record company would likely take the master tape out back and burn it. It took more than talent to get a record on the air. If the WLAC jocks did play the record, however, it could mean the gravy train. There were as many as fifteen million potential record buyers out there on a given night listening for the latest on WLAC.

While digging around in Nobles's castoffs, Hoss pulled out "Please, Please, Please." Though he had never heard of the Famous Flames, he decided to give it a test spin on a playback machine in the closet that served as their record room. The

Hossman fell hard. The record blew him away. He had never heard anything quite like it, but it did put him in mind of those Sundays when his black nanny had taken him to her church. Its congregation would rock little Gallatin with the Lord's own music. Hoss played the song for two weeks, and when Nobles returned from the track, he played it too.

Although Hoss Allen has always felt that he discovered "Please, Please, Please," he is not the WLAC deejay generally credited with doing so. John R., who had also turned down James Brown's gospel record the first time Brown came to WLAC, always claimed he found "Please, Please, Please" and rode it hard. Most folks, including James Brown, believe that he did. Hoss, who is not given to claim-jumping, is willing to concede that John R. may have had his own copy of the record tucked away and that he may have fallen in love with the song on his own. It could have happened, just like maybe Henry Ford in the U.S. and that fella in Germany or France or wherever invented the automobile at the same time. Simultaneous sweet inspiration.

At any rate, John R. took the record and began playing it on his nightly show. Over the years, the deejays changed positions on the nighttime programming at WLAC, but Richbourg is best known for his late-night work, from one A.M. to three A.M. on Program 10. Because few other stations of such power were on as late as WLAC, Richbourg's show was incredibly influential. Other late-night deejays around the country tuned their radio to John R. while they were driving home from work. Musicians did the same while packing up and hitting the road from one gig to the next. And of course blacks and hip young whites tuned in, too, during their romantic interludes on lovers' lanes or for impromptu sock hops staged on paved country roads or city street corners.

John R. played almost nothing but dubs, records that no one else had yet; he also mixed in a few of his favorite tunes (made dearer to him by regular payments from record promo men in the standard practice of the day). The strength of the

WLAC signal, his charismatic radio voice, and his skill as probably the best product pitchman in radio made John R. one of the big muscles in the music business. When he went on the air "hittin' and gittin'" with records, hundreds of thousands were listening. If Richbourg and the other deejays who prepared a generation for rock-'n'-roll latched onto a record they liked, they had the freedom to play it for hours on end, building its audience. In some cases, the boost was provided for profit as much as for personal pleasure. But whatever his motives, Richbourg stayed with the unusual gospel/rhythm-and-blues hybrid "Please, Please, Please" when few other deejays in the country were playing it.

Hoss Allen, of course, was sticking with it, too, but his early-evening show did not have the prestige or the audience of Richbourg's post-midnight broadcast. By April of that year, Ralph Bass, the record promo man who had been fired for signing James Brown's record, was back on the job and cackling. "Please, Please, Please" reached number six on the rhythm-and-blues charts and became the first of James Brown's 114 charted singles. It also became, over years of steady sales, Brown's first record to go gold, reflecting sales of more than a million copies. From that point on, James Brown was a man to be reckoned with in the music business, and the Nashville deejay who had stood by his song and played it across the county had a friend for life. Richbourg rode "Please, Please, Please" for weeks, gave it an audience, and made it a hit. Every deejay in the country wanted a piece of that record once John R. got on it. James Brown knew a hard worker when he saw one, and it was John R. whom Brown came to think of as both a father and a brother.

John R. was not the first deejay to play Brown's premiere hit. Hamp Swain in Macon and Hoss Allen — and perhaps others around the country — had played it before him. But John R. had the highest profile and the biggest audience, and he would forever be known as the man who broke James Brown's first hit. In much the same way, John R. would overshadow the

The legendary WLAC *deejays — (seated, l to r) John R. Richbourg, Gene Nobles, Hoss Allen, Herman Grizzard; (standing) Don Whitehead*

more private Gene Nobles and become known as "the daddy of rhythm-and-blues radio" even though Nobles and his *Randy's Record Shop Show* had played the music before Richbourg. Of such tenuous fiber, legends are woven.

It would probably be impossible to trace a single source for the staccato explosion that occurred when raunchy rhythm-and-blues blew out of the back-room bars and black-and-tan clubs into the streets and sock hops of white America, where it was cleaned up a bit and called rock-'n'-roll. Little Richard's flagrantly homosexual lust call, "Tutti Fruitti" (which even *he* diluted a bit for general consumption), became Pat Boone's namby-pamby "Tutti Fruitti," no more threatening than "Mares eat oats and does eat oats and little lambs eat ivy. . . ."

Gene Nobles, John R. Richbourg, and Hoss Allen were the first deejays to play rhythm-and-blues for a large listening audience of both whites and blacks. No doubt there were dozens of deejays in smaller towns like Macon's King Bee, Hamp Swain (who played with and promoted not only James Brown and Little Richard but also Otis Redding), who were playing the music, too. Before there were rock-'n'-roll deejays, there were these pioneering disc jockeys who played rhythm-and-blues and became the role models for all who followed. They were also the guiding spirits for their listeners.

They played black rhythm-and-blues music because that is what their listeners wanted to hear. It sold. The jocks may have loved it, but if rhythm-and-blues on the radio had failed to sell baby chicks or Bibles or Royal Crown hair dressing, the deejays would have been playing something that did: gospel, jazz, bebop, country-and-western, whatever worked. They played to their listeners' taste.

Most white rhythm-and-blues deejays of the time sounded black, either because they had grown up with blacks in the South or because they worked at it to win favor with their black audience. John Richbourg was such a master of black phrasing that his listeners generally assumed he was black. But Richbourg's phrasing was all part of his act. At home and off the air, he spoke like the very distinguished descendant of French Huguenot settlers that he was. A trained actor, Richbourg developed his black inflection to communicate better with his primarily black audience. He eventually proved himself a friend of the black man as well, but his black idiomatic radio voice was very much a calculated tool. John R., as beloved as he would become, seldom ventured out into the community of his listeners. Except to those who sought out this generally solitary man as a mentor and friend, he was primarily a warm and welcoming voice on the radio, fostering affection and loyalty just by playing the music.

Like John R., Zenas "Daddy" Sears was a failed actor who wandered into radio, found a huge following among the black rhythm-and-blues audience, and, over time, began attracting white listeners. And, like John R., he was a white man who adopted black speech patterns to appeal to his audience.

But Zenas Sears, unlike Richbourg, offered more than his voice and radio presence to the black community. He became an advocate and an early champion of civil rights in Atlanta and the South. He provided career support for Ray Charles, Chuck Willis, Gladys Knight, and Little Richard, among others, and moral support for Dr. Martin Luther King, Jr., Hosea Williams, and other prominent black leaders of the civil rights movement in the South. Before his death in 1988, the professorial deejay would be recognized as one of the forces that held Atlanta together when racial turmoil was ripping up other cities around the country.

Slightly built, almost scrawny, with the bookish look of, in his son's description, "a lost paleontologist," Sears realized early on in his acting career that he was never going to make women swoon as a leading man, and that character actors didn't make enough money in those times to feed a family. Sears came to Atlanta looking for work as an actor after his run at the big time on the East Coast went nowhere. Once the partner in a comedy team with Garry Moore, Sears was left behind when Moore went to television as a game-show host and emcee. Zenas (the name was a family heirloom) worked for a time as a barker at the Gayety Burlesque Theater in Baltimore before landing in Atlanta. His first radio job there was at WATL, where his marching orders were to play a Bing Crosby record every third song. His civilian announcing career was interrupted early on by military duty in World War II, where he served as an Armed Forces Radio announcer in India along the Burma Road. The troops in his audience were 85 percent black, and he played the music they liked to hear, even when he couldn't get the records. "When I was in the Army, we had a lot of black troops, so I played the stuff I thought was black music, but there were a couple of guys who were in a gospel group there, and that's what the troops were requesting," he told Hugh Merrill of the *Atlanta Journal.* "We couldn't get any gospel records over

Zenas Sears, the intellectual deejay

there, so I started playing these groups live." Some of the soldiers brought their own records to Sears, introducing the boy from Baltimore to the gutbucket blues and soulful rhythm-and-blues of the South. It wasn't just an adventure; it was an education.

After the war, he returned to WATL in Atlanta, among the smallest of the city's stations. There, he began slipping in some of the black music early in the morning. It was difficult even to find the records back then, so he would search out black record shops and buy them himself, which made his show all the more popular with blacks. Ad sales picked up. "I never really tried to sound black, oh, I guess I might have picked up one or two jive phrases to throw in, but it wasn't an effort to imitate," he told Merrill. "I just liked black music and that's what I played."

Unlike other pseudo-hip white deejays of the rhythm-and-blues and early rock-'n'-roll era, Sears came by his hepcat nickname legitimately. He was on the air in 1948 when word came that his wife, Clare, was at the hospital ready to give birth to their second child. It was late at night. He was alone at the station. A record was playing. He took off for the hospital in a mad scramble, forgetting everything else. The record played itself out, and for what seemed like a long, long time, the only thing the station's listeners heard was the hiss and tick of a needle looking for a way out of a record groove. When Zenas Sears returned to the station red-faced but proud to be the father of not only his second but his third child as well—Clare had given birth to twin boys—Zenas was dubbed "Big Daddy" by his friends at the station. The "Big" eventually became more than this slight, owlish man could carry around, so the moniker was whittled down to Zenas "Daddy" Sears. His friends knew him as "Zene" or simply "Z."

Zenas Sears played rhythm-and-blues for his primarily black audience until the station owner down in Columbus, Georgia, got within earshot of the signal one day and heard what was coming out of his station. The next day, Sears was out of a job. A pattern was developing. Bill Lowery, who would become a sort of southern godfather to rock-'n'-roll and pop music in Atlanta, hired Sears as a deejay at WQXI-AM, but after a short time Zenas switched over to state-owned WGST that broadcast out of the Georgia Institute of Technology, commonly known as Georgia Tech. He talked Lowery into coming with him in 1948. "Zenas was very serious about his black music, and he had a lot of whites listening to his shows too because they were catching on to it. I was liable to go on the air unprepared, but he would have his entire show ready, from the first record to the last," says Lowery, who would later become one of the top record producers in the South, working with Gene Vincent, Joe South, Tommy Roe, the Tams, Mac Davis, and Ray Stevens, among others.

WGST was in the dumper financially when Sears and Lowery arrived. It sat on the edge of a large, primarily black public housing project, Techwood Homes, and the station management was hopeful that Sears and his music would draw listeners. Sears, who always knew his way around the halls of government, checked in with Governor Herman Talmadge about being brought in to play black music on the state's own radio station. The governor told him he could play the music, but to stay away from community-action nonsense like voter registration for the Negroes or promotions for the NAACP. Sears went back, played the music, and ignored the governor's admonitions about social issues.

He played it straight with pop tunes on his *Corner Drug Store* show from nine-thirty P.M. until ten P.M. and then, when all the judgmental white folks were tucked into bed, he unleashed the black demons and their rhythm-and-blues. "We did all the get-out-the-vote-stuff anyway. Nobody white listened to the radio after the news at ten o'clock. We started at ten-fifteen P.M. and would run as long as we could sell it, which was usually about two A.M.," the deejay told Bill King of the *Atlanta Constitution*. "We were playing Dinah Washington, Lonnie King, and Louis Jordan was real hot. My theme song was a record by Fats Waller. Artists like Louis Armstrong, Ella Fitzgerald, and Duke Ellington were what was known as 'white acts.' They're becoming more popular with blacks now but weren't during their heyday."

Sears, whose social consciousness was always stronger than his not-insubstantial drive for business success, rapidly became known as a friend to the black community in Atlanta and also as a friend to black performers in the South. Jerry "Iceman" Butler remembers Sears as a "salt-of-the-earth kinda guy. There was hardly a time when I went to Atlanta that I didn't stop by to see him. It was business, sure, but I liked the guy. His station was the voice of the black community, and when there were problems, he would go to the mayor of Atlanta and say, 'This is what I am hearing, and this is what we can do.' He served the people in the black community."

Sears became active in Atlanta's black community and its causes

At the time, there were few recording studios in the South, and not many record companies were eager to record blacks. The New York-based companies would pack their equipment up and come to Atlanta, where they often taped sessions by local artists in WGST's studios in the Dinkler Building on the edge of downtown. Often, the record company talent scouts were summoned by Sears, who served as a talent scout and manager for black artists in the days leading up to eruption of rock-'n'-roll.

In 1951, as the major record companies began to sense the growing audience for rhythm-and-blues music, RCA in New York telephoned Sears and asked if he knew of any black talent in the South. He put the word out, and a performer named Billy Wright told him of a very strange, but very talented kid out of Macon — Little Richard. The eighteen-year-old performer, who claimed he "looked like Tarzan and sang like Jane," came into the studio on October 16 with Wright's band playing backup. The session was not regarded as one of his best. He may have been nervous at his first time in a studio, but it resulted in a small local hit called "Every Hour," which Daddy Sears played until the needle wore through the groove.

Back in Macon one night, the Penniman family was sitting around their radio listening to the biggest late-night radio show in the South, *Randy's Record Shop* on WLAC, when Gene Nobles put on a tune he'd heard that Zenas Sears was doing well with in Atlanta. It was the first time Little Richard heard himself singing on the radio. He says in *The Life and Times of Little Richard*, "It came on, I jumped up and started screaming and running through the house and shouting, 'That's my record, my record, my record. That's my record!'"

WGST was also home to the first hit recording of another black musician destined to become legend. In November of 1954, Ray Charles was in town with his band at the Royal Peacock Club, the center for black music in that part of the South, when he decided he wanted to get a few new songs he'd come up with on tape right away. He called Atlantic Records, which two years earlier had bought his recording contract for two thousand dollars, and told Jerry Wexler and Ahmet Ertegun that he had a little something for them if they could get down to Atlanta. Sensing that Charles was on the verge of breaking free of the constricting Nat King Cole crooning style that he had developed early in his career, the top executives of Atlantic got on a plane.

Charles had been working in New Orleans with blues singer Guitar Slim before coming to Atlanta. The record company execs, considered to be two of the most enlightened in the business, thought that this musical sponge may have found his own style down there and brought it home to Georgia (he was born in Albany, in south Georgia, in 1930) for a revelation. When they arrived, they headed for the only studio in town, the control room at WGST, where they met up with Zenas Sears. Normally, Sears would set these sessions up for late at night when the station was off the air, but this time it was done in the studio control room during regular broadcast hours. "Ray had been hanging around here with a trio and was trying to sound like Nat King Cole, and then I got him this session and he finally cut loose," Sears would recall. Years later, Wexler too would recall that recording session as one of the strangest he produced in his long career with Atlantic. They had to stop their taping every half-hour to let the local news announcer do his spots. It took three hours just to get set up, but by the end of the session they had four songs on tape: "I Got a Woman," "Come Back, Baby," "Greenbacks," and "This Little Girl of Mine."

The WGST session was memorable for several reasons. A background singer walked out because, as a religious person, she felt it was wrong to sing the way Charles was singing — he was giving gospel a blues treatment. It was also profitable for Atlantic. It was the first time that a major artist had blatantly dared to put an essentially gospel sound to a raunchy rhythm-and-blues beat. Charles had rewritten the gospel song "My

Jesus Is All the World to Me" into a soulful hit that defied the classifications of the day.

The song was also perceived by the stricter church-going folks in the black community as blasphemy. Many of them reacted as if they had found girlie pictures pasted in their family Bibles. Ray Charles was condemned for bringing the devil into God's living room, and Zenas Sears caught some heat for opening the door. Still, it was a major step for Charles's career, one that gave him the confidence to play the music that was deep within rather than imitating what he heard outside. Many in the music business believe that Zenas Sears helped Ray Charles uncover "soul music" in that WGST studio between regular broadcasts of the news, weather, and sports.

Sears profited from his relationship with the "blind genius," as Atlantic called Charles, a few years later when the singer performed at a two-day concert festival promoted by Daddy Sears at Georgia Tech's Herndon Stadium. The crafty deejay recorded Charles's performance — with a single microphone — and sent the tape to Atlantic. The record company made an album from Sears's recording and paid him royalties that put his twins through college.

Daddy Sears made a big impression on Ray Charles, but an equally legendary woman performer made her own impression, a black-and-blue one, on the deejay very early in her career. Sears was emceeing a gospel show in Atlanta featuring "The Man with the Million-Dollar Voice," the Reverend C. L. Franklin, a powerful Detroit minister guaranteed to pack the house. The righteous reverend brought his little girl with him, and he asked the deejay please to make sure and introduce her. The minister said his daughter, who was about five years old, was the world's youngest gospel singer, but she would not be performing that night. All of the acts were on the stage and Sears introduced them, but he forgot about the reverend's daughter. So she took it upon herself to walk up to the deejay and kick him in the shins. At that point, he remembered to show R-E-S-P-E-C-T to little Aretha Franklin. He introduced her.

She took a bow, walked up to Sears, kicked him again, and sat down.

Like many deejays who saw talented performers falter and their careers wither and die because of poor management, Sears was unable to resist the opportunity to try his hand at managing a performer when one fell into his lap, or at least when one put a ladder against his house. Chuck Willis was a nineteen-year-old house painter who impressed Sears by singing soulfully while applying a fresh coat to the deejay's house. Sears raved about the kid one day to Danny Kessler, a producer for the Okeh rhythm-and-blues label of Columbia Records, so Kessler went to Sears's house to see Willis. The producer signed the singer to a contract. Willis proved to be a national hit-maker, a singer, songwriter, and producer who was one of the first blacks to be invited to perform on *American Bandstand*.

Sears also helped Willis get his own television show in Atlanta. The deejay wrote the shows, and Willis performed. Willis was with Okeh from 1951 to 1955 then moved to the Atlantic label, at which time he left Sears's management. Willis wrote "Oh, What a Dream" at Atlantic for Ruth Brown, and Patti Page covered it for a hit. His 1957 rendition of Ma Rainey's "C.C. Rider" was a national hit, and when the dance fad "The Stroll" became popular in late 1957, Willis became known as the "King of the Stroll." He was also dubbed the "Sheik of the Shake" after he began doing the dance wearing a turban. Two more songs, "What Am I Living For?" and "Hang Up My Rock-and-Roll Shoes," were released together and were climbing the charts when Willis was killed in April of 1958 in a car crash in Atlanta.

Sears left the state-owned WGST radio station in 1954 when there was another wave of racist complaints about his music selection. His friend Bill Lowery said Sears dodged racial epithets most of his career. "He was threatened a number of times by the KKK. I remember we would get phone calls late at night. My secretary at WGST answered the phones for Z, and she said that many times there were challenges for him to step outside because somebody wanted to blow him away. He was a pioneer for black music in this part of the country, and he was a friend to the top echelon in the music business in those days. He worked on me to play black artists like Fats Domino, but I was afraid my listeners wouldn't like that kind of music. It was mostly young kids who were diggin' it then. Some guys played Pat Boone covers of black songs to appeal to that audience, but Zenas would not play covers. I didn't really get involved in that kind of music until Elvis came along, and I took flak for playing him. I'd get terrible phone calls for playing Elvis," Lowery says.

When his black music got him in trouble at WGST, Sears left, joining former WGST ad salesman Stan Raymond at his original Atlanta radio home, WATL. Under an agreement with management there, Sears and Raymond ran the station under a new name, WAOK, with all-black programming. At the time, Atlanta was only 35 percent black, and many predicted that the two new station executives would never make a go of it. But Raymond was a canny businessman and Sears knew radio programming. He had also become a champion in the black community, and wherever he went his audience followed. At WAOK, Sears played a mix of gospel and rhythm-and-blues, featuring tunes such as Joe Turner's "Shake, Rattle, and Roll" and "Sweet 16." The station's owner, James Woodruff, one of the many wealthy heirs to the founder of the Coca-Cola Company, found it socially embarrassing to be associated with the black programming on his station, so he sold it to Raymond and Sears for only one thousand dollars down. That was in 1956; by 1963, they had paid off the $500,000 purchase price with their profits from the station. Sears did not mind living well. He bought himself a Mercedes coupe and kept a flower in a crystal vase on the dashboard, but he was also loyal to the black listeners who kept his station on the air.

"Zenas was not your typical radio jock. He was an intellectual, and he was much more community-minded than business-minded," says Raymond, who noted that he and his partner often clashed because of Sears's liberal tendencies.

When Raymond would rail about certain deejays, particularly Pat "Alley Pat" Patrick repeatedly reporting late for work, Sears would side with the deejays. He was adamantly pro-union and sided with his employees against his partner when they wanted to unionize. "I'd say, 'Look, Z, you're not talent anymore, you're management,' but we finally ended up with a union," Raymond recalls.

In the mid-sixties, when civil rights demonstrations tore up much of North and South, Atlanta remained relatively calm. Many have credited WAOK and Zenas Sears with helping to ease tensions by keeping the lines of communication open between black and white leaders. "When the movement started, we devoted ourselves to it even though it was very controversial," Sears said in a 1979 interview. In the early 1960s, there was an Operation Breadbasket boycott of the Atlanta Coca-Cola Bottling Company because blacks felt they were not being promoted fairly. "It wasn't mentioned anywhere in the press in Atlanta except on WAOK," Sears said. "Coke took its ads away for a while, but when it was over, they came back doubly strong."

Raymond also remembers his former partner as a scrupulously honest man, who didn't take payola—at least in its most blatant forms—but who tried to make sure that those who did take it accepted only their share. Raymond and Sears owned several radio stations during the years of their partnership, but their efforts to buy a station in Orlando, Florida, were thwarted because Sears had once admitted to the Federal Communications Commission that he had taken payola as a deejay. Raymond was furious, not that Sears had taken payola, which few in the business considered a crime, but that he had been so stupid as to admit it.

His anger dissipated, however, when Sears told him what he had confessed. He had discovered that the top disc jockeys at their Atlanta station were getting regular monthly payments from record companies to play their records. He knew that the deejays still played only what they wanted to play, so he didn't mind the payments so much. It was the fact that not all of the deejays were getting them that bothered him. Daddy Sears corrected the situation by instructing the record companies to send all of their payola money to him so that he could make sure it was fairly and evenly distributed. "I don't think he took a nickel of it for himself," says Raymond, who is now a radio and television station broker with offices in Atlanta and Florida.

Sears's son Chuck recalls that his father regarded the entire payola controversy as something of a joke. "The only payola in our house was the salad bowl we got from RCA every year at Christmas. They weren't very nice salad bowls at that," he says.

Daddy Sears had a fling at the big-time market shortly after he became a partner in WAOK in Atlanta. In early 1954, radio station WNJR in Newark, New Jersey, just outside of New York City, went after a market neglected by the big network stations in Manhattan and began programming nineteen hours of all-black music: rhythm-and-blues and gospel. Zenas Sears in Atlanta, Alan Freed in Cleveland, and Hunter Hancock of Los Angeles—three of the best-known white deejays playing black music—were paid to tape shows for the Newark station for rebroadcast to the New York audience. Around this time Zenas also began emceeing five or six shows a year at the Apollo Theater in Harlem, where he managed to win over his audiences even though many were shocked at first to see the puny white guy behind that big voice. And it was certainly a big voice.

Chuck, his oldest son, recalls that his father's voice commanded attention although those outside the family often wondered where the sound came from. Certainly not from that little fellow with the thick glasses and bald head? Chuck says, "He was slightly built, not very impressive to look at, but when he said something in that voice, it sounded like it had the authority of three well-known gods behind it. It made him a hard man to intimidate. If he turned on that voice, he could make you feel inadequate to breath the same air as him." There were efforts to intimidate Zenas Sears, particularly during the civil rights movement when he and his station took stands that were not shared by the racist segments of society. Sears's sons felt some of it in school, where they had to endure hoots of "son of a nigger-lover" and other razzing from a small group of schoolmates. "It was only a few, I think in part because it was hard to hate and holler like that, then go home and listen to James Brown," Chuck Sears says.

The deejay's son recalls a more frightening encounter with racism that his father braved in the early 1960s, when the Ku Klux Klan in full white-robed regalia assembled across the street from the radio station and burned crosses one summer night. Chuck, then a teenager working part-time at his father's station, remembers running to his father to tell him about it, only to be admonished to ignore the entire assemblage: "He said, 'Don't give them any credit by recognizing them. They'll go away.' And that is what happened." The son also remembers receiving his own lesson in racial understanding whenever he slipped up around the house and referred to blacks in stereotypes. Chuck says, "If I didn't like a kid on the football team who was black, for example, and I would say something like, 'They always act like they're better athletes,' my father would push through the words, asking me who 'they' were. He didn't believe in judging an entire race by the actions of an individual."

The deejay did have his pragmatic side. When his son's Northside High School was about to be integrated and it appeared there might be trouble at the school, Sears transferred the boy to a private school. He apologized but explained that he was concerned for Chuck's safety. When it turned out there were no problems at Northside, the deejay told his son he could return the next school year. "He said I could have gone sooner, but the private school had collected the year's tuition in advance, and they didn't give refunds. He seemed to feel pretty guilty about the whole thing," Chuck remembers.

Sears was inducted into the Georgia Music Hall of Fame and had an award for black broadcasters dedicated in his name before he died of respiratory failure in 1988, following a series of strokes. The Yankee who ran a black radio station endured catcalls of "nigger lover" most of his life, but he was greatly respected for his strong-willed support of blacks and their music. Unlike most deejays, Sears was an intellectual committed to racial equality because of his strong moral beliefs, not because blacks bought the records and products he pitched.

"There was no phoniness about Zenas. A lot of people are liberals in name, but he was truly interested in the welfare of the black community. He was involved in the black community," says Stan Raymond.

WLAC in Nashville and WAOK in Atlanta were the big outlets for rhythm-and-blues in the South, but Memphis was home to many of the musicians who played it. WDIA, a low-power but high-profile station there, was the first in the country to feature all-black programming. Most of the deejays at WDIA were black, but one of the first, Dewey Phillips, was a white man who played rhythm-and-blues for his primarily black audience in the late forties and early fifties. Phillips was there at what many consider the formative moment of rock-'n'-roll when black rhythm-and-blues met up with white rockabilly in the form of a young Memphis hepcat named Elvis Presley.

Former station engineer Sam Phillips, no relation to Dewey, had worked at WLAC and in Memphis at WREC in the mid-1940s, but he found himself drawn more to the small recording studio he had built in a former radiator shop. He recorded whatever people would pay him to record — speeches, weddings, funerals. But his primary interest in opening up the side business was to record the black music he had grown up with on a small Alabama farm at a bend in the Tennessee River. Black performers were practically lining up in the streets to be recorded, and Phillips was glad to oblige even though his association with "niggers" brought racial taunts from white coworkers at the radio station. While still working at the radio station in early 1951, he recorded nineteen-year-old Ike Turner, a one-time teenage deejay at WROX in Clarksdale, Mississippi.

Turner and his band, with Jackie Brenston singing, produced "Rocket 88," which many regard as the earliest rock-'n'-roll record. It had a driving beat, a hot sax, and a raunchy fuzz guitar sound that Ike had created accidentally when his amplifier fell off the top of the car when a trooper stopped them en route to the studio.

Sam Phillips didn't have a distribution system for his records, so he sent "Rocket '88" to Chess Records in Chicago; they had great success with it. The sound captivated hip young people around the country and inspired a young deejay at WPWA in Chester, Pennsylvania, Bill Haley, to add the song to the play list of his rockabilly band, the Saddlemen. They even recorded it on a Philadelphia label, but Haley's first "cover" of a rhythm-and-blues song went nowhere. He would do better later. Meanwhile, Sam Phillips, who had once been a deejay himself in Muscle Shoals, Alabama, quit the Memphis radio station in June of 1951 and began recording full-time at his Sun studio. He recorded black artists almost exclusively, including Rufus Thomas, another WDIA deejay, who gave Phillips his first hit song, "Bear Cat."

Later in his career, Thomas would become disenchanted with Sun's founder and record for the Satellite label. He and his daughter Carla, then a senior at Hamilton High in Memphis, cut a duet that would become recognized as one of the first "Memphis soul" hits. Released in 1960, "'Cause I Love You" was guaranteed airplay on WLAC when the record company cannily gave John R. publishing credit and thus a financial stake in the record's success. He played it religiously, Atlantic Records picked up rights to distribute it, and doors were opened for the father and daughter that might never have been unlocked otherwise. Rufus Thomas, like most black performers, has taken his licks from white men in his business, and he calls few of them true friends. But he counted John R. as a friend, and he too performed at his benefit. He says, "As far as I know, there were only three, maybe four, white deejays who were loyal to black musicians. Dewey Phillips, who was the best white deejay in

Memphis was one, then, in Nashville, John R., Hoss Allen, and Gene Nobles."

Rufus Thomas split with Sam Phillips when the record producer began concentrating on white musicians to the exclusion of the blacks who had given him his first successes. Phillips had always been a dedicated nonconformist, and when the big record companies began moving in and signing black artists after they had a hit on his label, he redirected his talent search. He was still looking for that elusive "different" sound of soulful blues, but now he was looking for it from white performers around Memphis.

Phillips decided the key to success for his small studio would be to find, as he often said during that period, "a white man who had the Negro sound and the Negro feel" to his music. He found that man in Elvis Presley, who wore Royal Crown Pomade hair grease and bought his clothes at Lanskey's Men's Clothing Store. Phillips got Elvis's sound on a dub and went looking for a deejay to play it.

In Memphis, he went to Dewey Phillips, who was not kin but was a kindred spirit. Dewey Phillips began playing rhythm-and-blues on Memphis's WHBG in 1950. He built up a strong following among not just blacks but whites as well. When Elvis came up with a version of "That's All Right" that gave Sam Phillips goose bumps on July 5, 1954, the record producer got a dub of it almost immediately to Dewey, who had the *Red Hot and Blue* show that was geared toward Elvis's hipster crowd. The deejay played the dub thirty times in one night, and when the telephone lines lit up after each play, he put out the call for the singer to come into his studio for an interview. The story goes that the nervous kid had gone to Suzore's No. 2 Theater to watch a movie rather than listen to himself, even though he tuned the dial to WHBG on his parents' radio before he left so they could hear.

Vernon Presley tracked Elvis down and dragged him to the station, but he was so nervous that Dewey Phillips had to trick him into an interview. He told him to sit down and get comfortable, that the interview would begin shortly. Elvis said he didn't know anything about being interviewed. The deejay told him not to say anything dirty and asked him several questions about himself, particularly what high school he attended, since Dewey wanted everyone to know that Elvis was white. After several questions, Phillips rose and thanked Elvis for coming in. The singer was surprised. What about the interview? he asked. The deejay told him he had just done it; the microphone had been open the whole time. Elvis broke out in a cold sweat, but he had his first interview—and his first hit— under his belt.

By the time Sam Phillips had real records of the song pressed, there was a back order of five thousand copies. It eventually sold about thirty thousand and made number one on the country-and-western charts. But most deejays around the country who received a copy threw it away. Some said Elvis sounded too black. Others said he sounded too country. Dewey Phillips thought he sounded just fine, and he continued to play Elvis Presley whenever his friend Sam came around and even after Elvis moved on to a larger record company and a bigger-than-life career.

Most of the white deejays who played rhythm-and-blues in the late 1940s and early 1950s were based in the South because that's where the musicians and the audience were most plentiful. Among the first white deejays outside the South to play rhythm-and-blues was Jumpin' George Oxford of KSAN in the San Francisco and Oakland areas. He was a hambone jock who broadcast high on the frenzy scale while plugging E-Z Credit furniture stores and dropping veiled innuendos about his lust for his female listeners.

The real pioneer in playing rhythm-and-blues to large audiences on the West Coast was Hunter Hancock, a hit-making white deejay whose radio voice bordered on shrill. Hancock lacked the classic pipes of John R. or Hoss Allen, but he had a big reputation as a hit-maker. He prided himself on his ability to spot talent. His show began with the sounding of a hunt bugle. "Let's go a-huntin' with Hunter," said an announcer, "huntin' around for some of the very best popular Negro musicians, singers, and entertainers in the world. You'll hear music which runs the gamut from beepbop to ballads . . . swing to sweet . . . and bluuuuess to booogy . . . records which are the tops in popularity around the country along with some of the newer records whose popularity will be determined by you, the listeners. So now let's go huntin' with Hunter."

Between pitches for Dolphin's of Hollywood record store ("If it goes around and makes a sound, you'll find it at Dolphin's"), Champion Sparkplugs, and Robert Hall clothing stores, he played the Olympics' "Hully Gully," the Coasters' "Charlie Brown," Chuck Berry's "Almost Grown," Dinah Washington's "What a Difference a Day Makes," and other rhythm-and-blues tunes. He spun "sepia" or "race" tunes originally at sundown-sign-off station KFVD in Los Angeles in the early 1940s. Hancock claimed that he was the first deejay, white or black, in that part of the country to specialize in rhythm-and-blues.

He began with a Sundays-only show in May of 1943, playing mostly jazz, and on June 14, 1948, he began a daily show six afternoons a week. He was again playing mostly jazz, but a promoter for Modern Records suggested that he switch to rhythm-and-blues to attract more black listeners. Hancock told Arnold Shaw, author of *Honkers and Shouters*, that a black deejay named Joe Adams, who later became Ray Charles's manager, did have a daily show on the air just a few months before his, but Hancock described Adams's radio program as primarily a pop music show. Another white deejay on the L.A. late-night scene in the early fifties was Dick "Huggie Boy" Hugg, whose opening lines on KRKD were "Keep alive and listen in! All night long! Hi! *Huggie Boy Show!* All night long from Dolphin's in Hollywood!"

Hunter Hancock, however, was the biggest jock and probably the first white one to play rhythm-and-blues for the Watts residents of Los Angeles. A native Texan, Hancock began in radio at KMAC in San Antonio during World War II. Four months later, he moved to a sister station in Laredo, stayed there just three months, then headed for California and KFVD. The station changes its call letters to KPOP in about 1954 because of too many jokes about its being the station that transmitted news, music, and a social disease. Hancock knew little about black music when a big advertiser, Todd Clothes, bought an hour slot six days a week to advertise and appeal to Watts residents. The deejay got right into the swing of rhythm-and-blues, however, with his *Huntin' with Hunter* and *Harlem Matinee* shows. He staged talent contests at the Watts night-club owned by singer Johnny Otis, the Barrel House, and hosted amateur shows at the Club Alimony. He also picked up a nickname, "Old H.H.," and his own record labels: Swingin' Records and Magnum.

Hancock knew that the real audience for rhythm-and-blues was at night, so he got permission from KFVD to do another show for a nighttime station, KGFJ, in about 1952. He bounced around L.A.'s radio dial for years, working at various times for KPOP and KGBF (both were reincarnations of KFVD) and back to KGFJ with his friend Art LeBoe—another white deejay who became renowned for his broadcasts from Scrivener's Drive-in on KCLA—for an evening program until July 27, 1968. He generally refused to play white musicians on his program, and until white teens began turning to rhythm-and-blues in the early fifties, his audience was all black. When station management began dictating that he play white artists' records in 1966, Hancock decided that the fun was gone out of his job. Two years later he quit and left radio altogether. "It used to be a ball playing what you wanted to play and what people wanted to hear—saying what you wanted to say," he told Arnold Shaw.

The East Coast generally lagged behind the other regions of the country in playing rhythm-and-blues, but Phila-delphia has always been a big radio market. White Joe Niagara of WIBG's "Wibbageland" began playing rhythm-and-blues in the late 1940s. The South Philly hipster arrived at WIBG after military service in Panama and one year of bouncing around the radio dial at several of the city's other stations. Between 1947 and 1957 he had the highest ratings of any deejay in Philadelphia, and there was plenty of competition. "You hear the word from this rockin' bird!" came the call from Niagara, who had an erratic speech pattern that kept the listener on his toes. Porky Chedwick in Pittsburgh at WAMO billed himself as the "Daddio of the Raddio, a porkulatin' platter-pushin' poppa" who had "more jams than Smuckers." Chedwick claimed he had a Ph.D. in insanity from the University of Spinner Sanctum and confessed to always having a grape in his ear "to make my head ferment."

In the early days of personality deejays, there were few in the country, especially among the white deejays, who could match the trio at WLAC for their selection of hot new rhythm-and-blues records, the power of their signal, the length of their broadcast day, and their ability to pitch products. They were the three kings of early rhythm-and-blues radio. When rock-'n'-roll emerged in its earliest incarnation as rhythm-and-blues played by whites, often with a strong rockabilly influence, they wouldn't have much to do with it. They generally preferred playing black artists unless their sponsors mandated otherwise. Even thought they professed disdain for rock-'n'-roll, in truth Gene Nobles, John R., and Hoss Allen had everything to do with it. They opened the door.

They were one wild bunch, the legendary three deejay boys of WLAC. Starting in the mid- to late-1940s, these white men played black records for an audience of blacks and whites and lived like parentless children in the Music City. They had some times, particularly Gene and Hoss. Especially Hoss. Gambling, skirt-chasing, drinking. Drinking some more. And losing money just as fast as they could make it. John R. was the best known and the most beloved in part because he was on at the key time, late at night, with a voice that sounded like every listener's closest friend, black or white. And he was best known also because he took an active part in the music, promoting and managing acts and furthering its reach. In the early years at WLAC, Gene Nobles was the man to be reckoned with and, by the account of most who were present, he was the first at the station — and perhaps in the country — to give black music a big radio audience.

Although he was slightly crippled on one side from a lifelong battle with rheumatoid arthritis, Gene Nobles was a high-spirited, feisty fellow when he arrived at WLAC in 1943. Nobles worked a split-shift at the station, which enabled him to host three shows, the *Sterling Dance Hour*, the *Midnight Special*, and *Gene's Record Highlites*. He had come to WLAC from stations in Mobile, Alabama, Dalton, Georgia, and Chattanooga, Tennessee. His first radio job had been in his hometown, Hot Springs, Arkansas, where he worked free just for the experience and, he notes, would probably still be working free if he had not decided to seek more gainful employment elsewhere. He had been a carnival barker for two years with American Model Shows, which he followed each summer from Macon, Georgia, to La Crosse, Wisconsin, and back. He worked the bingo games, mostly, in those Depression years. He was known for his quick tongue and his quick hands. He could make change lightning fast, counted as a primary skill in the bingo business. It also served him well in the deejay trade, where he was known to make a fast buck given the opportunity.

In those early days, Nobles had a ten-fifteen-P.M.-to-midnight show, and in the wee hours, in response to requests from listeners, he began mixing in a little black gospel between the tunes that most deejays of the forties played — big-band sounds, such as those of Tommy Dorsey and Glenn Miller. He has no particular plan in mind, but he got so much fan mail from black listeners that he slowly began playing more and more of their music. After all, most of his advertisers made products for blacks, Royal Crown hair dressing, for one, so it made sense to play what they wanted to hear, even if a few of his white listeners complained. And they did. "But my controller answered the phone, so he got all the cussing," says Nobles.

Some of the angry calls and letters came from white parents, who had caught their teenagers listening to black music under the covers. Parents were not thrilled with their children's listening to suggestive rhythm-and-blues, the double entendres that this music inspired from the deejays, or the fact that Nobles pretended to drink Sterling Beer on the air. A local minister campaigned to have him fired because of that, but his boss, E. G. "Blackie" Blackman, who spent much of his twenty-eight-year career at WLAC defending his deejays, noted that just because a kid sees a beer sign doesn't mean the sign should be chopped down. Besides, Nobles never drank beer in the studio. He preferred Seagrams V.O. He brought a bottle of it — at least — and a few cans of Coca-Cola into work every night. Every single night. He rarely drank alone.

His most frequent drinking partner was a man known to him only by the name of "Skull." Skull ran a strip joint, the Rainbow Club, and when things were slow there, which was a good deal of the time, he would come to the studio to drink and play gin with Gene. The only interruption in their fun came when Gene had to get up and put another damn record on or do a bothersome commercial. Nobody said being a deejay in those early days had to be hard labor. Of course, there were distractions. WLAC had all sorts of distractions in the same manner that Sodom and Gomorrah had distractions.

The deejays at WLAC were celebrities in Nashville, and their celebrity reflected on the station and those who worked there. Many of the staff members — deejays, engineers, technicians, secretaries, elevator operators — were young and single, or at least they were locked into that frame of mind. In such an environment, things happen. Sometimes, they happened quite fast. This was radio, after all. As Nobles, an avid student of WLAC's sybaritic side, noted, there were no casting couches at WLAC, but there were audition rooms, one of which was equipped with a six-foot divan covered in a plush, inviting fabric. There was a large loudspeaker over the divan, and most who entered the room assumed that sound came only through the speaker, but due to the wily ways of radio technicians, this speaker could also pick up sound and broadcast it back to a limited but enthusiastic audience.

The audition room was kept locked and, according to management decree, only a select few received keys. And then a few more, and a few more, and a few more. The nearby hardware store did a thriving business in key-copying. About the only station employee without a key to the reception room was a certain receptionist, and, Nobles notes, she didn't need a key because the door was always opened for her. "As a matter of fact, someone suggested we install a revolving door for her convenience," Nobles says.

Saturday afternoons, when the management types were tucked away for the weekend, were bawdy times at WLAC. A three-hour *Hillbilly Jamboree* featured "anyone who could twang a guitar or shout through his nose." The young talent often brought around liquid courage to help them prepare for their radio debuts and generally a boyfriend or girlfriend or two as well. One thing often led to another, and that often led to the discovery of the audition room and its comfortable couch. It seemed such a cozy, private place. When word went out from the engineering booth that an "audition" was underway, the big speaker would be adjusted and the primal utterances both broadcast and recorded on a special reel suitable for private parties. Nobles often threatened to play the audition tape as background to a tune on the air, something like "John and Marsha" or "Silent George," but remarkably, in a rare show of restraint, he never did. There was so much other mischief to get involved in, he really didn't have the time.

Nobles was the station's chief prankster. When he received a detailed letter from a man and woman, both of them professional wrestlers, telling how their once-stymied sex life had been reversed by his playing of what turned out to be the first big hit of that romantic crooner Little Richard, Gene

Nobles went to the mat for them with that record. Per their directions, the deejay began playing his advance copy of the moody ballad "Long Tall Sally" seven or eight times straight at exactly the time of night requested by the pin-mates while asking that musical question "Havin' some fun tonight?"

Always an enthusiastic sportsman, Nobles especially enjoyed horse racing. Management assumed, no doubt, that the high-powered binoculars he kept in the office were merely for track use, while, in fact, the deejay used them to participate in WLAC's most renowned off-the-air programming. The unofficial slogan for the station in those early years could well have been "WLAC, Home of the 50,000-Watt Peeping Toms." At the time, WLAC was located on the tenth floor of the Third National Bank Building in downtown Nashville, directly across the street from the Noel Hotel, which, as luck would have it, happened to be nine stories high.

At night, when only the late-shift deejay and his engineer were present in the studio (ostensibly), the station management turned the lights off everywhere else on the floor and the darkness, combined with the elevated vantage point, made for some interesting views across the street. The hotel served a randy clientele that included tourists, musicians and record-business folks, and soldiers from nearby military bases and their girlfriends, dates, and casual acquaintances. It was also a not-so-secret rendezvous point for locals in lust. Nobles always felt it was amazing that there was generally more home-town talent checked into the hotel than at any of the Nashville amateur-night competitions.

The station did not pay night differential, but there were certain benefits on that shift, among them membership in the nocturnal "Bird Watcher's Society" that met each evening in a well-windowed hallway facing the hotel. The society had only a few rules. No matches could be struck because the flame might frighten their quarry into shutting the drapes. Bring your own binoculars. The founding members of the society were station employees, mostly engineers, deejays, and a few salesmen who stuck around for the show. But as word got out around town — and radio stations have no secrets — the ranks swelled with friends, friends of friends, and even visiting record promotion men, who always found WLAC a good-time place to hang out. Some research was involved. Members of the group befriended and bought off bellboys in order to learn the room-numbering system and to inspire them to phone whenever a promising couple, flushed with passion, checked in.

It was important to know the room number not only for calling attention quickly to a particular location so that all could focus their attention, but also for contacting attractive young women who checked in alone and, even more importantly, for playing pranks on philanderers and other birds of prey. The observers at the radio station would generally wait for a cheating couple to be fully engaged before ringing them up. The caller would say, "This is the bell captain downstairs. There is a man down here who says he wants to come up, and he seems quite angry. Should I let him . . .Wait! He's on his way!" Click! The mad scramble that ensued was generally good for several weeks of cackling. On one night of surveillance, a rather obese man, obviously lonely for companionship, was spied in the window of his hotel room with himself in hand. He was allowed to proceed with his self-satisfaction for a while, but then his telephone rang. "AREN'T YOU ASHAMED OF YOURSELF???" boomed the hellfire voice on the other end of the line.

It was difficult for a deejay to work, knowing that all the action was going on down the hall, but most records lasted only three minutes, providing little time for the platter-spinner to take part. Nobles overcame that handicap, however, after discovering a recording of Glen Gray's song "No Name Jive." This particular transcription ran for seven minutes, enabling the deejay to escape for quick peeks at the action whenever his fellow night-stalkers alerted him to particularly interesting viewing opportunities. All was fine then, for a time, until word got out about his tactics. Then whenever "No Name Jive" was heard on WLAC, the informed public would come racing to the station, squealing tires to a stop out front, and scrambling to the viewing deck to see what they could see. At such times, the station's hallway had a higher occupancy rate than the hotel.

The after-hours observatory was temporarily shut down at one point, after a straight-laced female employee showed up unexpectedly one night and walked into the blackened hallway unaware that there, in the darkness, were more than a dozen hotel hawks. She made it only a few feet before she tripped over a ladder, knocking two men from their perch, and nearly broke her leg. Shortly after that encounter, the station management endeavored to fix it so that the lights in the hallway could not be shut off. But station engineers are an enterprising bunch, and in a short time the nocturnal bird-watching society was back in business. Only a move of the entire station to the less strategically located Life & Casualty Building put an end to what had become one of the top attractions for WLAC employees, their friends, and visiting record-business executives from around the country.

Record-business executives and promo men were drawn to WLAC not just for the intriguing nightly views but also for what went out over the air. Nobles, the old bingo-barker, had come across a winning formula by the fall of 1946. Black listeners wrote to WLAC and told Nobles that they especially enjoyed the rhythm-and-blues records he played. Some of those records were brought to the station by students at Fisk University in Nashville. Fisk was the school of choice for the sons and daughters of the emerging black middle and upper-middle class of the South. When they came to Nashville to learn, the Fisk students brought their music, which they passed along to WLAC to be played on the radio. Nobles's deftness with double entendres also made him a favorite of college students: "I have to hurry tonight. I'm getting a little behind."

He got away with some fairly risque lines for the times, including a few twisted around commercials for Gruen (rhymes with screwin') wristwatches: "If your girlfriend is mad at you, why don't you give her a good Gruen?" He had particular fun

Hugh Jarrett (l) backed up Elvis as a Jordanaire

with commercials for White Rose Petroleum Jelly, which he advised his young listeners to keep in the glove compartments of their cars "for whatever might come up." The Federal Communications Commission got hold of a tape recording of that particular line and "it really hit the fan," Nobles recalls. "FCC attorneys asked the station to 'show cause' why the broadcast license should not be revoked. The lawyers in Washington talked to the lawyers here. The sponsors talked to the station manager. The manager talked to the sales manager. The sales manager talked to the program director. Nobody was speaking to me. Finally, the FCC voted not to take away the stations's license, the boss promised not to fire me this time, and I agreed to cut out my tongue."

Several years later, another popular WLAC deejay would get cut out of his job for taking the petroleum jelly jokes too far. Hugh "Baby" Jarrett, a former member of the Jordanaires group that backed up Eddy Arnold and Elvis Presley early in their careers, came to WLAC in 1960. He filled a vacancy created when Hoss Allen left the station for a short fling on the other side as a record promotion man for Chess Records.

Jarrett, a native of Gallatin, had grown up in the Nashville music scene. As a bass singer in high school, he performed live on the air at WLAC, where the risque Nobles was one of his early heroes. The Jordanaires sang as a studio backup group around Nashville for five years, three of them with Elvis. When he arrived at WLAC as a deejay, after taking a course under John R.'s tutelage at the Tennessee School of Broadcasting, Hugh Baby was considerably younger and hipper than the other deejays at WLAC, and he did not share their purists' passion for rhythm-and-blues. They played white "covers" only when they had to because a sponsor, like Randy's Records, was hawking a tune (since Randy's Dot Records produced Pat Boone, they had a lot of his covers to sell).

Hugh played everything that the younger kids wanted to hear, especially rock-'n'-roll. He was particularly inclined to play those artists who used his group as backup singers, a fact that was well known around town. Jarrett got around town a lot. His Hugh Baby Hops for high school and college students were immensely popular throughout the area, sometimes creating a stir because many parents were not thrilled by the sight of their young dancing wildly to the live music of black performers. But Jarrett created the biggest stir with his blue humor that, because of his hipper and younger audience, went beyond the sort of corny double entendres favored by Nobles. He felt then, and even still as he looks back, that he was merely following Gene's lead, but his chief sponsor, Randy Wood, and the station management decided that he had taken it too far.

His alleged sins on the air would be, by today's standards of shock radio, tepid stuff. But in Nashville in the early sixties, Jarrett went over the line. He pushed it with one of his standard bits, a play on the popular novelty song "The Bird." Teens would call in and request that the deejay give a "Hugh Baby Bird" to someone, or he would offer to dispatch a fifty-

Jarrett was eventually fired from WLAC for using "coarse language"

five-gallon drum of White Rose Petroleum Jelly to "all the beaches at Fort Walton Beach." Many of his young male callers would request that he send assorted and sundry things to Belmont, a local girl's school. "The kids loved it, it was a little risque, but it was real popular," recalls Jarrett.

But in August of 1963 he said something that was recorded by a listener and presented to the Federal Communications Commission's good-taste monitors. It did not meet their standards. "It was nothing more than a double entendre," says Jarrett, who is still sensitive about the matter more than twenty-five years later. "I honest-to-God don't know exactly what it was. I was using 'The Bird' thing and the White Rose Petroleum Jelly thing, but I honestly don't know exactly what it was that got me fired. It broke my heart at the time because nobody had ever warned me."

Jarrett's line, whatever it was, brought a formal letter of warning to the station from the FCC, saying that it had allowed Jarrett to use "improper and suggestive language." The federal regulators warned that if the station did not exercise tighter controls over its programming, it would stand in jeopardy of losing its license. The commission said that the reprimand would be made part of the station's file for consideration during its next license renewal hearing. That kind of warning left the station with little choice but to fire the offending deejay in order to show the FCC that the reprimand was taken seriously.

The FCC reported that Jarrett had been known for using "coarse language, some of it susceptible to double meaning" and that management had not monitored him adequately. One big WLAC sponsor of the era said that Jarrett's shows had brought protests from parents who considered him "vile and tasteless." Few stations could afford to have both the FCC and its big sponsors angry with their announcers. Hugh Baby was fired, and Hoss Allen, who decided he liked sitting in a radio studio as a deejay more than driving all over hell and back as a record promoter, came home again. Jarrett left Nashville for Atlanta, where he established himself again as a hot deejay, working several stations over the years and even today as an oldies deejay on a weekend show at radio station WSB.

Jarrett and others have pointed out that his was not the worst offense at WLAC. That credit would go, surprisingly, to gentlemanly John R. The incident occurred after he had given a long introduction to a brand-new record. When he went to play it, he couldn't get the turntable to work. In a rare lapse of technical skill, John R. neglected to shut off his own microphone when he let loose in anger. "What's wrong with this motherfucker?" he said. The "m-f word" went out over fifty-thousand watts.

The lapse did not escape the attention of the barmaids on Printer's Alley in Nashville, who began calling up the station to report what they had heard. But apparently no one from the FCC was listening because not a word was heard from the feds. When asked how the transgression slipped by his notorious twenty-four-hour tape monitor, Blackie Blackman, who is still a sly dog at eighty-two, says, "We must have had a bad engineer on that day. I think it got lost."

The same offending phrase was spoken on the air on another occasion when veteran WLAC deejay Herman Grizzard, one of the pioneers of baseball broadcasting, used it as punctuation while telling a joke to Hoss Allen. Both thought they were off the air, of course. "We still don't know how it happened," Hoss says. That slip-up did draw the attention of the FCC, which sent agents from the FBI to investigate. The agents came to Allen's home and interrogated him about the incident, which they had heard about but did not have a recording of. (Must have been that same dagblamed bad engineer, Blackie says.) When they asked Allen if he had said the offending word, he truthfully replied that he had not. "On everything that is holy," he swore that he was not the offender. And he claimed that he could not really recall if Herman had said it. The agents then went to Herman and asked him only if Hoss had used the phrase. Herman said no. For some reason, the agents neglected to ask Herman if he'd said it himself. After bouncing around for several days, the FBI dropped the matter, and Herman and Hoss escaped, as John R. had.

The deejays at WLAC generally tried to keep it clean on the air, but when it came to pushing products, they were shameless. They were hucksters for Bibles and billfolds, soul-brother and soul-sister medallions, and diet pills that would take it off or put it on. They sold enough bad razor blades to bleed the world dry. Sometimes they sold them so well, they even sold themselves. The station had an advertiser who offered one hundred razor blades for one dollar. After weeks of pitching the blades as high-quality steel at a price that could not be passed up, Nobles could no longer resist sticking his own neck out. He did what he had told his listeners to do. He wrote the station where he worked and ordered one hundred razor blades, enclosing a check for one dollar plus C.O.D. charges. When the blades arrived, he could hardly wait to shave. But after several bloody confrontations between blade, beard, and innocent neck, he went out and bought an electric razor. And like countless numbers of consumers before him, he did not bother to take advantage of the "money-back guarantee" so cheerfully offered by that damn WLAC announcer, himself.

With WLAC's powerful reach, their announcers were called upon to market all sorts of mass-produced folderol. Nobles and his coworkers pitched men's socks by the barrelful then listened to their public complain that the product was fine, except that the socks could be entered from either end. Hot-rod mufflers were another big seller: "Give your car that distinctive sound. Save on gas consumption." They sold by the thousands. But they were also illegal in many states, and it was not unusual for the WLAC studio to look like a muffler graveyard, with the angry mailbacks strewn across the floor.

Nobles also pioneered the marketing of another unusual product, one that became a standard item advertised on WLAC and by other deejays around the country who followed the Nashville station's lead: baby chickens from the Carter Hatchery in Eldorado, Illinois. The chicks were "scrub" roosters that had hatched and therefore were of no use as omelet fodder. But the hatcher didn't want to keep feeding them until they were fryer-ready. These henhouse products had been simply and cruelly drowned before someone got the idea of selling them by the boxload on WLAC: "Get one hundred baby chickens for just $1.98. Friends, raise your own fryers and broilers. Cut down on the grocery bill. Have chickens and eggs to sell to friends and neighbors. Order one hundred baby chickens, only $1.98. If any of these baby chickens die within the first thirty days after you get them, they will be replaced at one half the price. SEND NO MONEY. Send your name and address to CHICKS, care of this station."

The orders poured in from all over the United States and, according to Nobles's memory, about ten million were sold during his tenure at WLAC. In addition, Nobles recalls, out of the 100,000 orders that figure represents, he received approximately "99,999 complaints, or thereabouts." The chicks seemed to be psychic, he says, because they generally lived more than the thirty days guaranteed, often to the ripe old age of thirty-three or thirty-four days. Nobles continues, "The foolish people expected chicks that would grow into fat, juicy, edible fryers or egg-producing pullets. Instead, they usually found themselves raising, in one buyer's words, 'Bantam-like roosters that could fly like an eagle, and, in gangs of twenty-five or thirty, swoop out of trees to attack dogs, cats, and unwary human beings.'" Another chick-buyer wrote, "My one hundred baby roosters seemed to thrive for eight weeks, then die at the rate of eight or ten a day, for which I am truly grateful. They were the most frustrated, flyingest, queerest chickens I have ever owned. They were constantly pecking and spurring each other, or anybody or anything that ventured into the backyard. I was afraid to go outdoors unarmed. They were roosters that never learned how to crow, but, with no hens about, I don't imagine they had anything to crow about. PLEASE DO NOT SEND ANY CHICKENS TO REPLACE THESE."

Nobles was the first to pitch birds by the box, but the other WLAC announcers were called upon to hawk the chickens, too. John R., the smoothest pitchman on radio, might follow up a live interview with singer Percy Sledge by sliding into his baby-chick spiel, which was well-greased with black dialect to make it all the more appealing to his audience: "I wish I had some more time to talk to Percy, but we got so many things to do here, man, it's pitiful, oh yeah. Now we've got to talk about some of them chickens. Now you like fried chicken, I know, everybody does. How would you like to have fried chicken on your table just about anytime you wanted it? Now look here, baby, you can if you just listen to ol' John R. I got an offer for you that would put that fried chicken on your table in no time, the Reich Poultry Farms (out of Lancaster, Pennsylvania) will send you 110 of the finest baby chicks you ever saw for the low, low price of just $2.95 plus fifty cents handling charge plus C.O.D. charge. Now these are fine, big, husky red-top chicks, and the Reich Poultry Farm guarantees your baby chicks must be in good condition on arrival and for three months after you get them or they will replace any of your baby chicks that fail to survive for half-price. How 'bout that? Ain't that a mess? Now this low price of $2.95 per 110 baby chicks may be withdrawn at any time. Don't delay friends, get your order in the mail right now. All you have to do is write a postcard or a letter addressed to Red Top — Red Top or John R. — WLAC, Nashville, Tennessee. Remember now, they're only $2.95 for 110 baby chicks plus fifty cents handling plus C.O.D. Because of this low price, the chicks will be primarily cockrows, no sex or breed guaranteed. Send no money, just your name and address to Red Top or to me, John R., WLAC, Nashville, Tennessee. Do it right now and think about that good eating you gonna have on your table when your baby chicks become fryin' size. Lip-smackin' good there, man. Awlright, let's go with Sir Latimore Brown, he got one that's breakin' out crazy like, you know, it's gonna be a great record, I think, one called 'It's a Sad, Sad World.' Latimore, tell us about it."

John R. and the other deejays realized that in the sad, sad world they had to deal with a lot of half-cocked complaints from dissatisfied baby chick customers. One night, John R. was on the air when the local news line in the studio began ringing. Normally, neither Richbourg nor his news announcer, Don Whitehead, answered that phone at night, but this caller would not give up. The newsman made the mistake of answering it. It was a listener from Louisiana wanting to talk to John R. Whitehead told him the deejay was on the air and could not be bothered. The newsman identified himself. You'll do, said the caller, who then explained that there had been a fowl foul-up on his order of six hundred baby chicks. The chicks were supposed to be sent to his mother on her farm. The bill was supposed to come to him, at his city apartment. Instead, Mom got the bill, and he got the birds. "We aren't even allowed to have a dog in these apartments," the caller lamented, "and right now my entire hallway is full of baby chicks!"

Oh, yes, and there was music too at WLAC. Between pitches for black hair-care products and delinquent roosters, not to mention hands of gin rummy and sips on his Seagrams and Coca-Cola, Nobles played the early boogie blues recordings of Roy Milton, Amos Milburn, and others. And the black students were not the only ones who liked what they heard. One Nobles fan was a salesman for Capitol Records trying to drum up business for a struggling record store in Gallatin, a few miles outside of Nashville. The store, Randy's Records, was owned by Randy Wood, a local boy who had come home from the war with training in electrical engineering and a love for quality sound equipment.

At first Wood went into business as a radio and record player and amplifier repairman, but he discovered that there wasn't much equipment around. Instead of servicing it, he was soon building it for customers. Whenever he completed an amplifier, his customers would ask if he had any records for them to test on it. The only records he had were a few by Frankie Carle, the pianist, so after a while Wood drove into

Nashville and bought one hundred records at 15 percent off from a jukebox operation. He put them in his shop and advertised by playing them over a speaker placed outside on the street. On the first day, his customers cleaned out his entire record inventory. He took that as a hint.

Soon he was on the telephone to RCA, Capitol, and Columbia records, telling them to send him whatever records they had available. He knew he could sell records, but he wasn't so sure which ones people wanted to buy. "That's why I ended up overstocked," he recalls. A good chunk of his stock collected dust on the shelves until the Capitol salesman invited him along on a trip to Nashville in late 1946 or very early 1947 to meet the salesman's favorite deejay, Gene Nobles. Wood liked what he saw in Nobles's witty, highly charged delivery. The deejay had invented his own language, dubbed "Slamguage," and he spoke, as he was fond of noting, "from the heart of my bottom." Nobles was always engaged in a running repartee with his engineer, George Karsch, whom he called "Cohort." The engineer's responses came back in the form of a recorded Tarzan yell.

Wood immediately took a liking to the little cynic and asked him if he thought he could sell records on the air by offering them through the mail. When Nobles said he could give it a try, Wood was game except for one small problem: it cost money to advertise on the radio. "I didn't have two cents. Not even one cent," he recalls. "I was just out of the service with two babies. I had nothing. But the next thing I knew, Gene called me and said he had a spot for me. Before I could say no, I was paying five dollars a night, which I could not afford, to advertise on WLAC for Randy's Record Shop."

It was only about a thirty-second spot at first, aired around midnight on Nobles's show, which at the time consisted of a wide range of popular music, including some rhythm-and-blues. Wood is a worrier, by his own analysis, and he fretted no end over the extravagance of advertising on the radio. When he had received only one record order after five days of advertising—and twenty-five precious dollars gone forever—Wood called Nobles and told him to get that spot off the air immediately before he and his wife and two kids had to take a room in the poorhouse. "Then," Wood says, "the following Monday, my man came in from the post office with all the mail he could carry. It was all record orders off the radio spot. I called Gene and woke him up at home and said 'Put that ad back on.' And from there it was pandemonium."

Wood and Nobles became virtual partners in the business, with Randy's Records sponsoring forty-five minutes to two hours of programming in the deejay's time slot. The record-store owner and the deejay also shared responsibility for selecting the records to be played on the show. "We were a team," says Wood, now seventy-two, and a multimillionaire with recording studios and a real estate investment business in Los Angeles. "It took a while before Gene trusted me to select records for the program, but eventually I would make them up one week at a time, and when he heard something good, he would call me. It was almost a family affair."

The records they selected most often in the show's early days were rhythm-and-blues numbers. "Gene Nobles was *the* deejay pioneer in playing black music for both black and white listeners," in Wood's history book. "Believe me, he was the first, he was so far ahead of everybody else, not just in the South but everywhere in the country as far as playing rhythm-and-blues on a major station, at least in my mind. Other guys rode on his coattails and tried to take credit, but Gene was the first."

Richbourg, who is often referred to as the "Daddy of Rhythm-and-Blues," actually first began playing those records when he filled in for Nobles while he was vacationing—at the race track as usual—in 1947. With a gruff but neighborly baritone that ranks among the best broadcast voices in radio history, Richbourg established himself as a personality while filling in. One of Nobles's other record store sponsors, Ernie Young of Ernie's Record Mart in Memphis, was aware of Gene's closeness with Wood so he asked Richbourg to do for him what Nobles had done for his competitor. Richbourg did the deed.

Eventually, he commandeered the late-night spot and captured a vast listening audience. But even today many who grew up with WLAC refer to all the former deejays and even the station itself as "Randy," as in "I remember listening to Randy as I grew up." Those who did refer to Richbourg by name in writing to him had a difficult time. Hundreds of letters arrived at the station addressed to "Richard Bug" or "John Are," so after several years he shortened his name to John R. Many of his listeners after that assumed that the *R* stood for "Randy."

The third member of the ruling deejay triumvirate at WLAC, Hoss Allen, came along in 1949. Saddled with the nickname "little Hoss" by his grandfather, he played drums in a hot local combo and harbored dreams of making it in show business as a young man. He got a taste in the Air Force, where he played drums in the "Flying Varieties" USO show that toured the U.S. and the Caribbean. In 1946, Hoss returned to his studies at Vanderbilt University, which had been interrupted by military duty after only one year. He took a speech course because he thought it would be an easy mark for a guy with a fine speaking voice. He was correct. His success in speech led to acting roles in the Vanderbilt Theater production of *Othello* in his senior year and brought an offer of a scholarship to a theater in Plymouth, Massachusetts. But Allen's family was not enthusiastic about his interest in acting, and, even though he was twenty-six years old, he abided by their wishes and took his grandmother's advice to take a job with a new thousand-watt station, WIHN in Gallatin.

The station opened in August of 1948 and Allen, who had never before sat in a radio studio, just put his mouth beside the microphone and did what came naturally. Having been raised by his black nanny, Allen identified closely with blacks — in fact his downhome speech and tanned skin often led people to mistake him for a light-skinned black man — so it seemed natural to play the music of Cab Calloway and Count Basie on his afternoon radio show, *The Harlem Hop*. This show became a hit, even with the folks in Nashville, who wrote in and said they listened to him in the afternoon and Gene Nobles on WLAC at night.

Hoss was a fan of Nobles's show, too. In fact, he and a friend used it to advertise a product they had developed. The friend sold specialty items to drugstores, and he'd gotten stuck with a large number of odd-looking, wire-rimmed, round sunglasses that had cost him about ninety-eight cents apiece. At the time, Dizzy Gillespie and Charlie Parker, the bebop jazzmen, were hot, so Hoss and his pal decided to try and unload the little white elephants by marketing them as "Bop Sunglasses" on WLAC. The idea turned a tidy profit—they sold thousands of the things—and Allen realized that WLAC was the place to be. After only nine months on WIHN, he convinced the management of WLAC to hire him as part-time host of a talk show aimed at women listeners. He went from that job into full-time work in sales for three years and then into production.

All the while, Hoss served as the backup deejay for Gene Nobles, whose vacations to the horse track provided ample opportunities for his fill-in. In 1955, when Nobles took a sabbatical to the race track for a few years (only to come back later), Allen took over his show. Allen himself took a three-year leave to taste the record business from a fresh angle in promotion and talent development for Chess. He was more than happy to leave the hard road of record promotion in 1963 when WLAC invited him to return. He is still with the station even though it has switched to a primarily news-and-talk format. The Hossman does a popular gospel show.

The addition of the Hossman to the staff at WLAC set the stage for some wild times in Nashville radio. Hoss was a bit younger than Nobles and Richbourg and much more of a carouser. Nobles was a hard-drinker and a gambler, but the little carny never seemed to get drunk even though he put away a bottle of Seagrams V.O. nearly every night he was on the air. Richbourg was not known as a hard drinker in public and seemed devoted to his work at the station. He also had six children at home with his second wife, Margaret.

Hoss Allen, however, was a wild man who drank until he couldn't stand, then sat down to have some more. His behavior made for some colorful, outrageous times at the station, but eventually it caught up with him and nearly killed him. With the help of his family and friends, Hoss got a handle on his alcoholism in 1971 and now looks back on those times as his "lost years." He regrets the drinking and some of his behavior no end. But those years are also rich with legendary stories about the hellcat called Hossman.

Allen, according to WLAC news announcer Don Whitehead, was the "devil" in those years. Whitehead came to WLAC in 1968 from Tennessee State University's drama department. He was inexperienced, but he was black, and the WLAC management was anxious to have a black face (even if on a Whitehead) among all those white men with black-sounding voices. A native of Richmond, Indiana, Whitehead had grown up listening to Nobles, Richbourg, and Allen and the music they played. He was in awe when he found himself working with them, even if he was somewhat surprised to discover that they were all white. (He was not the only one. The singer Jackey Beavers recalls that he was stunned when visiting WLAC to meet Nobles, Richbourg, and Allen, all of whom he had believed to be black, and then Whitehead, who he had assumed, because of his northern accent and last name, was white.) "Those guys talked the lingo as deejays," Whitehead says, "but as a newsman I had to be serious, and I didn't have a southern accent."

Whitehead may have been surprised by the color of the WLAC deejays, but he was not disappointed in them as men. They accepted him, helped him, and befriended him. "They took me under their wings. Even though they were very powerful men, each in his own way, they were very humble in person, and they each taught me what they knew and gave me insights," says Whitehead, now fifty-two and head of his own insurance claims adjusting business in Atlanta.

John R. was Whitehead's primary tutor, as he was for hundreds of aspiring radio men, black and white. Nobles, who generally taped his shows at that point and didn't spend a lot of extra time at the station, worked mostly to indoctrinate the new guy in performing under duress. He delighted in walking by Whitehead's booth during the newscasts and slowly disappearing downward as if walking down a flight of stairs. Nobles was also notorious for taping a picture of Adolph Hitler to the seat of his pants and parading in front of announcers to crack them up on the air.

Hoss also tutored the young news announcer, although his lessons were more in the wicked ways of the world than in the broadcasting business. When Whitehead arrived at the station clean-cut and collegiate, the wise station management issued a strict order to Allen that he was not to corrupt their prize "ambassador" to the black community. Hoss accepted the challenge. At first Whitehead didn't know Hoss well enough to understand the ban on associating with such a friendly fellow. "But then I found out he was the devil, so I used to sneak out with him all the time," he remembers.

On one of their first excursions to a private gambling and juice club, the two were nearly arrested when the police raided the joint. Everybody else scrambled out doors and windows to escape arrest, but Hoss was slowed by a bum knee that had long required the use of a cane and Whitehead stuck by him. Fortunately, the raid was conducted by the liquor license watchdogs rather than the vice squad so the two WLAC employees were not publicly exposed. Whitehead would find himself standing by Hoss many times in their covert adventures together. At one point, early on, it cost the young newsman his most prized possession, his car.

Allen remembers that episode vividly: "When Don first started at the station, I used to send him out to get me a bottle of booze all the time. He was either scared to say no or just didn't realize it was not part of his job. One night, he lent me his last ten dollars to get a bottle, and then I made him go get it. While he was in the liquor store, the police towed his damn car, which he had parked illegally. Neither one of us had any money since he had already spent the last of his money to buy my bottle, so I went down with him to the lot where they had taken the car. The guy running the place recognized us from the station—he was some redneck cop—and I told him Don would lose his job if he didn't get his car back. I said it was my fault because I'd sent him out for a bottle of booze. The cop finally said 'Gimmee a drink of the booze and you can take the car.'"

The station managers eventually gave up trying to protect Whitehead from Hoss's evil influence; instead, they tried to pump him for incriminating evidence on Allen's wayward behavior. Sales manager and vice-president Blackie Blackman rode herd on the deejays by monitoring a twenty-four-hour-a-day master tape of their on-the-air performances, known as "Blackie's Bible." It was well known that Hoss's radio act increased in liveliness in direct proportion to the reduction in the Nashville gin supply, and if Blackman suspected that Hoss was deejaying under the influence, he often called Whitehead in to see if he would confirm the suspicion. But Whitehead was no stoolie. He says, "He'd play the tape for me over and over again, trying to get me to say that Hoss sounded drunk. It was like being brainwashed. I'd just say that he sounded like always to me, but he would pick at me and pick at me and pick at me. But I'd always say, 'Blackie, I just don't think he sounds drunk.' Even when I knew Hoss had been high as a bird."

In the late forties, station management took a rather "lenient" view of deejays drinking and carousing, figuring it was all part of the package, but as their roles became more important and the advertising revenue greater, the management types sought to keep them under tighter control. They tried, anyway. Hoss kept his cache of gin in a file cabinet in the deejay's lounge, and one day a station executive discovered a drawer filled with empty gin bottles. Hoss was called in. But the one thing he could do better than drink was talk. He explained that he had a friend who was making his own wine and required bottles for his product. Hoss was only collecting them and storing them in the office for him. Somehow, that explanation got him off the hook. Hoss was adept at slipping out of hand-cuffs because he had plenty of practice.

One of his closest calls came when he decided late one night to escort one of the building's more accommodating elevator girls ("No ballot box was ever so completely packed as her sweater was," according to Gene Nobles, who remembers the girl fondly) on a private tour of the radio station. With a bottle of gin under one arm and the elevator operator on the other, Hoss first took her to the station's primary love nest, the infamous audition room, but they found that it was already in use. Nine P.M. was a popular time for auditions at WLAC. The off-duty deejay and his friend next found their way to the office of the station's chief engineer.

The door closed, but a half-hour later, it was yanked open again by one frantic-looking young man out of Gallatin. It was all the normally loquacious Allen could do to manage a loud grunt in the direction of Nobles, who was on the air, and to point a finger into the chief engineer's office. Nobles threw a record on the turntable and, with Cohort fast behind, went to investigate. The office resembled a slaughterhouse in every bloody way to Nobles's eyes. The elevator girl was sprawled in an arm chair with a long, deep gash in her forehead. The chief engineer's desk and all the papers on it were soaked in blood, as was a good part of the floor. Murder, Inc., came to mind. Before Nobles could take any action, he heard his record play out and the clunk, clunk, clunk that indicated career problems if not promptly addressed. He raced back to his microphone, blurted out a commercial, and threw another record on before returning to the gory scene. Hoss had recovered enough to explain what had transpired.

He and the sweater girl had a few shots of gin and traded snappy repartee. Hoss expressed a certain fondness for her. She played hard to get. They began the traditional mating-game rite, chasing 'round the chief engineer's desk. She slipped, slammed her forehead on a sharp corner of the desk, and went down bloodied. Nobles heard the explanation between sprints to his turntable. The downed elevator girl, in the meantime, was beginning to go pale and stiffen in shock. Nobles thought she had died and rigor mortis was setting in. Visions of the homicide squad, district attorneys, grand juries, and a hangman's noose played out in his jangled brain. For a fleeting moment, he entertained thoughts of where to hide the body. Hoss was nearly as stunned as the girl on the floor. Nobles made a sprint to put on another record. When he returned, Hoss was preparing to flee in panic. Cohort suggested dropping the girl, whom he too believed was dead, down the elevator shaft to make it appear that she had died in the line of duty.

In their flabbergasted state, the three men rejected that idea, not out of compassion, but because it might mean interruption of the elevator service, which would require them to walk down ten flights of stairs to go home. The gin bottle moved from one mouth to the next. Suddenly, the girl moaned. She lived! The two deejays, who were well known around town, persuaded the lesser known control engineer to escort the victim to the hospital in a taxi. An ambulance was out of the question, they decided. Magnanimously, the deejays sprang for the taxi fare, hush money to the cab driver, and medical expenses. At Nashville City Hospital, ten stitches closed the wound, and the girl recovered. She attributed her injury to an automobile accident and, to the undying gratitude of Allen and Nobles, never threatened them with blackmail (although she might have been less of a sport had she overheard their scheming when they thought she was a corpse).

The chief engineer's office received an emergency mopping and scrubbing. The bloodied papers were burned, and the engineer was heard to remark years later that he must have left the documents in a bar somewhere. The elevator girl never again got off on the tenth floor.

Like the deejay portrayed by Clint Eastwood in *Play "Misty" For Me*, the Hossman occasionally was just too alluring for his own good. His dulcet tones so infatuated one poor South Carolina mama that she wrote regularly to him expressing her adoration. Her letters were standouts even among the hundreds that Hoss and the other jocks received each day from their fans. Hoss relished her fawning letters, until he received one in which she announced that she had tossed her husband out and put his clothes on the front porch. She was on her way to join her Hossman, she wrote. Her baby and her bags were packed, and she was headed for the bus station. Hoss was alarmed, but there was little he could do to head her off, particularly since he was scheduled for yet another operation on his damaged knee.

He was recuperating when the woman called the station. Whitehead fielded the call and got Hoss on another line. "Please don't tell her where I am," the Hossman begged. "Just get her out of town." Whitehead was on duty that night and wouldn't be getting off until after dawn. He asked John R. to drive by the bus station and sweet talk the woman after his shift, but Richbourg was too smart to get involved in this mess. "I'm a married man," he said on his way out the door. Whitehead had little choice but to handle yet another one for Hoss. He went to the bus depot after work and found the woman with six suitcases and a baby. "She was a real heavyset black woman with a mental problem," he says. Whitehead told her that Hoss sent his apologies, but he had been taken ill. He gave the woman bus fare and eating money and told her to return home and Hoss would be in touch. Whitehead says, "She got on the bus, but she kept saying she thought she had seen Hoss get off another bus. Of course, she had no idea what he looked like, or even that he was a white man." After several months, the woman quit writing, apparently resigned to the fact that the Hossman would never be exclusively hers.

Although Hoss Allen and Gene Nobles had their appreciative fans, John Richbourg was probably one of the most popular radio deejays of his era. John R. arrived at WLAC in 1942 as the news announcer for the *Esso Reporter* spots, doing four newscasts a day. Richbourg grew up in Manning, South Carolina, near Charleston, the oldest of five children. He first got into show business at eighteen while living in Chattanooga, Tennessee, where he acted in local theater. He went to New York to try acting and stuck with it for twelve years, hoping one day to land on Broadway. His first small part came in a play that opened and closed the same night in New Haven, Connecticut. Another of his early acting stints was in the play *The Trial of Mary Dugan*, once performed in a little New Jersey town in the dead of winter before an audience of three people. There was no heat in the theater, and with the cold shoulder at the box office, the actors tried to give the three in the crowd their money back, but they wanted to see the play and the show went on.

He also performed in plays by Eugene O'Neill and a few Shakespearean offerings before looking to radio as a more financially rewarding outlet. There he found more work, and over the course of two years he performed in the radio soaps, including *Our Gal Sunday*, *Lorenzo Jones*, and *Second Husband*. He also appeared as a thug in *Gangbusters* and auditioned for a role in *Mr. District Attorney*. That part went to another actor, and an actors' strike so discouraged him that he took a job in "automotive finance," or to use the more common term, as a repo man. He was shot at twice and chased with a knife—and it wasn't acting—so, in the summer of 1941, while vacationing near his hometown back in South Carolina, Richbourg went to Charleston and auditioned at radio station WMTA. He had returned to New York by the time the results were in, but he decided to take a cut in pay to try radio back home. He did news announcing and spot news reporting for about a year at WMTA before signing on at WLAC in June of 1942. He worked there as a newscaster only about a year before he went into the Navy, but he returned after a three-year stint in the Visual Aids Department and stayed for thirty-two years. When he returned from the service, Richbourg resumed his newscasting but also filled in for Nobles on his popular nightly rhythm-and-blues show. The former actor's well-trained baritone and down-home deejay manner quickly won him favor with listeners and advertisers. His name became synonymous with WLAC and rhythm-and-blues music. People everywhere were saying, "Y'all listen to John R. last night?"

He received over 250,000 pieces of mail each year, and even ten years after his retirement on August 1, 1973, WLAC was still receiving letters addressed to John R.; sometimes that is all the envelope said, "John R.," or "John R., Nashville." In the 1950s at the height of his popularity, which mirrored that of rhythm-and-blues music, as many as fifteen million people listened to his show each night. He is credited with being the first deejay to introduce dozens of performers to a national audience, among them Otis Redding, Aretha Franklin, Gladys Knight, B.B. King, Chuck Berry, Jackie Wilson, James Brown, Bo Diddley, Wilson Pickett, Joe Simon, Marvin Gaye, Ike and Tina Turner, Little Richard, and Joe Tex.

John R. also helped many a young deejay get started, including a rough kid from Brooklyn, Bob Smith, who would later jack up the John R. gravel tones a few notches and become Wolfman Jack. Smith, like many of John R.'s apprentices, just showed up one day unannounced at the station to meet him. Richbourg, though not comfortable with a crowd of fans, never seemed to mind if kids like this showed up alone or in pairs. For several years, John R. and Hoss Allen taught classes at a school owned by Nashville country disc jockey Jud Collins of WSM. His Tennessee School of Broadcasting catered primarily to ex-servicemen educating themselves on the G.I. Bill. Collins taught the day classes, and John R. and Hoss had the night shifts whenever they weren't doing the real thing. Because the school did not allow blacks, John R. and Hoss rented a little office space and did private tutoring in broadcasting for them.

When WLAC brought on Don Whitehead as its first black news announcer in 1968, all of the deejays worked with him, but because John R. was the one who spent the most time at the station, Whitehead learned the most from him. He says, "I had listened to him growing up, and if someone had told me I would be sitting next to him in the studio one day, I would never have believed it. But then I never would have believed he was a white man either. John taught me a whole lot. He did so much to help young people in his day. He was a professional. He was a living dictionary, too. He knew words and studied the dictionary no end. He tried to get me to read it and study words, but I didn't have the discipline. I spent a lot of time with him and got to know him well. One on one, he would open up to you, but he shied away from crowds. He didn't like them coming up to the station in big groups, but if you came by yourself, he could deal with that. He loved people, but crowds weren't his cup of tea."

While Nobles taped most of his shows and rarely spent a lot of time at the station and Hoss was a blur, and in a blur, much of the time, John R. seemed to exist only at the station; the fact that he had six children at home was testimony that he obviously had a life outside the broadcast booth, but those who worked at WLAC would swear that he never seemed to leave the building. Unlike Nobles, John R. became deeply involved in the music business. He managed and promoted a few acts and for a time had his own record label. His word was good in a business where even contracts with lawyers smeared all over them cannot be trusted. He stuck by black performers as few white men ever did, shunning even Elvis because he felt he was just a chalky imitation of James Brown or Bo Diddley. He was the first white deejay to play B.B. King's 1952 debut hit, "Three O'Clock Blues."

There were many others. Joe Simon was a broke soul-singer selling fourteen records a year when he came to town and met John R., who offered to help him out with his crawling career. The result of their handshake collaboration was hits that included "Hangin' On," "The Chokin' Kind," "Drowning in the Sea of Love," "Power of Love," and "Get Down on the Floor." In 1969 Joe Simon won a Grammy, and in 1985 he still remembered John R. as the deejay who had helped him get started and kept him going. He explained his love for John R. to *Tennessean* reporter Robert K. Oermann, saying, "He was the first guy I ever met who could swing that much weight yet be so nice. I had never been to Nashville. I was just passin' through. He said, 'Well, man, I've got this label called Sound Stage 7; why don't you give me a chance with your career?' John R. introduced me to the Nashville lyrics. I've written some good songs, some hit songs, myself. But to this day, I can feel the country songs so much better."

In the late 1960s, as he was trying to get his own singing career moving, Jackey Beavers, of Cartersville, Georgia, made the pilgrimage to the door of WLAC. He quickly learned that these legendary radio men were just as accommodating in person as they were on the air. Beavers's career as a singer and songwriter included stints with Motown in Detroit, where he performed and also wrote songs for Marvin Gaye, Tammi Terrell, Junior Walker, and Joe Simon. Among his best-known songs is "Someday We'll Be Together," which sold more than five million when it was recorded by Diana Ross and the Supremes. Beavers eventually left Motown and the music business to become a minister and then a community leader in Atlanta. He has also served as executive assistant for minority affairs to Georgia Governor Joe Frank Harris. In his office beside the governor's in the Georgia State Capitol Building, Beavers, fifty-two, remembers John R. as his "personal coach."

Beavers says, "He was too good a man for the trade. When I was in that business, I was not yet saved, and you have to be almost ruthless to exist in that environment. John R. was too good a man for the record industry. He was one of the most kind-hearted fellas you have ever met. When we dropped off our first record with him, 'Lonely and Blue,' by Johnny Bristol and me, I kept sending postcards to John while driving back up to Detroit. 'I'm listening to you,' they said. Well, when we got back to Motown, he called and said, 'You don't have to hype on me. I like the record, I'll play it.'"

John R. played their records, kept playing them, and, maybe even more important, he treated them with respect and kindness. Rarely has a movement had such an unlikely champion. He was actually a shy, private man, who was much more

Gentlemanly John R. on the air

comfortable one-on-one than in a crowd. Unlike most deejays of his era, John R. was no hepcat hipster. He could play the role, to be sure. But he also projected a warmth that disarmed anyone who might otherwise catch a hint that he was a white man playing a part. John R. got into radio as a pitchman, a pro, but he stayed with it because after a time it worked its way into his heart and soul. Over time, he came to love the medium and the people who were its life's blood.

His trademark nightly opening line, delivered in a warm, understated manner—"This is John R. comin' at ya from way down south in Dixie"—was recognized throughout the country. He was proud to tell of the Chicago cab driver who picked him up on Michigan Avenue and recognized his voice as soon as he offered his destination.

John R. retired from WLAC, signing off for the last time on August 1, 1973. He quit rather than play rock-'n'-roll and pop hits as the management at WLAC wanted. "Okay, that's about all the time we have, I guess. . . . Thank you so much all you good people for calling. . . . God bless you all, you've meant so much to me, all of you, your wonderful mail, particularly in these last few weeks, it has been fantastic and I want you to know I am gonna answer as much of this mail as I can. It may take me a few weeks, but I'm gonna do it. Thank you so much. This is John R., way down south in Dixie. WLAC, Nashville, Tennessee, saying that for the last time. Good night."

He planned to devote some time to traveling in a camper and working with his J.R. Enterprises Production Company. "I'm going to miss it. I know I will," he told Nashville reporter Bill Hance. "You can't do something for thirty-two years, stop, and then forget all about it, but I'm going to try. I feel like I've just got to quit. I feel dragged out all the time and at my age, sixty-two, I need to slow down a hell of a lot," he said. At the time of his retirement, he was still broadcasting six nights a week. "The type of shows I have done are very demanding—the shouting, the commercial pitch shows. I can go home after doing my bit at night and feel like I've been plowed under. There's a lot of tension involved. You have to think so hard, push so hard, project so hard, and think of so many things that at times it really can become grueling. It's all ad lib." Then why, Hance asked, did he keep at it so long? "I guess it's the ham in me," he replied.

A dozen years later, John R. was failing badly both physically and financially. His business problems were similar to those suffered by many small record producers; the successes were greatly outmatched by the failures. "John R. was a wonderful man, but like many in this business, he got carried away with the ability to make records. He thought air time alone would make records happen, and you can't rely on that," says record mogul Randy Wood, whose success with Dot Records in the fifties was followed by a long career in the recording industry in California. At age seventy-two, he kept his hand in with Studio Masters, operated by a son, in Los Angeles. "There is no little skill involved in making a hit record, and even more divine intervention," Wood says. "It really is a miracle when a record takes off, and if you miss with one record, the money that went into it is gone. Then you make another mistake, have another bad record, and you panic, your judgment becomes hazy. John R. had some good records, but they just didn't make up for the bad ones."

John R. was also a notorious soft touch in a town in which the extended palm might be the city tree. One local musician was said to owe John R. about seventy thousand dollars. The deejay's health was failing fast as well. A heavy smoker most of his life, John R. suffered from chronic emphysema, and cancer was attacking his body on several fronts. The doctor bills for his liver medicine alone were running nine hundred dollars a month. His real treasure, that booming, incredibly rich voice, was also gone, reduced to a faltering rasp. The chamber from which it had broadcast, his powerful barrel chest, was sunken and depleted.

In 1984, Jackey Beavers received a telephone call from John R.'s wife, Margaret. She was weeping. She said the doctors had given up on John and pushed him aside to die. Beavers said he prayed hard that night, and his music mentor survived the scare and seemed to regain some of his lost strength. That spring, the deejay was well enough to get around a little, but he came near to death again in May, this time in a bizarre accident. Just after a tremendous Sunday morning downpour of rain, he went for a drive by himself in his Ford Escort. He drove across the Sugartree Creek Bridge, noting that it appeared to have a little standing water on it.

The next thing he knew, he had the sensation that his car was floating. The tiny creek had actually swollen to a depth of more than ten feet, and John R.'s light car had been swept into its torrent. "I was calm, I didn't panic. I was staring death right in the face when the car began filling up with water. . . . But then I started hearing somebody yelling for me to get out of my car," he told reporters afterwards.

Two members of the 401st Military Police Army Reserve on their way home after a meeting had spotted Richbourg's car. One of them, Robert Ellis, dived into the water while the other, Brian Johnson, ran for a rope. In the meantime, as water crept to within six inches of the top of the car's interior, Richbourg escaped through a window and into the current. "I'm really not sure how I got out of there," he said. Ellis saw Richbourg escape and, since he was upstream, grabbed on to a tree and waited for him to float his way. Ellis grabbed the disc jockey and held him against a tree in the middle of the surging stream until help arrived about fifteen minutes later. Johnson dived into the water with a rope and fastened it to the deejay, and Richbourg was hauled to the side of the creek where an ambulance waited.

Jackey Beavers and others among Richbourg's friends believed he had twice escaped impending death, but they were concerned about him and about the medical bills that were rapidly depleting his limited savings. They began to plan a benefit for him that would bring together many of those whom John R. had rescued in his day. The music and musicians played for him one last time on that night in the Grand Ole Opry Hall. With two hundred hit records between them, the sixteen acts on hand owed him, and they knew it. The benefit show was called "The Roots of Rhythm & Rock: A Tribute to the Legendary John R.," but it was just as much a testimonial to all the jocks who played that music in the forties, fifties, and sixties at WLAC in Nashville.

The diverse musical elements that had come together to ignite the rock-'n'-roll era were represented at the tribute concert held March 26, 1985. Soul, blues, New Orleans funk, country rockabilly, flesh-pressing beach music, and, yes, Lord, take-me-to-my-maker gospel. James Brown, the Godfather of Soul, wailed like he had not wailed in years, summoning it up from the heart. B.B. King and his guitar named Lucille brought the blues over from Memphis while up from New Orleans came the Neville Brothers telling it like it is, was, and always has been. Long-haired country boy Charlie Daniels peppered the mix with some redneck rock and kick-your-can country. The Coasters, the Tams, Jackey Beavers, and Billy Scott and the Georgia Prophets packed a little something from the beach, maybe "Poison Ivy." And Bobby Jones represented the gospel truth. Brown's performance in particular astounded, ranking among the greatest in his life.

Five hours into the show, just after midnight, following a blues guitar duet by B.B. King and Charlie Daniels, in which the country-rock star showed that he knew a bit about the soulful blues, B.B. brought it home. "So many great artists have been out here on this stage tonight," he said, giving a thumbs-up sign with both hands. "This little song will speak for most of us — in fact, all of us," he said. The first few words of the song, offered in a gentle, bluesy style were, "Somebody really loves you. Guess who?" By the time King finished the first chorus, he was joined on stage by fellow bluesman Rufus Thomas, who stepped in and said, "Give me some of that, B.B." The old Bear Cat sang the same lines and then passed them on to his daughter Carla. She in turn was joined one at a time by all those who had performed that night — a sort of living history of the birthing of rock-'n'-roll.

In his wheelchair John R. was pushed onto the stage for that final song. Margaret Richbourg recalls that it seemed like everyone onstage and in the audience wept. John R., who by that point had difficulty even speaking, told her that he had never realized that he had meant anything at all to them as a person.

This was not the manufactured stuff of Hollywood awards shows and celebrity love feasts. No Bob Hope hugging Brooke Shields through the plastic wrap here. Nobody, nobody, ever accused James Brown and Rufus Thomas of glad-handing to any man, especially to a white one. They were there, as were the others, because they wanted to be there, because they respected this man, because he had been there for them and their music.

Gene Nobles, the little carny with the cutting wit, had retired in 1974 and was just too crippled up and sick to make it that night; he had never been one for crowds. The Hossman was off somewhere, too, letting John R. stand alone in the spotlight.

Almost exactly a year after that benefit show, Jackey Beavers received another late-night telephone call from Margaret Richbourg summoning him to Nashville. John R. wanted to plan his funeral, and he wanted Jackey to help with the service. Beavers flew out of Atlanta at five-thirty the next morning. They spent a day together in John R.'s Nashville home, planning every detail. John R. said he wanted it to be a short and simple affair. "He was weak, but his mind was still strong," Beavers recalls. A short time later, on February 15, 1986, the voice of John R. was silenced. The funeral held the following Wednesday was a celebration of the music he had loved. Jackey Beavers sang "His Eye Is on the Sparrow," a song John R. had asked him to perform. Gospel singer Ella Washington, another of John R.'s protégés, offered "Amazing Grace" and "Because He Lives."

"John R. loved black music more than I did," says Beavers. "Some of the stuff I had to learn to like after he introduced me to it. He lived the music, and he believed in what the musicians were doing. He was too good and too honest for the record business, but I know he had to make a whole lotta points in heaven because he helped a whole lotta people down here."

THREE

Rhymers and Rappers

I stash me down to cop a nod, if I am lame I'm not to blame, the stem is hard. If I am skull orchard bound don't clip my wings no matter how I sound. If I should cop a drear before the early bright—when Gabe makes his toot— I'll chill my chat, fall out like mad with everything alroot.
> —The Lord's Prayer, according to Dr.
> Hepcat of KVET in Austin, Texas

To: Major Yuri Gagarin
*   Congratulations, I'm glad you made it. Now it's not so lonely up here.*
From: Jocko Henderson. Rocket Ship Commander. Radio station WDAS, Philadelphia, Pennsylvania, USA
> —Telegram exhibited in Hall 19 of the
> Museum of the Soviet Armed Forces
> in the Kremlin, Moscow, USSR

The nation's first black-owned radio station, WERD in Atlanta, went on the air in 1949 with the voice of Jack Gibson, who had given up plans to become a gynecologist—his father was a physician—in favor of a career in radio. He had worked previously as a gofer for popular Chicago deejay Al Benson and had also acted in radio soap operas in Chicago, particularly on *Here Comes Tomorrow*, the first authentic radio serial based on the life of a black family. The trials and tribulations of the black Redmond family were aired three times a week on WJJD, and the plots often featured attacks on prejudice, which was just dandy with the outspoken Gibson, who has never been any white man's model for a bowing-and-scraping, complacent black man.

When Gibson turned on his microphone for the first WERD broadcast forty years ago, he was winging it. The station had no real format when it went on the air. On that first day, Gibson read the black newspaper, the *Daily World*, and copycatted whatever the other Atlanta stations were doing. He was assisted by the first black married deejay duo, Dave and Mayme Bondu, "Mr. and Mrs. Swing." Dave played Mr. Milquetoast to Mayme's dominatrix. Gibson says, "He would say, 'Dear, can I play this Joe Turner record?' And she would say, 'I don't want to hear any more of that. We are gonna listen to the Drifters.'" WERD also featured a white deejay who sounded black, Johnny "Red Hot & Blue" Martin, and Herb Gershon, who was Jewish and who teamed with Gibson for the *Herb & Jack Lunch Call* at noon each day.

Later, in a well-traveled career, Gibson would make the rounds of most major radio markets in the country. He also became widely known as "Jockey Jack" during a stint in Louisville, Kentucky, because he wore jockey silks as a promotion. He later took on the moniker "Jack the Rapper" and, in 1976, began publishing a loud-and-proud trade publication with that name to encourage promotion of black deejays over their white rivals. The man who would become the defiant dean of black broadcasting and an outspoken foe of discrimination in the business learned the first of many hard lessons at WERD. Lesson one: even payola was prejudiced.

Rap, Jack: "In those days it was acceptable for record companies to pay you as a consultant. They'd give you fifty dollars a month to play their records. At tax time you'd get a W-2 form so it wasn't illegal. I remember I went to visit a New

York record company, and I got my little fifty-dollar check. Before I left, one of the guys gave me another envelope to take back to Johnny Martin in Atlanta. But the secretary forgot to lick it. Curiosity got the best of me. I opened the envelope before I got back to the hotel and discovered he had gotten a check for one hundred dollars compared to my fifty."

When he got back to Atlanta, Gibson telephoned the New York record promoters and inquired as to why he got half of what his white partner was paid. Gibson says, "The guy said, 'Jack, it's time you learned the facts of life. You are a Negro, aren't you? You play to Negro audiences and only Negroes listen to you. Johnny Martin is twice what you are because he is white and both white folks and Negroes listen to him.'"

It was that kind lesson that radicalized Jack Gibson. His experience was shared by most other black deejays, male and female, who pioneered on rhythm-and-blues and rock-'n'-roll radio in the fifties and sixties. White deejays tried to sound black. They played black music for white kids who danced black dances. Black was cool. Unless, of course, you actually happened to be black.

After World War II, there was a brief period prior to the settling in of Cold War paranoia when racial discrimination eased, due, in part, to the role of black soldiers serving in the war and the fact that the war was fought against a racist enemy. In that brief window period, blacks began finding jobs on radio even as whites abandoned their positions in that medium for the new venue television. Although blacks had long been on radio, these new roles went beyond the janitor's closet or portrayals of shufflin' Uncle Toms and screaming black mammies in radio dramas. There was a demand for black announcers by the mid- to late forties, and it was due not so much to social enlightenment as to economics. With a big dollar sign. By the latter half of the forties, advertisers began to realize that significant black buying power was out there waiting to be tapped, just as they would realize in the mid-fifties that teenagers had a lot of lawn-mowing and baby-sitting cash burning holes in their jeans.

Although author Ralph Ellison won the National Book Award in 1952 for *Invisible Man,* blacks were beginning to appear on radio in greater numbers. That year New York radio station WLIB conducted a survey of black listeners and reported a "billion-dollar" market that had been virtually ignored. Between 1940 and 1952, another survey found, the average income of black families in the U.S. had tripled. Other figures showed that employable blacks were working at a high level and that more and more were reaching upper levels in education, according to J. Fred MacDonald, author of *Don't Touch That Dial.* The radio program that Jack Gibson joined in Chicago was written by Richard Durham, who also wrote *Ebony* and the *Chicago Defender.* Durham's earlier show, *Destination Freedom,* began in 1948 and for two years offered accounts of blacks as historical and contemporary figures of note. It was, according to MacDonald, "the most consistent and prolonged protest against racial injustice by a single talent in all the popular arts."

Chicago was also home to pioneer black broadcaster Jack L. Cooper, who is widely regarded as the first disc jockey, black or white. From the early 1930s through the 1950s, Cooper and his wife Gertrude played black music and offered black-oriented programming. Mark Newman, author of *Entrepreneurs of Profits and Pride,* describes Cooper as "the first black newscaster on radio, the first black radio executive, and the first radio announcer, variety-show host, and disc jockey."

A former race-track exercise boy and professional welterweight boxer, Cooper also wrote for the *Chicago Defender* and headed the Cooper-LaMare Musical Company vaudeville troupe. He first appeared on Chicago radio at WSBC-AM with *The All-Colored Hour* variety show. An enterprising sort, Cooper bought time on as many as six radio stations in Chicago and took his salary from the advertising he sold. He broadcast anything and everything, including Chicago American Giants baseball games, comedy serials (*Horseradish and Fertilizer*), and *Search for Missing Persons,* a show credited with locating thousands of people, according to Chicago writer Chris Heim.

Cooper's music show, *Rug-Cutter's Special*, made him one of the radio's first disc jockeys, though he disdained that term. He reportedly made $185,000 a year, Heim says, from his forty hours on the air on four stations. He also worked in his advertising agency, talent shows, and community benefits. He retired from radio in 1961 and died in 1970 at the age of eighty-one.

There were about three thousand deejays on the air in the United States in 1947, and *Ebony* magazine reported that only sixteen of them were black. The magazine's survey also noted that most of these were recent hires because stations with large black audiences had begun to realize that having a black deejay on staff was good business.

Ironically, most of the black deejays took pains to enunciate carefully so that they wouldn't turn white listeners off— while at the same time white deejays were trying their best to sound black in order to appeal to their listening and buying audiences. One of the most ludicrous developments in this situation occurred in a likely location, wild and weird New Orleans.

Another Chicago resident, Vernon Winslow, went to New Orleans in the early forties to make use of his considerable education. Winslow had grown up in a household run by two college-educated parents whose color had stifled their career growth. His father was a porter, or stock boy, despite having a degree from Wilberforce University in Ohio, a school Vernon's mother had also attended. Vernon attended Lindblom High School, a predominately white school, in Chicago and, afterwards, the Chicago Art Institute, while also taking classes at the University of Chicago. In 1936, he took a position teaching art at Dillard University in New Orleans, and after a while he began writing a column for the *Louisiana Weekly* newspaper.

In order to appeal to the widest possible readership, Winslow wrote his column in the black-oriented newspaper in harsher language than he was exposed to growing up. He began studying jive in the manner of an archeologist, researching the history of terms and mastering the inflections. "I had to learn the wonderful patterns of jive," recalls Winslow, now in his late seventies. "I heard it in pool rooms and in the neighborhoods and, when I was in school, at black rap sessions I attended. It was interesting. It was fun to be a Negro, in that sense. It gave me something to put in my pocket and secretly admire, a language that we could use in two ways, a hip language that in a sense could be called a masquerade. I thought it was a very interesting but sometimes dangerous combination of identities. I used to be able to jive when out in the neighborhoods. But I can't jive anymore."

A frequent topic of his "jive-lingo" column, as he called it, was the need for black voices in New Orleans radio stations. Black businesses should have a black voice speaking for them on the radio, Winslow reasoned. His columns caused a stir locally and prompted a perhaps well-intentioned but bizarre invitation from a white-owned radio station. Winslow recalls, "They asked me to write my jive column for radio, but they wanted to have a white deejay read it. They said I could train him to read what I wrote and to sound like a black person when he read it. They liked the business of black people rhyming things, so I wrote the column under the name "Poppa Stoppa."

Although he thought the setup unusual, not to say awkward, the professorial Winslow saw it as an interesting opportunity to put black thoughts on white radio, even if they had to come out of a white mouth. Rather than stomp out in a huff, he walked through the door opened to him. That door, by the way, was at the back of the Jung Hotel, where the radio station WMJR, like most in New Orleans, was located. The Jim Crow hotel doorman quickly determined that Winslow was a light-skinned, straight-haired, smooth-talking "nigger." "Once he learned that I was a nigger, he would stop me and show me right to the back of the building and direct me through there and up to the studio in a freight elevator," Winslow says, with more amusement than scorn in his voice.

So Vernon Winslow, articulate son of two proud college graduates, became a tutor in the art of jive for a succession of young white men who broadcast under the name Poppa Stoppa. Through practice and hard work, the white deejays mastered such endearing, hip, cool phrases as "Wham, bam, thank you, ma'am" and "Look at the gold tooth, Ruth." The setup actually worked out quite well for several years, until one day when Poppa Stoppa went on a break and did not come back in time to read the script set out for him by the black man who pulled his strings. Winslow did what seemed like the natural thing. He began reading his own script on the air. Big mistake, nigger. "I said something, and when they realized I said it there was a helluva falling out," he recalls. "I was fired."

Winslow went back to teaching at Dillard and the station kept white deejays in the role of the Poppa Stoppa character he had created, even franchising the name for deejays at the chain's other stations around the country. Six months after he was Jim Crowed out of radio, Winslow received a job offer from the advertising firm that handled the Jackson Brewing Company account. Their product, Jax Beer, is one of New Orleans's most famous. The brewery was going after the black market, and they wanted to sponsor a radio show with a deejay who could pitch their product in a way that would appeal to blacks. But instead of a white man in black voice, they wanted the real jive product. Winslow says, "They gave me a flattering salary and made me an employee of the sales department of Jackson Brewing Company. They asked me to think of another name for myself, dropping the Poppa Stoppa thing completely, and I thought of the name "Doctor Daddy-O." The company and their advertising agency approved it, and from then on I was Doctor Daddy-O on the radio, and there were others — all sponsored by Jax Beer — around the South, in Mississippi and Texas, and they all worked through me."

At first Doctor Daddy-O and his *Jivin' with Jax* radio show broadcast out of the New Orleans Hotel, but Winslow had had enough of the back-door treatment. The show was moved to the legendary recording studio operated by Cosimo Matassa, who recorded just about everybody and everything that came through New Orleans in that era, including Lloyd Price, Little Richard, Fats Domino, and Ray Charles. Doctor Daddy-O would do his show each day with an audience of four or five people and a white man sitting alongside him to operate the soundboard while Winslow, as Doctor Daddy-O, played early rhythm-and-blues.

Black businessmen got behind the Doctor Daddy-O show, and Winslow's affection for bluesy jazz helped steer New Orleans musicians into new fields of rhythm-and-blues. Soon Winslow was the brown toast of New Orleans. His success inspired imitators both white and black, including Ken "Jack the Cat" Elliott, Okey-Dokey, and, of course, a long tradition of Poppa Stoppas. Winslow stayed with the program even when he went to Detroit for a brief stint as program chief for WCHB, which was trying to inject more soul into its programming. Winslow, however, found things in Detroit "a little bit rough," what with payola running rampant there. He says, "There were a few things happening that, well, there were financial relationships that you could not write down without . . . well, anyway, I left there after two years and returned to New Orleans, where today I play gospel."

Nashville may have had the most powerful rhythm-and-blues radio station in the South in WLAC, and the most widely recognized r&b deejays in Gene Nobles, John R., and Hoss Allen, and New Orleans may have had Doctor Daddy-O, but between those two cities was Memphis, with the mighty mite of early rhythm-and-blues radio, station WDIA. The country's first all-black programming station went on the air on October 25, 1948. The Memphis station had an influential deejay lineup that included at least two who would become even more renowned as performers — B.B. King and Rufus Thomas — and one "take-no-prisoners" wild-woman who was way ahead of her time, Martha Jean "The Queen" Steinberg.

Memphis was a transport hub for rural southern blacks

and whites moving north to the industrial centers of Chicago and Detroit. It was also a crossroads where black southern blues and hallelujah gospel music met white southern hillbilly sounds head-on. By 1950, radio station KWEN in West Memphis was broadcasting programs featuring Chester Burnett, known professionally as Howlin' Wolf, the great giant, physically and spiritually, of the Delta blues. Rice Miller's *King Biscuit Time,* originally hosted by urban bluesman Sonny Boy Williamson, was so successful that Miller eventually started going by the name of the program's originator. Call him Sonny Boy II.

The primary rhythm-and-blues outlet in Memphis, and perhaps the very soul of the town's black community, was radio station WDIA, the "Mother Station of the Negroes." By most accounts, it was the first radio station in the country to have all black deejays playing all black music. WDIA's deejays were powerful but only in a limited area because their station's signal was weak and until the mid-1950s the station went off the air at sunset. It was loaded with talent, however. First on the air in 1948, using a frequency formerly occupied by country-western stations, WDIA was owned by white businessmen but aimed at the black market. Its aim proved true. In just a few years, WDIA picked up a huge following and was advertising itself aggressively as covering a "Golden Market of 1,237,686 Negroes — nearly 10 percent of America's Total Negro Population."

Nat D. Williams, a Memphis high-school teacher who had hosted talent shows at the Palace Theater (Memphis's answer to New York's Apollo Theater) for many years, led WDIA's programming with his *Tan Town Jamboree* shows. He is generally considered one of the first black deejays in the South. The sophisticated Nat Dee, as Williams was known, had help from the jiving Maurice Hulbert, who had more radio personalities than Sybil.

Hulbert started each of his workdays as a somber Bible-packing preach-jay, hosting a gospel program and reading from the Good Book early in the morning. Then, by midmorning, warming his pipes up as Maurice the Mood Man with *Sweet Talkin' Time*, he directed his program to the ears of lonely housewives. Late in the day, Hulbert did another shift with the *Sepia Swing Club*, where he became "Hot Rod," with a high-torque tongue that fired off so fast it was rumored that he'd nearly put his own eye out with it one day. Hulbert, who later became the biggest deejay in Baltimore, was one of the many early rhythm-and-blues deejays to invent his own nonsensical vocabulary of a "blah-blah-doo-oblee-dah" talk.

Another of Williams's disciples was Martha Jean "The Queen" Steinberg, whose maiden name was Jones. She was — and still is — a Memphis beauty, "high yellow and long-legged," according to Jack Gibson's fond assessment. At first, the male deejays dubbed her "Miss Premium Stuff," but her regal bearing soon inspired her ascension to the throne. She married a Jewish horn player, had five children, and one day strutted her way into the radio studio. She began announcing in 1949, working alongside Nat Williams.

Willa Monroe had been the first black woman to do a homemaker show on radio. But Martha Jean was not about to settle for banging a few pots and pans around the studio. She wanted to make music. "I turned it into more music and got a night spot going. It was what it had to be: the Queen sponsored by the King of Beers, Budweiser," says Steinberg. Martha Jean took some heat because women radio announcers were expected to play in the kitchen or play gospel. She played hot stuff instead. So hot that the owners of Michigan radio station, WCHB, stole her away when they came through town en route to a convention. She left her husband and his horn in Memphis.

She became the queen mother of Detroit radio, where she rules unto this day, introducing the Motor City to blues radio in the mid-sixties with its appeal to blue-collar workers. She addressed truck drivers by name on her *Tastin' Time* show and dispatched wives to the factory gates on payday so that the grocery money didn't get spent at the liquor store on its way

Martha Jean "The Queen" Steinberg heated up her kitchen show with rhythm-and-blues

home. Today she is vice-president and general manager of radio station WQBH in Detroit and minister of her own Pentecostal International Science of the Mind Church, "The Home of Love." These days, the Queen plays gospel, and her subjects had better listen up. God hath no fury like a woman deejay named Jean the Queen. "I grew up bold," says Martha Jean. "Survival made me bolder."

One of the best known deejay-musicians in Memphis was Riley B. King, who sang jingles at WDIA for Pepticon health tonic, signing "Pepticon, Pepticon, sure is good. You can get it anywhere in your neighborhood." He also hosted that station's *Sepia Swing Club* and *Heebie Jeebies* shows as well as a Saturday midnight amateur show broadcast from the Handy Theater. King made more of a name for himself while moonlighting as a guitarist in the city's nightclub, gambling, and whorehouse district, where he was known as the "Beale Street Blues Boy." The nickname was later shortened simply to "B.B.," and his guitar got its own full name, "Lucille."

When B.B. King scored a hit with "3 O'Clock Blues," he and Lucille hied off to the chitlin' circuit to perform. His replacement proved to be another record spinner and music maker, "The World's Oldest Teenager," Rufus "Bear Cat" Thomas, of "Do the Funky Chicken" fame. Thomas was a local legend in Memphis then and is still today. He is known as the "Daddy of Memphis Soul."

Thomas was born in Casey, Mississippi, on the Tennessee line, but his family came to Memphis when he was a year old, in 1918. When he was a teenager, his history teacher at Booker T. Washington High School was Nat D. Williams, and it was Williams who served as his mentor. Rufus launched his performance career on his teacher's amateur hour. After graduating from high school, he spent his summers working tent shows and carnivals as a tap dancer, scat singer, and comedian, first with the Rabbit Foot Minstrels and later with the Harlem in Havana Troupe, a black adjunct of the all-white Royal American minstrel show.

A fun-loving, funky trickster given to capes, penguin costumes, feathers, and frills, Rufus settled down in Memphis with a wife and started his family in 1940, when he also succeeded his teacher as emcee of the amateur, show at the Palace. In 1950, Rufus arrived at WDIA, joining Williams and B.B. King. "I started at a time when black deejays weren't cool," Rufus said just a few days before his seventy-second birthday. "The black deejays were not rock-'n'-roll like the white deejays. We were rhythm-and-blues. We didn't try to sound white like they tried to sound black. We didn't need that. We were already it."

WDIA allowed the black jocks to play whatever they liked, and when Rufus started his Saturday night show, he played Frankie Laine, Vaughan Monroe, Nat King Cole. When he took over for B.B., he moved to heavier sounds, and after the station went to twenty-four hours in 1954, he hosted *Hoot 'n' Holler* from nine-thirty until eleven every night. Mostly he played the blues, but Thomas was a lively jive deejay who opened with "I'm young and loose and full of juice. I got the goose, so what's the use?" Actually, he was not all that loose. He had a wife and four kids, and to keep them in groceries and clothing Rufus worked three or more jobs for twenty-two years, overseeing eight boilers at the American Finishing Company textile bleaching plant, spinning records at WDIA, and performing wherever they'd let him up in front of an audience.

A well-browned ham, Thomas recorded his first hit, "Bear Cat," for Sam Phillips. Sam had originally opened his Memphis Recording Service to provide a studio for the many local black performers. Rufus initially recorded "Bear Cat"—an "answer" song to Big Mamma Thornton's "Hound Dog"—in 1951, and Phillips leased it and five other Thomas songs to Chess Records for distribution. Two years later, Phillips included "Bear Cat" in the first crop of records ever released on his own Sun label. It made number three on the national rhythm-and-blues charts and helped established Sun as a serious outfit. By his mid-forties, Rufus would be a rhythm-and-blues legend, teaching members of the Rolling Stones, who are among his biggest fans, how to "walk the dog."

The evolution of rhythm-and-blues into rock-'n'-roll was moved along in Memphis when black musicians such a Rufus Thomas and B.B. King jammed with white performers in defiance of segregation laws. They gathered at the town's many nightclubs, such as Sunbeams, where they learned each other's music and playing styles and, in spite of deeply ingrained racial prejudices on both sides, became friends.

"We'd learn a lot from each other, and we'd be friends," B.B. King said of those times in an interview. It was not all ebony and ivory playing in perfect harmony, of course. The cry of "Number One" on Beale Street had nothing to do with hitting the top of the record charts, or even winning a sporting title; it was the warning that went out across Handy Park when the police squad car marked with that numeral came rolling through looking to break up ominous interracial gatherings of the musicians.

Whites were also banned from entering most black nightclubs, and even when they were allowed in, it was only into special roped-off sections in the worst possible area of the club. They were not allowed to dance. But they watched. And the young whites in Memphis in the early 1950s copied the way blacks dressed and danced, mimicking their straightened hair styles and buying clothes at the shops blacks frequented, particularly Lanskey's Men's Clothing Store.

If the white cats and their kittens — as this hip crowd was known — hung around until late at night when there was as much beer on the floor as there was in the crowd, then the rules and the ropes might come down. The white kids could pour onto the dance floor with the blacks and try to prove that they too had the soul for this stuff. Young Memphis hepcats like Elvis Presley, Jerry Lee Lewis, Charlie Rich, and Carl Perkins would all sneak into these clubs, wearing their cat clothes and trying to talk in the bebop manner of the black musicians. One of their role models was Rufus Thomas, the irrepressible deejay, comedian, bluesman, he of the mutton-chop sideburns, capes, and high-heel shoes.

The problem for black performers such as Rufus Thomas was that once Elvis and his slicked-up rhythm-and-blues came around, Sam Phillips and Sun Records concentrated almost entirely on white performers, to the exclusion of blacks. Phillips has always claimed it was a move motivated by economics rather than race. There were plenty of record outlets for black musicians by that time, and Phillips, always the dedicated nonconformist, was hunting for something different. He found it, with no little success, providing early hits not only for Elvis, but also for Jerry Lee Lewis, Roy Orbison, Johnny Cash, Carl Perkins, Conway Twitty, and Charlie Rich.

Rufus Thomas understandably resented Phillips's change in attitude, particularly since he felt he had helped get Sun Records rolling with his "Bear Cat" hit. It was several years before Thomas hit the charts again, with "Soulsville U.S.A.," on a new label, Satellite, which later became Stax. Thomas was forty-six when he had a string of novelty dance hits beginning with "Walking the Dog" in 1962, followed by "The Penguin," which he often performed in full penguin costume, "The Funky Chicken," "The Breakdown," and "The Push and Pull," which was a number-one rhythm-and-blues hit in 1970.

Rufus Thomas had some funky moves, but on the radio he had nothing on the blues-playin' piano man turned deejay down in Austin, by-gawd Texas, by the name of Lavada Durst, also known, if you please, as the one and only Dr. Hepcat. This bebop jock worked as a deejay on radio station KVET from the mid-forties into the early sixties playing rhythm-and-blues and rock-'n'-roll on the white-owned station. John Connally, one of the owners and an aspiring politician who would become governor of the state, wanted a black announcer on his staff to help him appeal to black voters.

He heard Durst's lively patter over the public-address system at an Austin Black Senators semi-pro baseball game

Lavada Durst, better known as Dr. Hepcat, published his own dictionary of jock rap

and lured him to the radio microphone. Durst, probably the first black deejay in all of Texas, was renowned for his incredible East Side Austin bop talk. "They wanted me to put on a program and beam it directly to the black people. That's the way it started. They thought that I had the voice and the ability to project and I did," he remembers. He wanted to be different from the white deejays he heard on the air, so he laid the black jive on thick as Texas barbecue sauce. He picked the name Dr. Hepcat out of the cosmos. To him it sounded wise and soulful, like "you know what's happening, you're not square, you're not dead in there like a man in the casket," in the doctor's own words.

While still holding down his day job as coordinator of

athletics at the Rosewood Recreation Center, Durst would check in on the radio about ten-thirty each night, exchanging his jock strap for a jock rap: "Hey there, chappie, hello, chicks, ... it's a real gone deal, but I'm going to reel so stand by while I pad your skull." He closed the show each night with "This is Dr. Hepcat, Lavada Durst, in the cooool of the evenin' wishing you a very warm good night."

"I played rhythm-and-blues, down-home blues, upstate rhythms, T-Bone Walker. I used Duke Ellington's 'Things Ain't What They Used to Be' as a theme song and went out with blues. I played Lionel Hampton and those Duke and Peacock records, Big Mama Thornton, and Gatemouth Brown," Durst told Alan Govenar, author of *Meeting the Blues*. He played it for a tuned-in audience of blacks in Austin and surrounding black communities such as Froggy Bottom, Stick Town, Buttermilk Flats, and Sugar Hill. Although Austin didn't have that many blacks at the time, students at two local black colleges and a large but covert following among young whites — who risked being dragged off to the woodshed if Daddy caught them listening to that "nigger music" — gave Dr. Hepcat a huge audience in the region.

The white deejays in Texas weren't playing black music around Texas, at least not in the early days, but they were listening. "You could hear me on the air all over on car radios," says Durst. "A lot of university students who have gone on to be lawyers and doctors, when I meet them, say they listened to my music at night." Dr. Hepcat also promoted concerts at Austin's Dorris Miller Auditorium, bringing in Ray Charles for a $750 performing fee.

Durst was a musician as well, a Texas boogie-woogie and blues piano player. He recorded his first tune, "Hattie Green," a blues number, on Peacock. He had a spiritual song, "Let's Talk About Jesus," that he says sold a million copies, but he didn't make a dime. "It was recorded by a group of Austin singers, the Bells of Joy. I gave them that name, and they practiced over at my house. One of the fellas wouldn't say that I wrote the song because I was in the blues business and people might not like it. So I didn't get any royalty from the lyrics, anything. That's it. I don't think I've lost anything," he told Govenar. His songs came out of the black community, with their particular lifestyles, their loves, their dislikes, their differences, Durst says. In that environment, you had to sing the blues. You couldn't get a job, and the law could pick you up as a vagrant.

To assist his radio listeners in understanding his words and music, Dr. Hepcat wrote and published his own dictionary, *The Jives of Dr. Hepcat*, which has become a collector's item among folklorists and fans. This is how Dr. Hepact would describe his intentions to get a job, avoid the police, earn some money, get his hair straightened, buy some shoes, drive down the street, and sweet talk a good-looking woman: "If I had a pony to ride, I'd domino the nabbers, cop some presidents, gas my moss, and maybe get togged with some beastly ground smashers. Then I'd mellow to puff down the stroll where I'd motivate my piecechopper to latch onto a fly delosis."

Dr. Hepcat delivered his last riffs of that jive jabberwock in the early 1960s when, for personal reasons, he left radio and become assistant pastor at the Olivet Baptist Church in Austin. His sermons are jive-free. He is called "Reverend" now, but when he preaches, they listen.

Close behind Dr. Hepcat as one of the first black deejays in Texas was a man who conducted his popular rhythm-and-blues show for more than ten years without getting out of bed, usually while wearing pajamas. His name was George Prater, and he became the hottest deejay in Galveston in 1949 or thereabouts and continued that popularity until his death in 1961. Prater's radio career began after an automobile accident severed his spinal cord and paralyzed him from the neck down. During his hospital recuperation, he became deeply interested in the radio broadcasts of the local thousand-watt station KGBC. A friend, announcer Harry Martin, arranged for Prater to be brought into the station on a stretcher for a tour.

Radio stations were just beginning to recruit black

announcers, as Lavada Durst had been recruited in Austin, and before long Prater was on the air. He became so popular that the station's owners built a studio around his bed at home and put a glass front on his house so that the local black and white teenagers could see him do his nightly *Harlem Echo Show*, which featured rhythm-and-blues and, later, rock-'n'-roll. For his daytime show engineers played the records at the station, and Prater was cued for commercials and announcing duties. But for his nightly show, which ran for two hours, ending at midnight, he had an assistant, Red Mitchell, who worked with him to spin the records in his home studio. Prater eventually became a big celebrity in the coastal town and served as a leader in the black community, even though his injuries required him to take large does of painkillers. Then again, more than a few deejays of that era where under the influence of one kind of painkiller or another.

Just up from Galveston, Joltin' Joe D. Howard got his start in radio in Houston in 1953 with KNUZ doing *The Beehive* show with rhythm-and-blues. Another pair of hot black jocks in Houston were Cesta Ayers, who was the town's Doctor Daddy-O franchise, and Houston's first black jock, Lonnie Rochon, a Louisiana Cajun, who started playing rhythm-and-blues at KNUZ around 1947. Rochon shared airtime there with Spinner Sanctum Joe. Paul Berlin was the top white deejay in Houston then and still rates among the city's top, now working on the FM side at KQUE.

The Houston deejay scene was further enriched with the presence of one Gladys Hill, known as "Dizzy Lizzy." A talented blues singer, she broadcast over KYOK in the mid-fifties under that name, a franchised model shared by many women deejays, including Novella Smith who succeeded Hill. KYOK was home to another hand-me-down deejay character, Zing-Zang, her name inherited from a deejay who had worked as half of a dance team known as "Tops and Bottoms." Joltin' Joe Howard moved to Detroit in 1956 to open the first station in the country to be built from the antennae up by black owners. The station was WCHB, and Joltin' Joe was the first voice heard over its signal on November 7, 1956.

One of the hottest deejays on Detroit's WJLB was a white jock, Frantic Ernie Durham, whose wild-child style won his acceptance on both sides of color line, to the point that he emceed jazz and rhythm-and-blues concerts in the Motor City. Another big white jock in Detroit was Jack the Bell Boy (Ed McKenzie) on WJBK, who would upset a few apple carts in his "tell-all" payola exposé in *Life* magazine. A top-rated soul deejay in Detroit in the late fifties was known as the Prophet Jones, who claimed to have predicted the coming of the atom bomb when he saw a puff of white smoke escape from a chicken leg on his plate during a church social. LeRoy White, whose *Rockin' with LeRoy* on WJLB was the top-rated show in Detroit in the early fifties, was a hard-partying pioneer who packed so much clout that he packed the halls of government with his cronies. One of them, Bristoe Bryant, was a deejay whom LeRoy backed as candidate for the state senate. Bristoe won, stayed in office only one term, and from that point on called himself Senator Bristoe Bryant while on the air. LeRoy followed that success up by getting his wife elected to the state legislature.

Another deejay with a Ph.D. in boogie-woogie, William Perryman of Atlanta, became known as both "Piano Red" and "Dr. Feelgood." An albino black man with milky white skin, pink eyes, and red hair, he was one of nine children in a sharecropper's family that moved by horse and wagon in 1919 from his Henry County birthplace on a farm near Hampton, Georgia, to Atlanta. William was then only seven years old.

The centerpiece of the household in Atlanta was a piano bought by his mother, and "Red" spent a good deal of his time squabbling with his brother Rufus, who became known as "Speckled Red," over playing time at the keyboard. Speckled Red was later known as a jazz pianist, but Piano Red played what he called "rhythm and roll." Until his dying day in the summer of 1985, Piano Red claimed to be the first man to have played what others called rock-'n'-roll. There is at least one expert witness to support that claim. Bill Lowery of Lowery Music Company in Atlanta, the white-maned big daddy of the southeastern music scene, credits Piano Red with making the first rock-'n'-roll record, called "Rockin' with Red" or "Rock, Rock Rock" ("She rocks me in, she rocks me out, she knows what it's all about") on 78 rpm in 1950. It was distributed by RCA Victor. The record went gold, but it was played only on black radio stations and never made the rhythm-and-blues charts.

There are hundreds of musicians, and more than a few deejays and record producers (and no doubt some truck drivers and hairdressers) who claim to have invented rock-'n'-roll, but Piano Red deserves a spot high on the list of likely suspects, for fun, if nothing else. "He was the first one I knew to use the term on the air as a deejay," says Lowery. "In 1948, he would say on his show, 'Let's rock-'n'-roll with Red.'" In his teens, Red become a local star on the rented house party circuit that was black Atlanta's night out. Since blacks were not allowed in most of the nightclubs and hangouts in the segregated city, black home owners would clear out the furniture, pull up the rugs — if they had them — and rent the joint out for two dollars a night. Their guests would roll a piano into the front room and stoke up a fish fryer at the back door.

Admission was a dime, and for the most part the music was bluesy, slow, and seductive. It was generally too crowded to risk home demolition by playing jump music. So Red and the boys kept the mood hot 'n' nasty so that the paying customers could "just catch around each other and drag across the floor," as Red liked to put it. "When I was playing all those house parties, you didn't play nothin' but blues," he once recalled. "Those little houses were so small you had to play slow, 'cause you had such a crowd." Red remembered it as a sensual, dangerous kind of fun.

When black nightclubs did open in Atlanta, Piano Red became a hot act in town. "I don't care what kinda music ya like," he'd tell them. "I can make ya pat your foot if ya listen." He played the Royal Peacock, the Hole in the Wall, and the 81 Theater. Eventually he was invited into the homes of white Atlantans, who were not afraid to go public with their love of black music. Piano Red also played country clubs and resort gigs. In the summer of 1933, Red and Blind Willie McTell rode a train to Augusta where they cut a record for Brunswick at a local radio station. It was there that he took on the nickname Piano Red, at the urging of the record company. The name fared better than the recordings.

There was no air-conditioning in the studio, and when the Brunswick man got back to New York with the results of their efforts, he found that Georgia in the summertime was not conducive to wax recording. "It gets real hot down there in Augusta, Georgia, and they was catchin' the records on a big thick wax plate. The wax got warped and they couldn't do nothin' with it," Red said. For several years he had to augment his piano money with work as a upholsterer, but in 1950 Piano Red had a national hit on black radio stations with "Rockin' with Red" and, on the flip side, "Red's Boogie."

He made three gold records in the 1950s, including "You Got the Right String, Baby, But the Wrong Yo-Yo," but none of them made him rich. He signed away all future royalties for an upfront payment. In the fifties and sixties, he toured with a band under the name Dr. Feelgood and the Interns — sometimes with Little Richard — and worked a regular job as a deejay on WAOK, under the direction of Zenas "Daddy" Sears, who had helped him record at WGST's studios in Atlanta. Red hosted the show broadcast live from his garage studio, but under the Dr. Feelgood name. The Doctor would tell his listeners to lay their hands on the radio. "I'm working on heart attacks and strokes today," he'd say. The next day it would be cancer patients. His healing act was taken seriously by many listeners who reported that he had cured what ailed them.

Letters from Dr. Feelgood's patients filled their own mailbag. Music was the best medicine, according to this physician's reference. "It's something to think about," Red would say. "I takes music and I cures more people than all the doctors throughout the universe. If you really want to feel good, just put your hand on the radio. And if you got any babies that's not feeling good, pull 'em up close to the radio. I takes care of everybody — riding or walking or sittin' down talking."

In the 1970s, Piano Red became a fixture in the Underground Atlanta nightclub district, where he played five sets a night for ten years in Muhlenbrink's Saloon. He became even more appreciated by younger fans when the Rolling Stones made it a point to stop by and see him whenever they passed through town. In Switzerland while on a performance tour of Europe, he met the group's bass player, Bill Wyman, who had been collecting Piano Red albums since his youth.

When Underground Atlanta was shut down in the early 1980s (only to be renovated and reopened in 1989), Piano Red moved to the local club circuit where yet another generation heard him boogie with his rhythm-and-roll sound. He died of cancer at age seventy-three in 1985 and was eulogized as a bluesman who never seemed to have the blues. Unlike many of his peers, he took care of his financial responsibilities and his family, which included a son, two daughters, and an adopted son and daughter as well.

Red described his music this way: "Lots of people don't know it, but blues is really the startin' of music from people's hearts. Because I tell ya, a long time ago when people didn't have nowhere to go, 'specially the blacks, they had nowhere to go, and they worked on farms and things like that, all they did was sit around and sing. They'd have a, well, it wasn't no good guitar, but they'd start to learnin' on those things and they couldn't play nuttin' but blues. Now the reason why they bring so many of the ol' guitar players over to Europe today is not because they are so great, but those people realize from the sound and tones what those guys have in their hearts, y'know. I have a unique style. It's ... it's something that's different and it's ... it's noticeable. I have to have music with a sound and feelin' so I tell people on my personal appearances all through Germany and Holland and Belgium and all, I would tell them when they come in, I'd say I don't know how ya felt when ya came in but I know how you'll feel when you leave here. You gonna be feelin' good 'cause the Doctor is here tonight."

Not all of the early jive-talk rhythm-and-blues deejays came out of the South. Among the most notable but least coherent was Al Benson, who dominated the airwaves on black-oriented radio in Chicago in the forties and fifties. Known as "Yo' Ol' Swingmaster" and at other times heralded as the "Midnight Gambler," Benson was controversial because of his undisciplined and arrogant personality and his almost unintelligible speech. He claimed he was a man of his people although, in truth, he considered himself superior to just about everyone.

Benson's delivery, which he called "native talk" (to the embarrassment of blacks everywhere) was so thick-tongued as to make his words indecipherable, which was just as well as far as the censors at the FCC were concerned since Benson had a tendency to say things like "All yo' drivers out dere be careful with dem' automobubbles, don't want yo' to drive over no penistreans." Often, his tongue was thickened by drink. According to those who knew him, Benson was a hard drinker, and his stumbling tongue was no act. He was not the Dean Martin of radio. He really did put 'em down.

Jack Gibson, who would one day become dean of black deejays across the country with his *Jack the Rapper* trade publication, broke into radio as Benson's gofer. Mostly, Gibson says, he went for Benson's fifth of Hennessey before every show. "I used to carry his records and play them for him and get him his Hennessey. He drank a whole fifth of that stuff every show," recalls Gibson. "Back then the engineers played the records, and the announcer really only read his lines between records. Benson would fall asleep all the time during records, and, since I was eager to be an announcer, I would sit in a corner and just hope he wouldn't wake up so I could run to the microphone and

Al Benson, Chicago's notable but incoherent deejay

say something. But, you know, he woke up every time. He never would miss."

Although Benson did set him up in his first job at WJJD in Chicago, Gibson remembers him as a flamboyant star who treated most people like dirt. Gibson is not the only one to characterize Benson that way. "Al Benson was the most illiterate, uncouth ... why, he fell asleep during his own television show. You couldn't understand a thing he said most of the time," says Jerry Butler.

Butler believes Benson played the fool to a degree, but he also thinks he had a natural inclination towards loutishness. According to Butler, "He was a powerful man and a good businessman, and he was really nobody's fool, but he was arrogant because he knew he could get away with anything he wanted to do in the black community. He had so much power.

He would walk into Veejay Records, where I recorded, and tell the secretary, 'I'm Al Benson. Tell 'em I'm here.' And if she didn't get him in right away to see who he came to see, he'd threaten to have her fired."

To know Benson personally was not always to love him, apparently, but here is no denying his appeal or his success. He was voted the most popular deejay in the city in a 1948 poll by the *Chicago Tribune*. The *Defender* newspaper named him "Mayor of Bronzeville" in 1949. Benson was born in Jackson, Mississippi, in 1908; his real name was Arthur B. Leaner. He worked in minstrel shows and musicals as a child before coming to Chicago in the early 1940s. At first he worked in an eclectic array of jobs: Cook County probation officer, interviewer for the Works Progress Administration, pastor at a non-denominational church, railroad cook, and Democratic precinct captain. His radio career began with a Sunday night religious show on WGES-AM.

A ban on advertising on religious programming at the station inspired him to move first to jazz and later to urban blues and rhythm-and-blues programming. By the late 1940s, he was a dominant radio figure in Chicago, on the air ten hours a day on a number of stations including WGES, which became WVON, WAAF, WAIT, and WJJD. His voice was also carried on WWCA in Gary, Indiana, and WIMS in Michigan City. Benson's shows included *Swoon, Sway and Swing, Spinning the Shellacs,* and *Five O'Clock Jump*. Like many Chicago deejays of the era, he came on the air in quarter-hour segments, giving away free record albums and hyping advertisers such as Leo Rose Clothiers, Canadian Ace beer, and Italian Swiss Colony wine.

At the peak of his popularity in the late 1950s, he employed thirty-three assistants and, in one three-year period, earned an estimated one million dollars. His power came from his ability to sell whatever products his station advertised. Gibson recalls Benson's selling out an entire shipment of imitation fur coats, which he called "mutton lamb fur," in a matter of hours just by mentioning the product and the clothing store,

Smilin' Al's on the air. Although his audience was not as wide as that of the deejays at WLAC or, later, of Alan Freed in Cleveland and New York, Benson was just as strong an advocate of black performers, playing Muddy Waters, Bo Diddley, and Chuck Berry and refusing to put a needle on the records of the white artists who covered their tunes. As a sidelight, he also headed up a fan club for Cuban outfielder Minnie Minoso of the Chicago White Sox and led a drive in 1951 to give the baseball star an automobile. Benson also had his fans among whites. Chicago deejay Marty Faye, who was white, proclaimed that Benson "made Alan Freed look like peanuts."

While Freed was drawing national attention and earning a spot in rock-'n'-roll history for concerts that featured black performers playing to racially mixed crowds of ten to twenty thousand, Benson (who also dabbled in recording with his Parrot, Blue Lake, Crash, and Blues record labels) was promoting blues and rhythm-and-blues performances at Chicago's Regal Theater for crowds of similar and even greater size.

Benson often told the story of the time he needed to rent a large hall for a bebop concert. When he approached the management of the Chicago Civic Opera house, they told him it was too large. One of the managers offered to bet Benson a new hat that he would lose money if he rented the hall. Benson took the bet and wore the hat regularly after he grossed fourteen thousand dollars and had to turn four hundred people away from the packed hall. "He bought me a good hat, too," the announcer said.

Benson could turn on the charm when it served him, and he attributed his popularity to a common touch — administered when he was not in one of his four cars or on his strawberry farm. "It's the native talk, I guess. I talk the way the common people of my race do. They understand me. That business about 'geets' and 'walk heavy,' for instance. *Geets* means money. *To walk heavy* means to throw your shoulders back, stride in as if you owned the place, and look the man right in the eye. *Talk heavy* means to speak right up, don't be afraid; be confident. My people know what I mean."

Benson did not back down from controversy at a time when blacks were expected not to challenge the status quo. In 1956, to publicize the U.S. Supreme Court's anti-segregation ruling, he hired two men to fly over his hometown, Jackson, Mississippi, and drop five thousand copies of the U.S. Constitution "to wake up the citizens of Mississippi." Allen English, a deejay for a station in Oxford, Mississippi, responded by ordering a plane to bomb Chicago with twenty-five thousand Confederate battle flags, but Chicago's city fathers put a quick halt to the aerial attack.

During the payola panic, Benson, who was closely tied to Chess Records and the M&S Record Distributing Company, took a great deal of heat because he admitted that he had accepted thousands of dollars from record distributors. He denied, however, that it was payola, saying that the payments were for advertising in his *Musically Speaking*, a bi-monthly magazine, and his weekly "hit-sheet" of top-selling records, both of which were distributed free at local record stores. "You could shake me up and down and one way and the other, and my income wouldn't be a thousand dollars a month from all the distributors in America," Benson told the *Chicago Tribune*. Benson died at age seventy in Chicago in 1978.

Probably the most renowned black deejay of the early rock-'n'-roll era was the handsome son of Baltimore's superintendent of black schools. His name was Douglas Henderson. His father, Elmer, had a Ph.D. in education and a strong desire for his son to following in his footsteps. In 1950 or so, he sent the young man off to Tuskeegee Institute for that purpose. But the free-spirit in Douglas went astray just one year short of graduation—much to his father's initial dismay. A Baltimore deejay at WBAL named Chuck Richards was a friend of the family. His big Chrysler Imperial, diamond rings, and well-dressed wife caught Douglas Henderson's eye. One night, while Douglas was home from college on vacation, Richards invited his friend's son to the station. Douglas noticed that the heaviest thing Chuck Richards had to lift was a record.

Suddenly, being a radio deejay seemed like an inviting career choice. The next night, Chuck Richards came to the station and found young Henderson waiting. Shortly after his introduction into the business with Richards, Henderson spied an advertisement for a radio deejay in a local newspaper. With visions of big cars and pinkie rings on his mind, he applied. He thought all deejays were rich. The station with the opening was the small, daylight, one-thousand-watt station WSID in Baltimore.

Henderson got the job after some quick coaching from Richards. Then he eagerly asked what his pay would be, figuring to put a down payment on that Imperial right away. One dollar an hour, said the manager. A joke, thought Henderson, it's a joke. It wasn't. Henderson took the job anyway because he wanted to learn about radio. The superintendent back at home was not all pleased. Had they been a wealthier family, disinheritance might have been in order.

Douglas worked at the station only two hours a day, six days a week, so his total pay each Friday was twelve dollars, minus tax. To supplement that meager income, he began selling cars at a local Ford dealership. His amiable manner and gift of gab served him well, and before long he was the top salesman in the area for Ford. He was nothing if not eager to please as a car salesman, offering to drive cars over to the homes of customers to show them. His work began to pay off. By 1953, he had a nice car, a brand-new Lincoln, and his radio show had picked up a sponsor, Gunther Beer, which bought a half-hour show, raising his pay to thirty-five dollars a week.

After only about seven months at WSID, Henderson received a telephone call from the manager of radio station WHAT in Philadelphia. Bigger station, bigger town. The manager offered him fifty dollars a week. Henderson said he would gladly take $120. An enterprising young man, he also negotiated a lease for twenty dollars a month on an eighty-dollar-a-month apartment, in exchange for advertising the building on his show, and regular free meals at a local restaurant under the same arrangement. He was a charmer. Around this time, he decided to take on a radio deejay name. Douglas Henderson was just too straight-laced. He came up with Jocko. He liked the *o* sound. Inspired by the antics of Hot Rod Hulbert, who by this time had left Memphis and was tearing up the air in Baltimore, Jocko borrowed Hulbert's "gugga mooga" catchline, put a "great" in front of it, and made it a part of his lexicon. The two would continue their rivalry later in New York when Hulbert worked for wov in 1960 and issued this admonition to his listeners: "Not the flower, not the root, but the seed, sometimes called the herb. Not the imitator, but the originator, the true living legend—the Rod!"

To spice his act up further when he started in Philadelphia, Jocko, like Hulbert, began rhyming nearly everything that rolled off his tongue, whether it was callers' names, song requests, or his own introduction: "Hello, hello, this is the Jocko Show!" His smooth speaking voice and natural knack for rhyming soon made young Henderson the hottest deejay in Philly, and in no time at all he found himself the willing subject of a bidding war among stations.

After only a few months at WHAT, Henderson was offered a job by WDAS, one of the biggest, most powerful stations in town. When he told the woman who owned WSID that he had been offered two hundred dollars a week at the bigger station, the owner almost cried. It broke her heart to think that a black fellow was going to be making that kind of money in radio, Jocko thought. She came up with a counteroffer that was less than impressive. Two hundred and five dollars a week. The manager at WDAS said two-fifty, and Jocko was gone. He was on the air at WDAS for twenty years.

"Jocko had a delivery that was unlike anybody else on the air. One thousand and one deejays have copied Jocko's style over the years," says another Philadelphia deejay of that era, Dick Clark, who joined the *American Bandstand* television show in Philadelphia, where it began as a local program. Philadelphia was a big radio town in the 1950s and 1960s. Jocko Henderson and Dick Clark are two of the most famous deejays to come out of the City of Brotherly Love, but there were several others who had vast followings among both black and white teenagers. Jerry Butler was given his "Iceman" nickname by Philly's Georgie Woods, one of the biggest deejays in town — and the man Dick Clark relied upon to tell him which records were hot in the black community.

In his autobiography, *Rock, Roll & Remember*, Clark says he relied on the radio stations and the deejays around Philadelphia to keep him abreast of the music scene when he first took over *Bandstand*. He writes, "Philadelphia was a strong radio town in the late fifties; it was known as a breakout market. There were huge radio personalities, powerful stations, and the chance that if a record hit on local radio, it would get on network TV."

The deejays at WDAS included Kae Williams, Leon Fisher, and the dynamic duo of Jocko Henderson and Georgie Woods. Woods had a lot of clout in Philly, more than Jocko, and when he saw Jerry Butler perform in his cool and collected style — as opposed to the jumpers and screamers of the day — he had to come up with a nickname to describe his performing style to his radio listeners. At first it was Mr. Cool, but after one particular performance, he came up with "Iceman." The name stuck so tightly to Butler that when he ran for a seat on the Cook County Board in Chicago a few years ago, he was listed as Jerry "Iceman" Butler on the official ballot. He won.

"If you wanted a hit record in Philadelphia, Georgie Woods was the man to play it," recalls Butler. Woods, who is still on the air at WDAS, promoted shows at Philadelphia's Uptown Theater, a big stop on the chitlin' circuit, often featuring acts from Barry Gordy, Jr.'s, Motown Records. Gordy would provide the acts for free and give Woods exclusive promotion rights in exchange for Woods's playing their records on his show.

Philly seems to have had more than its share of out-standing radio deejays, black and white, including a pair of black deejays with British bearing. One of them, John Bandy, was a tall, handsome, charming fellow who spoke with an English accent and called himself "Little Lord Fauntleroy." The lord found himself a real lady in Gulf Oil heiress Roberta Pew, whom he married. He then retired from the airwaves for a mansion in Villanova, a suburb of Philadelphia. The other black Anglophile came by his accent legitimately. John Christian, known as Sir Walter, grew up in a neighborhood of Cockney immigrants and naturally spoke like his boyhood playmates. His trademark radio phrase was "alrighty deighty."

But none of the other Philadelphia deejays, black or white, had the range of Jocko's Rocket Ship. Henderson was a star of radio, television, and stage all over the East Coast, from New York to Miami and inland to St. Louis and Detroit as well, for more than twenty years. Starting in the late 1950s, he spent seven years as a commuting deejay, doing a four-to-six after-noon shown on WDAS in Philadelphia, then, after a quick meal and a catnap, jumping on the train to New York, where his radio shows were even more of a hit, first on mornings at WLB and then evenings at WADO.

When modern-day jet-set deejay Tom Joyner was named *Impact* magazine's radio personality of the year in 1989, he cited Jocko Henderson as his inspiration. Joyner commutes daily between Dallas and Chicago to do top-rated radio shows in each city, but he would be the first to admit that Jocko had the roughest road to travel.

Here is Jocko's description of his commuting career: "We were doing a four-to-seven show at WDAS and the shows at WLIB in New York was from six to nine A.M. We would leave WDAS at seven P.M. and go home and eat. Then we had to catch a milk-run train at two-twenty A.M. It took two hours and forty minutes to get to New York because it stopped everywhere. We'd leave the station and catch a cab to WLIB in the Teresa Hotel. Then we'd get off the air there at nine A.M., catch the eleven-thirty out of New York, came home, and drive out to do the four-to-seven show.

"We did that for seven months, and a fellow at WADO asked if I would do a night show in New York on his station, which had a stronger signal—it reach Bermuda—so we did that. We were on from ten until midnight for twenty years, and we kept commuting, but many times I'd miss the train. I'd see it going down the tracks, so we would have to drive to New York City. All the state troopers knew me, and they'd close their eyes and say, 'There he goes.' It was a one-and-a-half-hour drive from the train station to fifth Avenue, and we'd do it at about ninety-five miles an hour. Finally, I said this is not good, and we bought equipment to do it at the house. I taped the shows from home and would just mail them to WADO and, after they became a Spanish-language station, to WWRL. That was so easy. Even when there was snow ten feet deep, I could do my shows."

After he became a stay-at-home deejay, Jocko signed on to do even more broadcasts around the country, all in the comfort of his own rumpus-room studio. He says, "I did daily two-hour shows in Boston, New York, St. Louis, and Detroit and a three-hour daily show in Miami, in addition to my Philadelphia show. That went on for two years until one day I looked in the mirror and noticed I was beginning to look like a microphone. I decide to cool it for a while." Of course, a cooled-off Jocko was still pretty hot stuff. He also had a television show, *Jocko's Rocket Ship Show*, on WNTA out of the New Jersey-New York area. It ran for about a year.

When Jocko first started on radio in New York, a black newspaper reporter wrote that he would not cut it in such a sophisticated city: "This strange new addition to the city's radio family with his noisy clowning and strange vocabulary will soon discover that New Yorkers are more particular about what they hear on radio than the folks in Philadelphia. This Jocko fellow won't last three months." The joke was on the jerk, not Jocko, of course. It seemed that even the most particular of listeners wanted to hear the deejay out of Philadelphia. The rhymin'

Jocko Henderson hosted Broadway's first rock-'n'-roll review

rocketeer managed to hit Boston, Baltimore, Washington, Richmond, Miami, St. Louis, and Detroit as well, with his taped broadcasts individually tailored to each city.

In addition to all of his broadcast work, Jocko found time to host 107 shows at the Apollo Theater and the first rock-'n'-roll show staged on Broadway, at the Loews State. Jocko was just as big an attraction as the acts on the venue at these live shows. The Impressions first played the Apollo with the Jocko show, and lead singer Jerry Butler remembers that the deejay nearly brought down the house even before the first musical group took the stage. " Jocko was a showman. He had it all with the rhythm and rhyme and the *Rocket Ship Show*. He'd start the show with a smoke bomb going off, and he'd start a rap as he came out: 'Eeee tiddly ock, this is the Jock.' He was ahead of his time, and there was not another deejay in the country as innovative as him," Butler says.

"In my mind Jocko was the number one deejay in the

country. His presentation was so unique. Other guys rhymed, but he was very articulate and handsome. He had a flare for show business, but he was in a city where he could pull it off. In Miami or Charlotte, black guys couldn't go so far," Butler continues. "Freed and Clark got the press because they were white. Jocko was, to my mind, the most creative of any of them. Georgie Woods was immensely popular, but not as creative as Jocko. John Bandy, known as Little Lord Fauntelroy, was creative, too, but Jocko was creative both on and off the air."

Jocko was able to compete at the Apollo, which was a perfect showcase for his theatrical talents. Each of his shows began with the sound of a rocket countdown, followed by a blast. Then Jocko would swing onto the stage on a rocket suspended by wires from the ceiling. The audience would then join him in his rhyme-and-rhythm introduction: "Daddy-O and Mommy-O, this is Jocko, engineer abroad the big *Rocket Ship Show*, saying greetings, salutations, oo-pappa-doo, and how do you do? Are you ready for a big ride with your ace from out of space? Well, good deal. Button your lip, comb your knowledge box. It'll be transcribed, recorded and tops. Al, close the hatch. Passengers, fasten your seat belts. Prepare to blast! Minus six. Five. Four. Three. Two. One. Take her sky-high ... well, eee tiddle dee dock, this is the Jock and I'm back on the scene with the record machine, saying ooo-pop-a-doo and how do you do?"

Jocko was doing just fine by the mid-fifties. It took him a while, but he eventually began to live the dream life that he had envisioned when he first caught the sparks off the diamond rings on Chuck Richards's fingers. "People looked up to you, you were a celebrity," Jocko says. "You had the best of everything. A lot of guys let it go to their heads. A lot of them drank too much. I never drank much because I have a natural high. I have a ball all the time. It was just the way I was brought up. My parents were not strict, but they knew how to keep me and my brothers—who are all beautiful guys—in line." (Jocko's oldest brother, Elmer, Jr., a lawyer, once desegregated an entire railroad line by demanding to eat with the whites in the dining car. It cost him a few lumps on the head, but he did it. He later served as national legal counsel to the NAACP.)

Jocko and his father made peace shortly after the deejay's career took off and his parents realized that he had found something that gave him joy. His father died after Jocko had been at WDAS just a year, but in memory of him Jocko seeded his broadcasts and personal appearances with a message to his young listeners: stay in school and get an education. The superintendent's son has been a secret educator all of his life. He says, "The thing that kept me going was that I knew everything I said meant something. I always tried to give a positive message: stay in school, don't go near drugs. To me it was the opportunity to help some people and possibly keep them on the straight and narrow."

He used the power of his celebrityhood and his influence with entertainers to carry that message into public schools, literally, until it backfired on him one day. During a concert date in New York, he took the entire lineup of stars, including Smokey Robinson and the Miracles, into Lefferts Junior High School in Brooklyn. But before the appearance there he announced that students who had missed a specific number of class days without excuse would not be allowed to attend. The school auditorium held about twenty-two hundred, and three thousand showed up. The locked-out truants stormed the doors. "All hell broke loose, so I had to stop doing that," says Jocko, whose thrust in recent years has been *Get Ready*, an education rap program distributed on tape and in booklets through school systems and job-training programs.

Jocko also considers himself a pioneer rap-master, and he has some convincing character witnesses. In 1979, he recorded a nonsensical song, "Rocket Ship," done in his trademark rhythm-and-rhyme patter. It was picked up and distributed by Philadelphia International Records and sold 250,000 copies. The song reached number four on the charts in England. Jocko calls that record the first rap song every recorded, and Glenn Hinson, a folklorist specializing in black traditions at the

Smithsonian Institution in Washington, D.C., agrees. "The deejay and his rhymed introduction to records is one of the most easily identified influences on rap, and deejays anywhere in the country will tell you that the father of that tradition is Jocko Henderson," Hinson says. "His popularity was spread far enough that Jocko had a real impact."

Jocko's childlike joy of life made him a favorite with listeners around the country. Kids on playgrounds all over Philly and New York chanted his rhymes. His instinct for good public relations seems inborn. When Jocko's 1961 telegram to Soviet Cosmonaut Yuri Gagarin was discovered in the Soviet military museum by U.S. correspondents, the message was written up in the *New York Times* and other major publications around the world. At one point during Jocko's heyday, his New York fan club has fifty thousand members, including one pistol-packin' mamma who nearly loved Henderson to death, he says.

Jocko would move into the Apollo Theater six or seven times a year to do two weeks of shows, seven shows a day. One night, as he was resting his weary bones backstage, a doorman announced that a woman fan wished to see him. Now adoring stage-door Johannas were nothing new to Jocko, a happily married man, and he was in no mood to decline such affection graciously on this night, so he told the doorman to give his apologies. But this woman was not the typical teeny-bopper type, according to the doorman. She was a woman in her fifties. Thinking a more mature woman would probably just want to say hello then be on her way, Jocko agreed to see her.

She came in, introduced herself as Helen Hunter, and closed the door behind her before she berated the deejay for not answering her many letters and telephone messages. "She said, 'You made a mistake in not calling me,' and with that she pulled out a gun," Jocko recalls. "I said, 'Miss Hunter, you're gonna kill me for what reason?' And she said, 'Because you never called me or answered my letters. Who the hell you think you are?'" Right then, the deejay figured he was about to become the late Jocko Henderson. Miss Hunter began walking toward him with the

Henderson is considered the father of rap

gun pointed at a particularly dear region of his anatomy.

He suggested that perhaps in future correspondence she could put a star on the envelope to attract his special attention so he could answer it.

"Are you lyin' to me?" she asked.

"No," he replied, "and I'll take you out and buy you a drink right now to prove I mean it."

He escorted her down the street to a Harlem bar, bought her a glass of wine, and, after an hour or two, kissed her good-bye. He escaped without a shot being fired, and the next week her first letter with a starred envelope arrived. Jocko never failed to respond to her notes after that, and he even made it a point to drop a birthday cake off at her fifth-floor walk-up on Eighth Avenue when she dropped a hint about the date. He visited her there five or six times over several years until Miss Hunter, who was a grandmother, apparently was content that she had made her point. "I guess I could have had her arrested, but she still might have killed my ass one day," Henderson says. "I often wondered what happened to her after we lost touch, but not enough to go back."

Jocko's popularity in Harlem got him out of trouble, as well as into it, on occasion. Another night after a hard day onstage, he was walking to the nearby Teresa Hotel from the Apollo Theater at three in the morning when he noticed three very large, menacing men approaching him in a deliberate stalking pattern. Then he detected two more men coming up from behind. Muggersville, he thought. The burliest of the stalkers, five feet tall and five feet thick, walked directly up to him, stuck his face into the deejay's, drew back, slapped him on the shoulder, and let out a surprised yelp: "Jocko!" The others dropped their menacing stances, shrugged, and walked away. Henderson could hardly forget the face that had filled his vision, and later he encountered him in the theater. With plenty of protection around, he asked the powerfully built resident of Harlem, whose name was Nero, what his intentions had been that night on the street. "He said, 'Man, we were gonna mess you up,'" Jocko reports. Nero later telephoned Jocko from prison to tell him he would not be around for a while, twenty to thirty years, with time off for good behavior. "Those guys were killers," says Jocko. "And I never went out that particular stage door again."

Jocko's popularity as a deejay give him great influence with record buyers and made him a prime attraction for record promoters and companies. Jocko, like most deejays of his era, made the most of opportunities, but he was smart enough to avoid the appearance of impropriety. The singing group Lee Andrews and the Hearts came to his WDAS office one day and performed a new song they had just written, "Long Lonely Nights." Jocko thought it had potential, so he telephoned the owner of a nearby recording studio and escorted the group down there. In a matter of hours, they had a dub of the song, which Jocko packed off on the train to New York City, where he played it four straight times that night. The next morning, a local record-store owner called him in Philadelphia wanting to know where he could find copies of the song. Within three or four days, most of the East Coast was clamoring for copies. In the end, Jocko took a cut as producer, and the Hearts sang it for Chess while Atlantic covered it with Clyde McPhatter. Both records sold well, piling up royalties of four million dollars. Jocko made out all right, and nobody could call it payola.

Another valuable package dropped at Jocko's door came early, very early, one Saturday morning in the fall of 1957. It was special delivery, care of legendary promoter "Bumps" Blackwell. Blackwell had just been fired from his position with Specialty Records because his volatile boss, Art Rupe, had caught him trying to record the label's top gospel singer as a rhythm-and-blues or pop performer—a move viewed as nearly sacrilegious by gospel fans, who perceived other forms as the devil's music. Rupe fired the singer, too, and he was the package dropped at Jocko's door. His name was Sam Cooke, perhaps the greatest singer ever. Blackwell brought Cooke, whose father headed the Church of Christ Holiness Church in Chicago, to

Jocko because they had taken one of his songs to a smaller record company and made a dub. Jocko, who had come to the door with a pistol in his pajama pocket because of the hour, let them in without firing a shot and played the record.

The song, written by Cooke's brother, was "You Send Me," a masterpiece perfectly designed for the deeply romantic and expressive voice of the singer, who was so handsome that even his gospel performances in churches caused women to swoon in the pews. For the suave and charming Sam Cooke to start singing songs that were actually sexy was almost tantamount to overkill in many eyes. Women would not have a chance. "I heard it and said, 'Oh, my God, what a record!'" Jocko says. "I went upstairs right away and got a blank contract to sign them up for an appearance at the Apollo three weeks later. Then I took that record and played it on my show, and it reached number one in a week." Never before had a song reached the top of both the rhythm-and-blues and pop charts, but "You Send Me" did.

By the time Jocko's Apollo Show opened in Harlem, Sam Cooke was a national phenomenon, and the lines for tickets went around the block — twice. "It was a bonanza. I had to give him a big bonus for that because I had signed him up for scale," says Jocko. "The women loved him." Cooke died in December of 1964 in an incident that has spawned many versions but boils down to the singer's being shot to death in a three-dollar-a-night Hollywood motel where he had gone with a young model. The manager of the motel said she shot him when he came to her door threatening her because the girl had fled the room. The official explanation of Cooke's death was long viewed with suspicion in an era overripe with conspiracy theories of all types. Some claimed that the mob had done Cooke in because he would not be controlled; others said that his death was racially motivated, that such a handsome, talented black man was too big a threat to the white-dominated entertainment industry.

Rock-'n'-roll did a lot to open communication between blacks and whites, but it did not erase the suspicions. Black deejays such as Jocko harbor deeply rooted feelings that, as well as they did and as big as they were, they might have gone even further if not for racial barriers. Jocko watched Dick Clark's Philadelphia teen dance show become a nationally syndicated cultural institution, while his own show, which featured a primarily black cast, remained a local program. "The whole television and radio industry was very racist. Sponsors would not buy time, for example, on Nat King Cole's television show, even though he was so popular among whites and blacks. If I had been a little further ahead in time, things might have been different for me. If I hadn't been black, *American Bandstand* might have been mine," Jocko says.

Jocko also watched a white deejay out of Cleveland move into New York and command a huge salary and fees for his radio and concert work. That deejay was the one that the national press focused on when they wrote about the biggest radio personality in the country, the one with the greatest amount of influence. Jerry Butler knew and worked with both men, and as a black man, he sympathizes with Henderson. "One of the tragedies of that time was that he was relegated to black programming, not because he was inarticulate, but simply because he was black. He would have been bigger than most of the jocks of the era because of his flair for showmanship," Butler argues.

In some ways, Jocko Henderson was lucky that he did not succeed as much as others in New York, where his competition for black listeners was comprised of a colorful crew that included Phil "Dr. Jive" Gordon at WLIB; Jack Walker, "The Pear Shaped Talker," on WOV; Joe Bostic on WBNX; and Willie Bryant, "The Mayor of Harlem," who broadcast from a store window on 125th Street on both WHOM and WOR.

Jocko also had to take on "Dr. Jive," Tommy Smalls, a pioneering black deejay on WWRL, who opened his show with "Sit back and relax and enjoy the wax, from three-oh-five to five-three-oh, it's the Dr. Jive Show." Smalls was a popular deejay on a small radio station in Savannah, Georgia, when he was hired for the New York job.

On his way to the Big Apple, Smalls stopped by to visit Jack Gibson and Joltin' Joe Howard at WERD in Atlanta. "We never did figure out how he got the job in New York," says Howard, now with the city of Houston's Department of Parks and Recreation. "Tommy was a country boy, a smooth-looking, brown-skinned dude, who had been on the air in Savannah about five years. He was one helluva jock with a real outgoing personality, but I don't know how they ever found him down there. He stopped by to say he got the job, and he borrowed money from me and from Jack to get to New York." Howard and Gibson have often wished they hadn't helped their friend leave the South. "The bright lights and big city drove him nuts," says Howard. "He got there, and the mob just gobbled him up as soon as he hit town." Organized crime had a hand in several record and music-publishing companies in New York, and many deejays and record-business folks around the country have stories of their encounters with them.

It was the mob that fronted Smalls's money to buy the landmark Harlem nightspot Smalls Paradise from Edwin Smalls, a prominent numbers operator who was no relation to the deejay, Howard says. Smalls turned it into a hot spot for rhythm-and-blues, but he was just the man at the bar, his friends say. "He was Dr. Jive, and he had access to valuable air time to play their records so they said, 'Here, this is yours,'" Howard says. "That spelled his doom, all the money, broads, and booze. They give him carte blanche."

At the height of his success in New York, Smalls was one of the first deejays involved in packaging big rhythm-and-blues shows at the Apollo Theater and other venues. He and Jocko and Alan Freed were probably the three most powerful promoters of their day. Dr. Jive, like the other deejays, ran six or seven shows a day over two-week periods so that thousands and thousands of fans could see the performers that they had been listening to on radio. In December of 1955, the WWRL deejay went head-to-head with white r&b deejay Alan Freed.

Dr. Jive had his show at the Brooklyn Paramount while Freed had his at the Academy. Smalls's show took in eighty-five thousand dollars in one week. He featured Ruth Brown and Clyde McPhatter while Freed had La Verne Baker, Count Basie, the Cadillacs, Boyd Bennett, and Joe Williams.

In early 1956, powerful CBS television variety-show host Ed Sullivan, who also wrote a newspaper column for the *New York Daily News*, hired Dr. Jive to put together and emcee a one-hour rhythm-and-blues show and also to oversee a fifteen-minute segment of similar talent on Sullivan's own show, *The Toast of the Town*. Dr. Jive brought in La Verne Baker, Bo Diddley, the Five Keys, and other heavy-duty black acts. The white producers of Sullivan's show worked with Smalls and the performers he brought in, but they didn't always get what was going on.

At one point, they decided that Bo Diddley should go out and play Merle Travis's "Sixteen Tons," which had just been recorded and released by Tennessee Ernie Ford. Since Tennessee Ernie wasn't available, they thought Bo Diddley could do it even though Bo insisted he didn't know the tune. They wrote the lyrics in big letters on cue cards since Diddley couldn't see worth a, well, diddley, and pushed him out onstage where he proceeded to perform, with great style and skill, his own theme song, "Bo Diddley." He explained afterwards to the flustered producers that all he could see on the cue cards was his name, so he played his song.

Smalls's radio career ended in May of 1960, when he was arrested by the New York District Attorney's office as part of the payola investigation. Then thirty-four years old, he was charged with forty-eight counts of commercial bribery for taking $13,385 from eighteen record companies. He died about ten years later "supposedly of natural causes while he was out partying or something," Howard says.

Smalls was not the most high-profile New York deejay to go down in that investigation. There was another small-town jock who made it big, only to fall under bad influences, be disgraced by payola, and die at a young age. He was a white man who claimed to have coined the term "rock-'n'-roll." At one time, he was known as the Moon Dog, but he died, broken financially and spiritually, as the former deejay Alan Freed.

FOUR

The Moon Dog

*When the history of all this is written in a definitive way,
when the true story is put together, Alan Freed will be a
giant. More than any other man, he brought us rock-'n'-roll.*
— The late Paul Ackerman, rock-'n'-roll
writer for *Billboard*

The street in the residential area of Shaker Heights in Cleveland did a split when it came to the small, park-like island of some grass, a gully, and a tree. The car coming down the street before dawn on that morning in 1950 did not follow the road. It took its own disastrous course straight ahead, across the grass, and hard into the tree. It was incredible that the driver, the lone occupant of the car, survived the crash, though some would say later that it did kill him slowly, over time.

Alan Freed was not yet a national figure when he nearly died that night. He was a small-time radio announcer and late-night television movie host for WJW radio and television in Cleveland. A few years earlier he had been a popular teen disc jockey in Akron, Ohio. But his bid to become the first "teejay" was a flop at WXEL-TV in Cleveland. He was a heavy boozer. He

163

was separated from his wife, with two young kids. A crash, then, seemed inevitable.

Years later, Freed would tell his children in great detail how his nose was ripped off in the accident and that a policeman from a nearby station found it at the scene, picked it off the ground, put it in a bag, and carried it to the hospital in the squad car behind the ambulance bearing the rest of his mangled body.

It was a toss-up whether Freed was worse off on the inside or the outside when they retrieved him from the wreckage of the car. His face itself was nearly torn off. His younger brother, David, ordered the emergency room doctors to find the best plastic surgeon in town and get him to the hospital immediately, which they did. It took at least five hundred stitches and several operations to restore his features. He would always wear heavy makeup to cover the stitches that reattached his nose.

The inventory of injuries on this one twenty-eight-year-old man totaled what normally might have been a week's worth of trauma at the Cleveland hospital: ruptured spleen, ruptured liver, punctured lung, collapsed veins, mutilated face, detached nose, both knee caps smashed. Doctors told him that unless he cleaned up his lifestyle considerably, his devastated organs were probably capable of functioning for only another ten years at best. His lungs were so weak that, from that point on, every cold turned into pneumonia.

Doctors warned him that even one drink of alcohol could cause serious damage to his depleted liver. He responded by avoiding driving cars but staying behind the bottle, outliving the doctor's dire warnings by nearly five years. The autopsy report confirmed that it was indeed his liver that killed him. He had shown so little concern for it, before or after the accident, that some speculated that those doing the autopsy must have discovered the initials J&B on the organ that finally gave in.

"My father used to say to me 'I am living on borrowed time. I shouldn't be here so I have nothing to lose.' I think he had a feeling that you should live your life as a meteorite, burning fast and furiously. His life was short, but he filled his years with a lot of activity," says Lance Freed, now a record company executive in Los Angeles.

When he died in 1965, Freed had lived up to most of his favorite motto: "Live fast, die young, and make a good-looking corpse." He failed on the last part, though. He was still talking a good game in those destitute years, but he looked just terrible, his brother says.

One quarter Lithuanian, one quarter Jew, one quarter Welsh, and one quarter Moon Dog, Alan Freed was born December 15, 1922, in Johnstown, Pennsylvania. He grew up in Salem, Ohio, one of three sons of Maude and Charles Freed, a salesman in a clothing store.

Alan, known as "Al J." was an average student but an avid and innovative musician in high school. He was top trombone in the Salem Senior High School band, a drum major in the marching band, and had his own jazz combo, the Sultans of Swing, a name he borrowed from a hot Harlem band. It would not be the last time he'd take his cue from the black side of town.

Growing up, he dug the suave big-band sounds of Glenn Miller and Benny Goodman. He once drove the twenty-five miles to Youngstown and stood in line for three hours to see Goodman perform. He also had an enduring appreciation of classical music, particularly Wagner. He would call his first son Lance Ray Mac Freed, the middle name taken from the drummer Ray "Ray Mac" McKinley in the Glenn Miller orchestra. His second daughter was named Sieglinde after a character in the Wagnerian *Ring* cycle of operas. The other two children, a son and a daughter, he named after himself: Al, Jr., and Alana. He took music seriously. He took himself seriously.

After high-school graduation in 1940, he enrolled at Ohio State University for a year, studying engineering. He never graduated although he would one day claim to have a master's in engineering. Freed was always reinventing himself and anybody else within range of his imagination. "In the course of my walks around campus, I passed WOSU—the campus radio station. The bug bit me. It was then I decided I wanted to be a radio announcer. I used to drive my folks batty reading the newspaper aloud for practice," he told New York columnist Earl Wilson. It might even have been true.

Around the time the Japanese dropped in on Pearl Harbor, Freed joined the U.S. Army where, for reasons he probably made up, he was assigned to the Ski Patrol. While training in Wisconsin and protecting Oshkosh from Asian hordes, he developed a serious ear infection. The U.S. Army sent him home with a cottonball in his ear. He returned to Salem to work as a government inspector at military plants. While on an inspection tour of an aircraft parts plant in Lisbon, Ohio, about ten miles from Salem, he came upon a familiar-looking final inspector on the assembly line. She was Betty Lou Bean, the mayor's daughter. "I'd known him in high school. He played the trombone in the Salem band, and I played French horn in the Lisbon band," she recalled. "We had seen each other around but never dated."

They started going out then, but the dates were not your typical nights out on the town, Freed's first wife recalls. "An awful lot of our dates consisted of his reading the newspaper aloud to me to practice his radio voice and him asking my opinion of how he sounded," she says. Between the news and sports, however, something happened. They discovered that both of them loved classical music. Freed already had an extensive record collection, but it was nearly all highbrow stuff. "He was definitely not into rock-'n'-roll when we first started going out," Betty Lou says. They were married in 1942, and Lance and Alana were soon born.

While working his government job, Freed enrolled in a night class at a broadcasting school in Youngstown, Ohio, a program similar to the Tennessee School of Broadcasting where John Richbourg taught in Nashville. Freed did love radio, especially when he was on it. He had carried a toy microphone around the house as a youngster, ad-libbing radio jabber alone in his room. He may even have banged on a copy of Mother Goose as he played.

After finishing the broadcasting courses, he talked his way into the local radio station to do sports. His first real job was at radio station WKST in New Castle, Pennsylvania, where he played classical music for about forty-five dollars a week. Even there, he tapped on a telephone book with the music, his former wife says. For several years, Freed played the bouncing broadcaster. He went to WPIC in tiny Sharon, Pennsylvania, as a news announcer and was so unhappy in such a small setting that he confided to brother David that the station call letters stood for "We Piss in Cans." He got out of Sharon quickly enough and to WKBN in Youngstown as a sportscaster and program director and then, for a short stint, to WIBE in Philadelphia.

Freed had high aspirations though he did not have a great deal of company in his assessment of his talents. In 1944, he went to the CBS radio studios in New York and auditioned for a job, "but they told me to find a better profession," he reported. A year later, he landed at radio station WAKR in Akron, Ohio, as a newsman, but after filling in for an announcer who failed to show up for work, he won that job, and the *Request Review* sponsored by O'Neil's Department Store was his. He worked there through 1950 and became a hit with the local teenagers, even playing a little of the rhythm-and-blues music that was so popular on stations like WLAC, which Freed could pick up at night in Akron.

David Freed, who was a student at nearby Kent State University at the time and later would become a truth-seeking county prosecutor, recalls that he heard his brother use the term "rock-'n'-roll" regularly even then because back then "rhythm-and-blues" meant "nigger music" to the unenlightened listener. Betty Lou recalls that her husband became so popular with Akron's teens that it was difficult for their family to eat dinner at a restaurant without being surrounded by young fans. She says, "I think his appeal was his sincere love of the music and the kids. Starting in Akron, he would get tremendous amounts of mail, and all of it was important to him. If someone had a problem, he would talk to them about it, even on the air. He really did care about his listeners."

Freed was always a good father, too, Betty Lou recalls. It was being a good husband that he found difficult. Another sponsor of Freed's Akron show was the local Arthur Murray dance studio. When Freed went in one day to pick up the advertising copy for his program, he instead picked up an attractive supervisor, Marjorie "Jackie" McCoy of Warsaw, Ohio. "It was love at first sight between Marjorie McCoy and me," he told a reporter later, neglecting to mention that he'd had a wife and two kids back home at the time.

When Betty found out about his relationship with another woman, she confronted him. But Freed did not want to get a divorce or, especially, to give up his children. She says, "He was a very loving father, but I think he had difficulty coping with success, and the temptations it brought. I was devastated when I found out. He did everything he could to block the divorce, but he was guilty, of course. Eventually, I realized it would have happened sooner or later."

Although Freed has been portrayed in some accounts as an insufferable egomaniac, his family life provides a somewhat more benevolent picture. He may have had trouble staying married to one woman over the years, but he did not abandon his former wives and his children. Betty remarried, to Tom Greene, who eventually went to work for Freed so that the deejay could keep his children nearby. Betty and Jackie eventually became close friends, and Freed had two more children with his second wife — Sieglinde and Alan, Jr.

By this time, Freed had polished his voice, which even with training sometimes sounded like a sink disposal digesting olive pits. He had continual problems with polyps on his vocal cords. Freed had also developed a performer's temperament. He was good. Humble, he wasn't.

By 1950, Alan Freed was a big deejay in small Akron, so

naturally he demanded more money. The management at WAKR did not share Freed's assessment of his worth. So he walked. But only a few steps away, to another station, WADC. He opened his show there the very same night. As had happened when he fell in love while still married, Freed forgot something. He still had a contract with WAKR. Lawyers were summoned, and Freed soon found himself banned from broadcasting within seventy-five miles of Akron for one year.

History would show that being banned from Akron and its environs was hardly a fate worse than death — or even a slight flesh wound — for Freed. After all, Cleveland, and its lively radio market was close, but just far enough away to be outside the limit set up by the legal agreement. So Cleveland it was.

There Freed tried to make the big leap into television by taking his *Request Review* show to WXEL-TV, but apparently the world was not yet ready for music videos, at least this raw stuff. The show bombed. "It may have been the worst television program in history," recalls David Freed in the kind of blunt assessment only a younger brother could make. "He would say, 'Here's a record,' and the camera would pan to the spinning record on the turntable and then pan around the room. It was awful."

Alan lost that show but stayed around hosting a midday movie for a while before he went to WJW where he at first hosted a classical music radio show and also did the late-night movie on their television station. Never a heavy drinker in his youth, Freed became a major consumer of J&B Scotch about this time. His routine generally called for a few drinks with the boys before returning home to his family each night, but he had probably been drinking through much of the day as well. Alan and his bottle were a regular couple. The near-fatal crash interrupted that routine only briefly. He continued to drink intently when he recovered from the accident in the spring of 1950. The alcohol did not seem to affect his day-to-day performance, even as it pickled his liver early on.

"It was like a stimulant to him. Alan could probably drink all night, and you wouldn't realize it," says his brother. Freed's broadcasting career was, in spite of or because of his drinking, rejuvenated thanks to the business sense of Lou Mintz, owner of the biggest record store in Cleveland.

In the summer of 1951, Alan Freed had recovered from his most immediate and serious injuries, but up to that point Akron had seemed like the summit of his career. Cleveland had not yet thrown itself at his feet. In most eyes, he was a small-time classical music radio deejay with a bad reputation. As a broadcast personality, Freed was beginning to look like all-ego, no go-go, and his tendency to hit the booze didn't help. He needed a good idea big-time. It came on a hypnotic guitar lick backed by a heavy bass beat. And it came out of the wrong side of town. The wave that Freed had been waiting to catch had been building way down south in Dixie in Nashville, in Memphis, Atlanta, Macon, and Muscle Shoals — and in the isolated urban ghetto funk factories of Chicago, Los Angeles, Detroit, New York, Newark, Baltimore, and Philadelphia. The music had been rocking black-and-tan nightclubs for several years to the heavenly horror of churchgoing black folk. God's own gospel music had been usurped by the devils of rhythm-and-blues, and now the white hepcats and kittens were falling into it while pawing at each other on the dance floor and on four-wheeled love nests parked on the side of the road. Lawdy, Miss Clawdy!

Rhythm-and-blues pulled into Cleveland after a long haul up the hard road from the Mississippi Delta, Nashville, Louisville, Cincinnati, and Columbus. It had been called many names: race music, sepia music, nigger music, and now rhythm-and-blues (r&b for short). It was black and sweaty, working man's music, poor man's music. It was hungry and full of spit. Southern immigrants found work in the factories, and their music found the ears of the local teens, who needed a beat they could dance to. The black kids picked up on it first, but, like Freed, white teenagers were bored with the big bands and bewildered by bop. They wanted something to shake their socks

at. They found it in the back bins at Leo Mintz's Record Rendezvous, and Mintz, a savvy businessman, found his pitchman
in Freed, just as Randy Wood had found Gene Nobles and
Ernie Young had primed the pipes of John R. Richbourg. It was
happening again, but this time the whole world was about to
tune in.

Mintz, owner of the biggest record store in Cleveland,
was already the sponsor of Freed's classical music show, named
after the store. As the legend goes, he invited Freed to his office
one day to watch the teenagers sifting through his record bins.
With the finely tuned cultural awareness of a retailer plugged
into his cash register, Mintz had noticed a trend developing.
The white kids were skipping past the big-label stuff, the Patti
Pages and lollipop tunes. Instead, they were scavenger hunting
through the off-brand stuff, the Negro music, the darkie tunes
that played low to the ground and rumbled up through your
soles until they reached the place where your legs met and
caused all sorts of unholy commotion. The children of bankers,
school marms, and shop foremen stole the 78s from safe stor-
age, put them on the demo player, and danced in the aisles like
young junkies shot up and orgasmic.

Freed saw it, but he was not sure he believed it or
understood it. Mintz, whose advertising paid Freed's salary,
was more of a believer. He saw the possibilities: they were
green, folded, and marked "Legal Tender." The beat was hypnotic. Even better, Mintz said, white kids could dance to it
without taking lessons.

Mintz told Freed that if the deejay would start a radio
show for teens, playing the music they liked, he would advertise
on it and get others to do the same. wJw had a fifty-thousand-
watt clear-channel signal that would reach kids not only in
Cleveland but across the Buckeye State and beyond. Way
beyond, as it turned out.

Freed recalled his tentative feelings about Mintz's proposal in a 1956 interview with a British publication: "I heard the
tenor saxophones of Red Prysock and Big Al Sears. I heard the

blues-singing, piano-playing Ivory Joe Hunter. I wondered. I wondered for about a week. Then I went to the station manager and talked him into permitting me to follow my classical program with a rock-'n'-roll party." Leo Mintz was buying, but that was apparently beside the point.

Freed knew that other deejays and advertisers had been successful with late-night barrages of rhythm-and-blues. Although Gene Nobles says he does not recall it, both Hoss Allen and station executive E. G. Blackman say that Freed had long been a listener of WLAC and that once he got his new show started, he would telephone Nobles and John R. frequently to ask them what was hot with their listeners. Everyone in radio was also aware that Hunter Hancock in Los Angeles had made some waves with his wild *Huntin' with Hunter* show. Freed knew there must be something to this stuff if the kids were digging it in Cleveland, too.

He went after whatever that something was at eleven P.M. under a June moon in 1951. Freed signed off on his classical program and put the needle down on Todd Rhodes's "Blues for Moon Dog." Something came over him. With his rasping voice he set off on a sandpaper solo, a yowling, howling duet with the record's raging saxophone. Like a baby being born, *The Moon Dog Show* was off to a raucous start. The born-again radio jock pounded out time on a Cleveland telephone directory, and rhythm-and-blues spewed from the radio like a contagious virus afflicting the young and the listless with the dancing dementias. WJW's after-hours slot drew ratings like it had never drawn before. Freed had caught a wave, a rocking, rolling wave.

"Freed became Moon Dog, a sort of mid-American Steppenwolf, with more than his share of hang-ups but sincere and believable, with his rock-'n'-roll records and gravelly jive patter. The King of the Moon Doggers became a Pied Piper of epic proportions," writes Arnold Passman in his 1971 treatise, *The Deejays.* "For eight years, three in Cleveland and five in New York, he illuminated the wide-open night on powerful fifty-kilowatt stations, and he became the most successful dance promoter in Ohio and western Pennsylvania."

Freed's inital audience was almost entirely black, and he played to that crowd, thinking that the white kids would find him just as they'd found the back bins at Mintz's record store. His ear was bad for the Army, good for music, and even better for dialects and language rhythms. He set up the mystery of his own identity, just as the deejays down in Nashville had. Was Alan Freed white or black? He was a wild-child on the ray-di-o. "When I first heard him on the air, it was like watching a new actor take the stage. He was like quicksilver with his warmth and his drive and his energy and the feel-good sound that few people can pump through a radio microphone," says Joe Finan, who was then an impressionable young afternoon deejay at wJw. "He was one hell of an air talent. I was just a kid from

In the early days, Alan Freed played to mostly black audiences

Sharon, Pennsylvania (never pissed in a cup). When I turned Freed on, I was listening to someone very different. He could have been playing polkas, and I would have listened."

Freed might not have known much before about artists like Sam "The Man" Taylor or La Verne Baker or Ivory Joe Hunter or about the unfamiliar twelve-bar tempo and the beat that rattled internal organs, but he learned quickly. Wagner it wasn't. Como? Who cared? This was his big-beat ticket to the big time. Freed was hip. A "white Negro" is the term author Norman Mailer used to describe the cross-race cultural mix underway.

"He was the kind of guy who could walk into a black-and-tan club on the east side of Cleveland, and the blacks would be very comfortable with him," says Finan. "He was idiomatic, certainly. But there was no pretense with him, and there were very few jocks who could do what he did. Of course, very few of them had any brains. They would try to do what Freed did. They would read a record label and find a telephone book and beat on it, but Freed used that telephone book for energy and to build the imagination of the listener. Most other jocks were just two-dimensional people; he was three."

With the success of his new show, Freed began to live the music as well as play it. He hung out on Cleveland's east side where hip whites and blacks mixed in the black-and-tan clubs. He was so popular with blacks he could go and drink where no honky had dared to tread. "He was almost like some white savior in the black neighborhoods," David Freed recalls. "We could go into black bars like Gleason's, where most white men could not get within one hundred yards of the place, but the place would open up for him, and the owner would introduce us around so we could spend time with whatever performers might be there. I really think Alan was color-blind in that regard."

Freed's influence on the black community did not escape advertisers. Erin Brew beer, a local product, signed on as a sponsor for Freed's show, and, as Finan says, "He put that damn beer on the map." The favorite beer of blacks prior to that had been a brand called P.O.C., but when Freed began popping the cap off Erin Brew in the studio, extolling its virtues as he guzzled, he changed the drinking habits of an entire listening audience. Erin Brew was soon the top beer in town.

At first most of Freed's listeners were blacks because he was playing their music, but he quickly picked up the young hipster whites, the "cats and kittens" who were tuning in to rhythm-and-blues and the late-night radio coven conducted by the mad Moon Dog. Freed managed to lure white listeners without turning off blacks. Many other deejays who hosted early rhythm-and-blues radio shows were not true believers, and listening to them pitch the sound was like watching Queen Elizabeth watusi. They just didn't have it. They were squares trying to reach a hip-cat audience. Worse, some of the deejays insulted their black listeners. A few would not give out the titles of the records they played. Instead, they assigned them numbers, and when they urged their black listeners to go to the local record store and buy the record, they told them to ask for "Number 13." In their own racist ignorance, they believed that blacks, the people responsible for this innovative soul-stirring music, were too stupid to remember their own song titles.

Even as Freed shot out of the dungeons of broadcasting to seats at the best tables in Cleveland's finest restaurants, he kept the bottle to his lips. A bottle was always around, even in the radio studio, where his drinking was tolerated. His microphone, his records, his telephone book, and his J&B Scotch were the tools of his tirade. Finan, who would seek help for his alcoholism much later, concludes that Freed's success frightened him and made him even more reliant on the anesthetic buzz. Though Freed dominated the radio waves and influenced the lives of a generation of young listeners, he was rarely in control of his personal life. Most knew him as a gentleman and a thoughtful man when he was sober, but his drinking hindered his judgment and, in the end, took his life. Only his incredible energy and his role as a champion of rock-'n'-roll carried him as far as he made it.

He may not have been a believer at first, but, by most accounts, he became one. He was a hustler and a con and a self-aggrandizer and everything else it took to be great at the manchild job of radio deejay. He may have made a few dollars off the sweat of black performers, but most of them are grateful to him for getting them up onstage where the sweatin' could be done. Freed was a deejay Elvis. White playing black. Taking a little away, giving them some back. In Harlem some black deejays raised hell because they figured Freed took a job away from one of them. Maybe. But Freed also made their jobs all the more significant. He helped the music find a greater audience. His fast, furious spin as the country's premiere rock-'n'-roll deejay set the tone of the time, and his collapse at the end of the decade matched the cynicism that would follow, until one day sweet, defiant rock-'n'-roll was nothing more than background music to a commercial message. Today "Pappa's Got a Brand-New Bag" full of Success rice (James Brown), Sunlight dishwashing liquid leaves us "Breathless" (Jerry Lee Lewis), and Shield soap and only Shield soap allows us to "Rock Around the Clock" (Bill Haley and His Comets). But for a while there, Alan Freed played sin on the radio while parents and preachers shouted "Nigger lover!" and "Sinner!" and teen-agers found each other and danced, danced, danced. Like the Miami deejay convention of 1959, it was one hell of a party until they turned on the lights.

Screamin' Jay Hawkins, a maniacal rocker of the fifties grew up in Cleveland and was home from his third stint in the military when he first heard Freed on the air in his hometown. "That cat was stone wild," Hawkins told Gerri Hirshey in *Nowhere to Run*. "I went to find out who we had in Cleveland that would dare. I mean, how could a black cat get away with such shit? So I go there, and I say, 'I want to talk to this Alan Freed.'" When a short, stocky white man walked out, Hawkins was stunned. "I says, 'Oh, no, you're playing black music on a white station?' and he says, 'That's me.' So I shook his hand, and I said, 'Well, thank you, you're doing us very good.'"

Hawkins would thank Freed again and again over his career. Freed was one of the few deejays who would play Hawkins's wildass records, which included the 1956 classic "I Put a Spell on You," a song that was not appreciated fully until Creedence Clearwater Revival covered it years later. Hawkins's other stalwart tunes include "Armpit #6," with Keith Richards on guitar, and "Constipation Blues," which was a big hit, he claims, in Japan.

It was Freed, Hawkins told Hirshey, who poked, prodded, and finally paid him two thousand dollars in cash to open his act from inside a coffin. It happened December 28, 1957, at the Paramount in Manhattan. There were protesters outside the theater proclaiming that Freed was the anti-Christ and Screamin' Jay Hawkins was a cannibal. There were two hundred cops on horseback and twenty thousand people wanting tickets to the six shows. There were also Freed and the cash and a quart of Italian Swiss Colony pink muscatel that got Hawkins into the coffin. When the time came, he leaped from it, his cape fluttering behind him, and nearly brought the walls of the Paramount down, which is exactly what Freed intended. The zebra-striped coffin with a three-minute air supply kept Screamin' Jay's career going strong years beyond its anticipated life span. The righteous deejay had been right again.

"History done Alan Freed wrong," according to Screamin' Jay.

Freed was not the first deejay at the rhythm-and-blues party, but he entered the scene at the right time in the right place, and he is generally acknowledged as the first to apply the term "rock-'n'-roll" to what was happening musically. One of the most often told versions of this many-versioned tale has it that Freed and Mintz were sitting around one afternoon in the spring of 1952 at the record store thinking up advertising copy for Freed's latest venture, concert promotions. This scenerio of the historic moment has Mintz suggesting that they say the concert "will really rock." One of them — both claimed at one time or another to be the one — came up with "rock-'n'-roll."

Even that was not a totally original thought, since rhythm-and-blues performers had long used those terms as euphemisms for passionate trysting, the dirty deed, S-E-X, as in "Good Rockin' Tonight," by Roy Brown, and "Rock All Night Long," by the Ravens and others. By the early fifties, it was also a reference to dirty dancing as in "We're Gonna Rock," by Gunther Lee Carr. Even earlier, gospel singers had used it to signify salvation, as in "Rock Me," written by gospel great Thomas Dorsey. That song became a pop hit in 1939 when it was recorded by famed gospel performer Sister Rosetta Tharpe.

Whatever the source of the divine inspiration, the name of Freed's radio show was soon altered to *The Moon Dog House Rock-'n'-Roll Party*, giving Freed the right to claim until death that while he may not have been the first to play the music, he was the first to put it all together in one package and peddle it to a big audience of both blacks and whites. Part of the package was notoriety as the leader of the rock-'n'-roll revolution. Donning his trademark louder-than-a-train-wreck plaid jacket, Freed was quick to take his success and his act out of the studio and on the road.

In no time, he was packing concert halls with racially-swirled crowds. At first he recruited area talent to perform. Later, he made excursions to Harlem and the South, peering into gospel churches and honky-tonk bars, one ear cocked for back-stoop pluckers and street-corner quartets, stars waiting to shine. When he became *the* deejay, of course, all he had to do was start the bus up and the biggest acts in the country would pile on, black and white, drunk and dangerous. Most of them performed free of charge, with the understanding that their next record would get plenty of air time on Freed's radio show with its fifty zillion listeners.

Gerri Hirshey, who now writes for *Vanity Fair*, described Freed's travelin' shows from the musician's point of view in her history of soul music: "All of them, his merry band, know him for a marauder, hauling buses full of creased and conked blacks in florid suits along with bands of Vaseline-slick white Romeos, all of them with lust in their hearts and lightning in their thighs when they hit a stage. Tonight is a representative sampling: Fats Domino, Chuck Berry, Jerry Lee Lewis, the Everly Brothers, Screamin' Jay. In addition, there are the groups: the Cadillacs, the Moonglows, Frankie Lymon and the Teenagers. Freed is packing more and more vocal groups into his radio play lists and stage revues."

He became the Man and the Target, both for the same reasons. He played raunchy black music and made white kids act crazy, stirring up every kind of racist white nightmare imaginable and horrifying the black gospel crowd as well. This was not just black music. This was black music that churchgoing blacks threw their Bibles at. Straight-laced whites, including the Roman Catholic Church, and particularly southern whites were the same way. Jerry Lee Lewis, who studied earnestly at the universities of both heaven and hell, had to be talked into performing "Great Balls of Fire" by Sam Phillips at Sun Records. The Killer thought it was too blasphemous for general consumption, but in the end he played it because he was the Killer.

Freed and his music also roared up the rear ends of established music businessmen. ASCAP, the licensing agency formed by music publishers, had been built primarily on white foundation blocks and had historically tried to keep radio stations from playing records because its members felt musicians would be forced out of work. Its only real competition was BMI, a rogue outfit of radio broadcasters who signed up small, independent record companies and even hillbilly, black, and Hispanic musicians to more favorable licensing arrangements as a way of generating music for their stations. The introduction of record singles and albums and recording tape threw ASCAP's empire into a tizzy, and Alan Freed and his rock-'n'-roll shook its nerves and rattled its brains. Composer Billy Rose called the music on BMI's list "obscene junk." This analysis came from a man, who—as Dick Clark of *American Bandstand* has pointed out—wrote that high-brow hit "Barnie Google" with his "goo,

goo, googlie eyes." The music played by Freed and Clark pumped millions into BMI while ASCAP clenched its fists, slammed doors, and kicked puppy dogs.

Freed made some powerful enemies and, like any fifties and sixties icon of rock-'n'-roll worth his doo-wah, he went down in a blaze of conspiracy talk. It was the era of the McCarthy "red hunts," the Dodd hearings on TV sex and violence, the quiz-show scandals, the Kefauver hearings, the Jimmy Hoffa investigation, and, of course, Howdy Doody.

The FBI watched Freed. The Catholic Church watched him. The mob watched him. The KKK watched him. The powers in the music industry watched him. The commie-watchers watched him.

And everybody listened.

"I don't think it was the FBI or the church single-handedly trying to bring him down," says Freed's oldest son, Lance, who has seen copies of the FBI's file on his father. "I would just say that I think, in a sense, he was victimized. In a sense, he probably was not a great businessman, and maybe perhaps he could have protected himself a little bit better."

Playing rock-'n'-roll became a sort of quest for Alan Freed, his son says. He was passionate about his work; he loved it and took joy in it. "When you feel like that about what you are doing, sometimes you lose perspective, or maybe you really don't care about anything else," says the son. "I was there, and I can tell you it was labor of love for my father. It was a passion."

Freed shook them all up with his first concert show on March 21, 1952, in the Cleveland Arena. It was called Moon Dog's Coronation Ball, and some have hailed it as the birthdate of raucous rock-'n'-roll.

The talent lineup was hardly the sort to drive mid-western teenagers into a crotch-grabbing frenzy: the Dominoes, Paul Williams, Danny Cobb, and Varetta Dillard were the somewhat dim headliners. But Freed had become hot stuff, and, through relentless hyping on his program and station, including handbills mailed out and distributed on the streets, the concert attracted a crowd well beyond the arena's capacity of ten thousand. Freed, who for once was on the conservative side of an issue, estimated that seven thousand gate-crashers showed up for his party.

Cleveland called out the police reserves. One person was stabbed, and five were arrested for public drunkenness. The concert was canceled midway through the performance, which was inaudible anyway, by firemen who decided that more than twenty thousand fans in the ten-thousand-seat arena was at least ten thousand too many. The fact that only a tiny fraction of the crowd was white may have had something to do with the decision.

The *Cleveland Press* said there was a mob of twenty-five thousand. The *Cleveland News* said that only eighty-seven hundred tickets were printed. The black newspaper, the *Call and Post*, which sided with those who thought Ray Charles was a blasphemer, called the concert's music "garbage, trash, a shocking display of gutbucket blues and lowdown rhythms. . . . The shame of the situation lies not in the frustrated crowd that rushed the arena, but in a community which allows a program like this to continue and to exploit the Negro teensters."

There were allegations that Freed and his fellow promoters oversold the concert, but he crossed his heart and denied it, blaming gate-crashers and rowdies for the trouble. Freed, Mintz, and another partner were charged with overselling tickets, but the charges were later dropped.

Freed went on the air the night after the concert and, on the verge of tears, said that he had been so upset at the outcome that he "went off by myself and cried. . . . If anyone even in their wildest imagination would have told us that some twenty to twenty-five thousand people would try to get into a dance — well, I suppose you would have been just like me, and you probably would have laughed and said they were crazy," he said. Freed said that only ninety-seven hundred tickets were sold before authorities ordered them to stop selling. "We were still some twenty-three hundred admissions short of the capacity of the arena," he claimed. He noted, too, in his radio counterattack, that the Harlem Globetrotters game a few weeks earlier at the same arena had sold thirteen thousand tickets without outraging anyone.

Freed appealed to his listeners for forgiveness and sympathy. Then the wily bastard promised to do it again soon—in a May 17 concert called the Moon Dog Maytime Ball at the arena. The Dominoes were again headliners. "Tell us tonight that you are with the Moon Dog," he said the night after the coronation calamity, calling for their telegrams, cards, and phone responses. He said, "I will make it right with you as Erin Brew, the standard beer, northern Ohio's largest-selling beer, brings you the *Moon Dog Show!*"

Although it slowed him down just a step for a short time around Cleveland, the riot at the Coronation Ball actually propelled Freed into the national news and probably led to his eventual conquest of the world, or at least New York City. His power as a radio personality and concert promoter was featured in stories around the country after the riot. Anything that could stir up that much excitement in Cleveland was bound to cause talk. After the Cleveland Arena concerts, Freed moved his shows to smaller halls with reserved seats. Soon he was drawing crowds of one thousand and more to concerts in Ohio and Pennsylvania. Most of the acts were black, but the audiences were increasingly mixed.

More than three thousand came to an August 1952 concert at the Summit Beach Ballroom in Akron, featuring Charles Brown and the Clovers, two New York acts. Moon Dog madness was as prevalent in his listening audience as Madonna-wannabes were for a time in the 1980s. Moon Doggers and crazy kittens, late-night looney-tunes. The music mesmerized teenagers and put scowls on the faces of their moms and dads. What was going on in there? Turn that cat fight down!

Cleveland quickly gained a reputation with record companies as a good place to break a new hit. Why Cleveland? For one thing, it was big enough to have several hip deejays but small enough for a record to make a very quick, easily measurable impact. "The thing about Cleveland was its instantaneous response," says Finan. "If a record came to town, we would know in two or three days whether it was a hit. That was how fast the action was in record stores. That was not the case in more sophisticated cities so that is why Cleveland became the place to break a record. Rather than doing market research and bringing people in to hear records, the record companies just came to Cleveland."

Among the deejays around Cleveland at the time were Soupy Sales, later reported to be a comedian, and Tom Edwards, an entrepreneurial jock who, with his wife, packaged record-hop promotions and put out a newsletter. Other Cleveland deejays included Phil McLaine, Carl Reese, Freed, Finan, and the more conservative but powerful Bill Randle. Freed was the only one playing rhythm-and-blues in that market, and he played it on a split-shift from five to six P.M. and then from eleven-fifteen P.M. until two A.M. (except Saturdays when he went until three A.M.). The others for the most part were pop-music jockeys who would slowly move toward rock-'n'-roll as it entered the mainstream.

Finan and Randle filled the same time slot on rival stations although Randle was on the air seven days a week to Finan's six. Had there been any more days in the week, he would have staked them out, too. Like most disc jockeys, Randle was possessed of a powerful ego, but unlike most others, he had, and still has, a daunting intelligence to back it up. The afternoon time slot and Randle's more mature audience made him a far more powerful figure to record company executives than Freed in the early going. In 1954, Randle dominated the time slot between six and seven P.M. to the point that 65 pecent of the radios in the listening area were tuned to him—the highest rating of any deejay in the country. In November of that year, he signed on with WCBS in New York to do a weekend stint for four hours each Friday night in addition to his work at

WERE, where he was a stockholder as well as an employee. Randle was also unusual in the business for his controlled performances, knowing exactly what he was doing each minute of his show. His young competitor at KYW, by comparison, was "into the glitz and superficiality" of the business, confesses Finan himself.

Randle and Freed had something that the upstart Finan did not have, Finan admits today. They had genuine ears for music. When Jud Phillips, brother of Sam, of Sun Records brought a controversial new artist's first record to Cleveland, he took it first to Finan (Freed played only black music and, in the early going, considered Elvis a country rockabilly singer), who was considered hipper than Randle. But Finan, like 95 percent of the deejays at first, was not that hip on Elvis. He said, "He played this record for me and I said, 'Jud, I am not going to play that shit.' He said, 'Joe, you gotta play it, this thing is big in Memphis.' I said, 'Who gives a shit about Memphis? Nothing happpens there.'" Phillips threatened to take the record to Randle, which prompted Finan to wish it on his rival. "I couldn't even tell if the guy singing was white or black," Finan recalls. Especially with a name like "Elvis." Randle got the record and began playing it every fifteen minutes. The resolute Finan predicted his rival would "destroy himself" by hawking the likes of Elvis Presley.

"The impact of Randle's spinning of the Sun discs in Cleveland was unforeseen and quite shattering," writes former record-company man Arnold Shaw in his well-regarded book, *Honkers and Shouters*. "Teenage listeners seemed to instantly go berserk and kept calling the station for repeat plays."

Word spread "like a contagion" to record-company executives in New York, Chicago, and Los Angeles that the hottest new performer in the universe was Elvis Presley. In two days, Finan was on the telephone, begging for copies of the song from Sun Records in Memphis. "Whenever I have needed a lesson in humility, I think of that," Finan says. Randle may have been a Bach and Beethoven man at heart, but he had an ear.

Among his other coups was Johnny Ray, whom he heard singing in a Cleveland nightclub and championed on the air, making him a star. Randle was also the mentor of a male quartet that was known as the Canadaires when he found them. He clipped their hair, changed their names to the Crew-Cuts, and lined them up with Mercury Records where their tunes "Crazy 'Bout You, Baby" and "Sh-Boom" became rock-'n'-roll classics. Randle, who was earning about $100,000 from about 102 sponsors, was not modest about his success. As he told *Time* magazine in February of 1955, "I'm constantly getting a mass of records. I weed out those that are obviously bad and play the rest on my program to get listener reaction. Then I feed the results into a machine. I'm the machine. I'm a Univac. It's so accurate that I can tell my listeners, 'This tune will be No. 1 in four weeks.'" Randle was primarily a businessman. He says, "I'm in the businesss of giving the public what it wants. This stuff is simply merchandise, and I understand it."

Others were not so understanding. Randle was primarily a pop deejay while Freed played mostly black music. Freed, then, was the one viewed as a disruptive force in society. Randle was just a good businessman. Senator Joe McCarthy of Wisconsin had Americans looking for Communists in every high-profile point of society, from politics to Hollywood to the military to literary circles. People who thought along those paranoid lines saw rock-'n'-roll as yet another hidden menace.

Freed was the mad hatter, the pied piper leading teens to the dance floor. "Banging home the beloved rhythm-and-blues records with the aid of a cow bell and phone book, Freed, moored behind just the flickering light of the VU meters in a dark studio, was perhaps the head witch-doctor McCarthy failed to burn," writes Arnold Passman.

The adult backlash against rock-'n'-roll served only to inspire teenage enthusiasm for the popularized version of rhythm-and-blues. Freed, whose receding hairline was the only hard evidence of adulthood, knew which side he was on. He drew ten thousand of the young and increasingly restless to the Newark Armory just outside New York in Newark, New Jersey, in May of 1954. About 20 percent of them were white. Freed was on the air in Newark by that time, too. Radio station WNJR, a small five-thousand-watt station, was programmed with nineteen hours a day of r&b and spirituals along with news and sports and thus became the first full-time black-oriented station for the New York market. The station offered three of the country's hottest deejays on tape: Hunter Hancock from Los Angeles, Zenas Sears from Atlanta, and Alan Freed out of Cleveland.

The taped programming on the Newark station began to bring in big-money national advertisers and some local sponsors from New York as well. Radio executives in the Big Apple were already tuned into Cleveland to a degree since the Cleveland Indians were making life miserable that summer for the hallowed New York Yankees. In much the same way, Alan Freed was hitting long balls to teenage fans compared to the short-hitter deejays on WINS in New York. Soon the big-league scouts were on the horn. And in July the most popular deejay in Cleveland was called up to the major leagues at WINS-AM. He went on the air September 8, 1954, and initially broadcast on the late-night shift but was soon promoted to the prime seven P.M.-to-eleven P.M. slot. Radio marketing wizard Rick Sklar, who was then with WINS, said Freed was offered seventy-five thousand dollars a year to come to the Big Apple. He bit. It was the largest amount ever paid to an r&b jock by an independent station at that time.

Freed bid good-bye to Ohio with a capacity crowd of thirty-one hundred at the Akron Armory and a show featuring Joe Turner, Faye Adams, Al Savage, the Joe Morris Orchestra, the Five Keys, and Joe Cooper. Then he put his second wife, Jackie, and his four children on a plane for New York. Sklar, who told of Freed's coming in his book *Rockin' America*, says that Freed also brought along hundreds of 45s that he "piled helter-skelter in an old five-shelf supply cabinet in our office."

It would become the most influential record library in

commercial radio, imitated everywhere, according to Sklar. It would change the sound of popular music in America and the world for generations.

WINS deejay Paul Sherman, who would become a friend and eventual successor to Freed as his "Crown Prince of Rock-'n'-Roll," told Arnold Shaw of his first impression of the wild man from Cleveland: "I see this guy sitting in the studio with a big telephone book in front of an open microphone, thumping his hand all the while the record was playing and making gibbering noises in the background, 'Go, man, go' and 'Yeah, yeah! yeah,' and accenting the beat. . . . We looked at each other, and Fisher said, 'Oh, my God, I give him three months.' I said, 'You're crazy. I give him one week.'"

Sherman ate those words, as Freed ate up New York. "The kids grabbed him right up," Sherman says. The badass Freed took over the nights at a time when the "good music" stations were dominant in New York. He pulled out a Manhattan telephone directory, put on a golf glove (he'd gotten wiser) to protect his hand, and pounded his way to the top of the ratings. WINS went with him and had to shut off the deejay's telephone lines because there were too many people trying to reach him. Freed fan clubs sprang up all over the East Coast. Moon Dog mania swept Manhattan.

Freed was golden. But then along came a crazy guy in a Viking hat saying he was nothing but pyrite. New York was a big city, but it wasn't big enough for two Moon Dogs, according to one Louis "Moon Dog" Hardin, a blind composer and major metropolitan character given to appearing on city streets clothed in Viking garb—or sometimes a monk's outfit—and often found leaning on a staff of the sort used in the shepherd, not the music, business. On December 4, 1954, *Billboard* carried the news. Freed was enjoined by New York Supreme Court Justice Carroll G. Walter from using the nickname "Moon Dog," or any variation thereof, on his radio show. The judge ruled that Louis Hardin had been Moon Dogging since 1947 and therefore predated the Moon Dog-come-lately Freed, who had been using the name only since 1951.

The judge did allow the deejay to continue using the "Moon Dog Symphony" song. Freed's golden-boy image was tarnished again when a mass meeting was held in a Harlem YMCA by folks who felt his jive-talking style was just another example of a white man making money off the black man's labors. The most vocal complainer was an established New York deejay, Willie Bryant, once voted "Mayor of Harlem" by a black newspaper, who felt like maybe he, as a real black man, should have Freed's imitation-black-man job.

A black bandleader, Lucky Millinder, defended Freed, however, praising him for "the fire and excitement of a Reverend Billy Graham," according to WINS executive Robert Smith, who attended the meeting. Freed kept on keeping-on, and Bryant played his own music in Harlem. Around the same time, a Harlem record-store owner congratulated Freed, in *Down Beat* magazine, for bringing black and white teens together, even if they danced on separate sides of the music hall. "Look," the store owner told a *Down Beat* reporter, "if the Supreme Court could get kids together as well as Freed has done through music, we wouldn't have a thing to worry about."

There were a few scattered protests from other corners in the early months of Freed's assault on New York. The *New York Daily News* ran a series of articles that linked rock-'n'-roll with juvenile delinquency, a popular theme of the day, particularly after Bill Haley's "Rock Around the Clock" was dubbed in at the last minute as the theme song to the 1955 parental horror movie *Blackboard Jungle*. Moms and dads were not reassured in the least when, in that same year, James Dean came out in black leather with a motorcycle and a knife in *Rebel Without a Cause*.

But in 1955, Freed's *Rock-'n'-Roll* show was hotter than Davy Crockett's coonskin cap (well, almost), and the deejay tried to protect his new name by copyrighting the term "rock-'n'-roll." But it was already too late to stake that claim. Ever the opportunist, Freed made a brief run at calling the music "The Big Beat" so he could again make it his own. No one was buying that nonsense, so he humbly accepted his crown as one deejay in a long, multi-racial line of self-proclaimed kings of rock-'n'-roll.

In its sixtieth-birthday edition, *Billboard* ran a front-page column seconding the deejays' ascension to the throne, proclaiming the radio disc jockey "the undisputed king of local radio programming." The proclamation was supported inside the entertainment newspaper with facts and figures from its annual disc jockey poll. The figures showed that the average radio station was programming 109.4 hours per week of which 63.8 hours, or nearly 60 percent, were devoted to deejay record shows. That was an increase of 13 percent over the previous year.

Television had weakened network radio, but in its place aggressive local radio stations emerged with deejays as their most powerful ratings weapon. "The disc jockey is vital to this type of operation, for there is no limit to the ingenuity he may use in his programming," the newsweekly concluded. There would be limits later.

The same edition of *Billboard* featured an inside story on the expanding influence of deejays like Freed. In another survey, *Billboard* found that these enterprising fellows were involved not only in broadcasting but also in owning retail record and music stores, personal appearances, performing, songwriting, managing artists, publishing music, and operating jukebox routes.

In Los Angeles, for example, *Billboard* found that the top five deejays at radio station KLAC were a mini-conglomerate. Alex Cooper promoted dances. Peter Potter had taken his Jukebox Jury radio show to television. Jim Ameche was a narrator for Capitol Records, Gene Norman had a nightclub, publishing company, record shop, and jazz concert tour, and Dick Haynes promoted local dances.

Bandstand's Dick Clark would set new standards in deejay entrepreneurship when his testimony during the 1960 payola hearings (called "Clarkola" by the *Washington Post*) revealed that he had interest in thirty-three companies, including his own record-pressing plant. By his own estimate the former Philadelphia deejay lost about eight million dollars when he divested himself of most of those to remove any taint of conflict of interest during the payola investigation. He proved himself very adept, and probably much smarter than his interrogators, during the hearings and afterwards. About twenty-five years later, *Forbes* magazine estimated Clark's fortune at $180 million. "The hearings taught me a lot about politics and business," he writes in his autobiography, *Rock, Roll & Remember*. "I learned not just to make money, but to protect my ass."

Clark was the clean-cut, too-cool-for-school, and ready-for-prime-time television deejay of the day, but Freed, who was contemptuous of the competition, had to be the undisputed and unabashed anarchic topcat of rock-'n'-roll radio. He operated on a high-voltage frequency, his wiry hair crackling with energy, his arms flailing and tongue wagging. He howled, bellowed, and pounded the *p*s out of the Manhattan telephone directory. He selected his own music from his favorite stash in the battered green supply cabinet, flipping through piles of records until he found what he was after. Then he would hand the record off to his young black producer, Johnny Brantley, who would find a request letter from a fan pining for that particular tune. Brantley would then arrange the letters and records in racks, Sklar recalls. There were no categories designated by marketing research, no program directors breathing down Freed's neck. He had four hours to fill, and he filled it the way he wanted. Fast tunes, slow tunes, male singers, female singers — he paced it by his own tastes, not the pseudo-scientific bullroar of some hired consultant.

While Clark showed no contempt for Pat Boone, Bobby Darin, Connie Francis, and Fabian, the purist Freed won the loyalty of most performers and listeners because he refused to play "covers" of black songs by white artists on WINS. He still thought Elvis was a country rocker. When the McGuire Sisters had a number-one hit and gold record with "Sincerely," Freed refused to play it, though he did play the original by the Moonglows. Although some claimed Freed loved money above all else, that decision cost him royalty fees. He was listed as a cowriter on "Sincerely."

Like most other top deejays, including Clark, Freed cut his own deals and reached his own understandings with the record companies, publishers, and performers regarding frequency of play. He claimed that he never took money to play a record because that would have taken away his freedom to program his show. But he never turned down a "gift" from a grateful source for favoring a tune on the air, he said. Payola was not against the law at the time—the law would be written after the investigation—as long as the income was reported to the IRS. Freed sometimes forgot to tell Uncle Sam. David Freed says his brother was careful, however, not to relinquish control of his show to the payola paymasters who flocked around the big jocks like pigeons about the peanut vendor. (Dick Clark, who has also denied that he ever played for pay, once had to shoo away a two-bit record-promo hustler who walked up to him while he was on the air at *American Bandstand*.)

David Freed says, "If the music was good, Alan played it. He told me that he would never take money to play a record because, if he did, his career would go down the drain. Anybody in the business back then would tell you that Alan was the toughest nut in town to sell a record to. If he didn't think it was good, he wouldn't play it." The opportunities for gratuities were always there for an enterprising deejay. Concerts were cash machines and the overhead ridiculously low when record companies provided their performers free of charge in return for the deejay's good will and future air time for their records. Six or seven shows a day for two weeks straight helped make the deejay a happy pappy.

Freed marched across Manhattan in 1955, and his *Rock-'n'-Roll* show jackhammered the competition in the ratings. He presented his first dance concert to the city January

14-15, 1955, at the Saint Nicholas Arena in Manhattan, drawing sixteen thousand. There was no trouble. The promotion for the concert was handled by Morris Levy, owner of the Birdland nightclub and Roulette Records. Levy has been characterized variously over the years as Freed's best friend and business associate or as a mob-affiliated wheeler-dealer who controlled Freed from the moment he landed in New York. In 1989 Levy, who also owned, among many other things, the Buddah record label and the Strawberries record-store chain at one time, was facing a ten-year prison sentence on an extortion conviction unrelated to his association with Alan Freed. Levy was convicted in May of 1987 as the result of evidence gathered in a three-and-a-half-year federal investigation into alleged organized crime infiltration of the record business. His conviction and $200,000 fine were appealed.

(Levy's conviction was for conspiring to extort a customer in the 1984 purchase of more than four million cutout or discontinued records. The FBI planted listening devices in Levy's Roulette office to gather evidence. The agency, according to an October 29, 1988, story by *New York Times* reporter William K. Knoedelseder, Jr., "has long alleged that Levy and Roulette have acted as a 'front' for Vincent 'The Chin' Gigante, reputed boss of the Genovese crime family." An FBI agent testified during Levy's sentencing trial that a convicted Philadelphia heroin kingpin told authorities that he purchased three to five kilograms of heroin each month from Levy, delivering cash to the Roulette office in a suitcase.)

Freed picked up an entourage in New York—including the husband of his first wife—but some of it looked an awful lot like the "crooked nose" crowd, according to Freed's family and friends. In *Rockonomics*, Marc Eliot's peek into the cash drawers of rock-'n'-roll, the author asserts that Levy "reportedly kept an underling assigned to Freed at all times." One of the underling's assignments, according to Eliot, was to keep the deejay well lubricated with J&B before business meetings, "presumably to make him easier to manipulate."

Freed, who had dabbled in the record distribution business with his brother in Cleveland, had joined Levy and his partner George Goldner in forming Gee Records to produce acts such as the Flamingos, Little Anthony and the Imperials and, most notably, Frankie Lymon and the Teenagers. Freed eventually sold out his share of the label to Levy, whom Eliot claims had muscled his way into Goldner's business and "quickly assumed formal managerial control of Alan Freed's career."

David Freed, who had done business with Goldner from Cleveland while operating Lance Records distributing company with Alan, is cautious in talking about Levy, as many people are. "When Alan went out East, there were a lot of guys hanging around who were gangster types," David says. "I know that Mo Levy was a friend, I never concluded that he was a gangster, and I don't know that anyone could have influenced Alan to change his pattern of playing records that he liked. I can't believe that Alan at any time, drunk or sober, would have done anything other than what he wanted to do."

In fairness, it should also be noted that Morris Levy has always denied that he is affiliated with organized crime. He says he knows many of its players because he began working in mob-owned nightclubs on Broadway in New York when he was twelve years old. A multimillionaire who breeds racehorses on his fifteen-hundred-acre farm in upstate New York, Levy is also a noted philanthropist and was named "Man of the Year" by the United Jewish Appeal in 1973. He has also chaired million-dollar fund-raisers for the Black Congressional Choir, the Foundling Hospital, and St. Patrick's Cathedral Choir. He has served on the boards of the Opera Company of Boston and the Columbia County Hospital.

Alan Freed was turning into quite the wheeler-and-dealer deejay in New York. He syndicated his radio show for play at other stations around the country, and his first customers were in Kansas City and St. Louis. His sponsor was Greisedick beer. In the fall of 1955, he returned to the

Paramount with another Levy production. This one grossed $154,000 and netted $125,000, even with a lineup featuring Tony Bennett, the Harptones, Nappy Brown, the Moonglows, the Red Prysock band, and, for the first time anywhere outside the chitlin' circuit of the South, ladies and gentlemen, Mr. Chuck Berry and his low-slung guitar. Obviously, talent came cheap when the promoter had access to a large radio station's turntable.

Berry and Freed were to have a close working relationship over the years although it would get rough when Berry realized that Freed had taken quite a bit of money out of his pockets. In his 1987 autobiography, Berry describes the first time he realized that Alan Freed had been listed by Chess Records, with which Freed had long had an affiliation, as a coauthor on his song "Maybellene"—a common deejay incentive in those days: "My first royalty statement made me aware that some person named Russ Fratto and Alan Freed . . . were also part composers of the song. When I later mentioned to Leonard Chess the strange names added to the writer's royalties, he claimed that the song would get more attention with big names involved. With me being unknown, this made sense to me, especially since he failed to mention that there was a split in the royalties as well."

Berry, who can be a very tough customer to deal with, eventually came to that realization, and nearly thirty years later recovered the full rights to his song from Freed's estate. The performer figures that he was robbed of half of his royalty money over the years, but when he received his first royalty check of ten thousand dollars, which was twice what he had paid for his first house a couple of years earlier, he never thought to question the practice of sharing writing credit.

Berry continued to work with Freed, and in 1958 they both appeared in a film entitled *Go, Johnny, Go.* Freed, coincidentally, played a New York disc jockey. Berry spent five days on the set with him in Culver City, California, and, as he writes in his autobiography, this was the first time he realized how heavy a drinker the deejay was. Berry thought at first that

Freed could drink a great deal without showing any effects, but "Just since I had known him, I could notice the physical deterioration of his body under the quantity of alcohol I assumed he was consuming. . . . Once before a Montreal concert and long before his ailment became critical, he invited me into his dressing room and fell on me, taking us both to the floor. I don't think he ever knew that I didn't drink, for he was constantly offering me a nip. I remember him being really stoned at the Montreal engagement, a condition he was in increasingly. This caused him to be interrupted by stage managers for reasons I call 'baby handling' because of his inability to carry out his obligations regarding announcements on his shows or on the business end of the paperwork and tour proceedings," Berry writes. At one of those "loose-lipped sessions," Freed told Berry that he intended to give him back the one-third writer's credit that Chess had given to Freed on "Maybellene."

Rock-'n'-roll muscled its way to the forefront of the music scene, the movie scene, and the scene of the crime in 1956. Deejays were top dogs in radio. In that year, deejays commanded 68 percent of the airtime on twenty-seven hundred AM stations across the United States. They were playing, on average, 16.4 records an hour, which came to 500,000 spins a day.

As leader of this pack, Freed was high profile. His syndicated show was even played over Radio Luxembourg on an English-language station that reached Americans working or stationed throughout Europe. Freed may have been bigger than even Elvis at this point, depending on which of them you asked. Presley (who was still "Mr. Rock-'n'-Roll" to Freed's "King of Rock-'n'-Roll") pushed the doors for rock-'n'-roll open even wider as a white boy with all the right, or wrong, moves. He made his first appearance on national television early in 1956, on January 28, on the *Dorsey Brothers Show* and followed that with his historic appearance on the *Ed Sullivan Show* in September. The former truck driver, who had signed a thirty-five-thousand-dollar contract with RCA, also made his movie debut that year in *Love Me Tender*. Its theme song had sold over ten million copies by the year's end.

Alan Freed, in the meantime, was not resting on his turntable. The lead drummer of the rock-'n'-roll movement came out with not one, but two, of his own movies that year. Both films were quickie productions that had echoes of Freed's ill-fated Cleveland television series in their crude presentation: a lot of music with little plot. The first was *Rock Around the Clock*, starring Freed and Bill Haley, another "King of Rock-'n'-Roll," whose recording of Ike Turner and Jackie Brenston's "Rocket '88" in 1951 was one of the first covers and marked the beginning of the transformation of black rhythm-and-blues into everybody's rock-'n'-roll.

Rock Around the Clock featured Freed back in his best Sultans-of-Swing mode with trombone in hand, fronting for an eighteen-piece orchestra with Bill Haley as his sideman. The movie was the centerpiece for riots by rowdy, working-class "Teddy Boy" teens in England. One hundred youths were arrested. The *New York Times* London bureau filed a wonderfully stuffy report in which it was noted that the "jiving" youths used a fire hose to drive the theater manager off the stage when he interrupted the show to "expostulate" with them about their behavior. The Brits were baffled, the *Times* reported. The teenagers were behaving is a most un-British fashion. The report wondered, in print, if it was the appeal of some "latent jungle strain ... or just another manifestation of their instinctive and youthful love of rhythm?"

The Bishop of Woolwich, obviously no Wizard of Oz, told the *Times* man that the hypnotic rhythm and wild gesturings in the movie had a "maddening" effect on the helpless youths. Sir Malcolm Sargent, conductor of the, ahem, British Broadcasting Corporation's Symphony Orchestra, described the music as only he could: "It is nothing more than an exhibition of primitive tom-tom thumping."

Another daring but unnamed official of a British youth group suggested that perhaps this dance music was nothing more than the present generation's rendition of the Charleston.

And the official noted that it certainly was not as vulgar as the Black Bottom dance craze of an earlier era.

In spite of all this posturing, the Queen Mother herself invited the hard-drinking Haley and his Comets to her castle for a command performance. Meanwhile, back at home, Haley was banned from performing in his native Pittsburgh because of increasing anti-rock sentiments among the monarchs of the establishment. Even old won'cha-come-home Pearl Bailey got into the anti-rock act when she cut a record entitled "I Can't Rock-'n'-Roll to Save My Soul."

Freed's second movie was an even bigger hit. *Rock, Rock, Rock* offered Connie Francis's voice coming out of Tuesday Weld's mouth but also featured authentic performances by Frankie Lymon, Chuck Berry, the Three Chuckles, Cirinio and the Bow Ties, six-year-old Ivy Schulman, the Alan Freed Orchestra, La Verne Baker, the Moonglows, the Flamingos, and the Johnny Burnette Trio. The movie resulted in the first rock-'n'-roll soundtrack album from Freed's friends at Chess Records and, allegedly, poured a lot of cash into Freed's pocket. *Billboard* reported in November of 1956 that Freed "should be rolling in the long-green once his second feature movie is launched simultaneously in seventy New York theaters on December 5. In addition to owning 10 percent of the film outright, Freed plays a leading role and publishes fifteen songs from the twenty-one-tune picture score." The industry journal said Freed also stood to collect lucrative performance credits for a unique deejay promotion in the picture. It was the first rock-'n'-roll movie soundtrack with performers from six different labels on a special promotional album that would be sent to six hundred top deejays around the country.

Rock, Rock, Rock provided a centerpiece for Freed's annual Brooklyn Paramount holiday show during Christmas. It broke house records and made headlines. Freed's concerts always seemed to make headlines. Thousands of teens began converging on Times Square around four A.M. even though the first show was not until noon. One hundred and fifty patrolmen and ten mounted police corralled the "seething bobby sox and leather jacket throngs behind temporary wooden barricades hustled to the site when policemen alone proved unequal to the job," according to the story filed by *Chicago Tribune* reporter Harold Hutchings, whose account ran under the headline "Rock-'n'-Roll Addicts Take Over Times Square." Hutchings estimated the size of the crowd at 10,500 by midmorning with seventy-five hundred outside and another 3,650 or so inside the theater. Two girls suffered leg injuries, and the glass windows of the box office were broken in the crush when the theater opened at eight A.M. The police established a command post under the theater marquee: "The police job was made tougher by sweat-ered girls—many in black toreador slacks or blue jeans—who darted under the barricades into the street. When young men got out of line, the cops unceremoniously moved them back, but catching a wiry blonde was not always easy."

"Alan Freed, thirty-five, a disc jockey, was the cause of it all," Hutchings wrote. "Freed is to the teenagers the founder of rock-'n'-roll. Freed contended that when youngsters sing, dance in the aisles, stand on the seats, and keep time to the beat, they are just having a good wholesome time and keeping out of trouble."

Freed was on a rock 'n' roll. His third movie opened in 1957, the same year that Clark's *American Bandstand* became a national show and federal troops were sent to Arkansas to force integration on Governor Orval Faubas. It appeared that the good guys were winning. *Don't Knock the Rock* was origi-nally to be called *Rhythm-and-Blues*, but Columbia decided not to rub the racial implications of the movie in the face of the edgy white establishment. After all, the towns of Memphis and Chat-tanooga, Tennessee, Columbus, Georgia, and Birmingham, Ala-bama, still had laws prohibiting white and black performers from appearing onstage together. The movie, Freed's reply to the anti-rockers, featured some of his greatest discoveries: the Cleftones, the Cadillacs, Bobby Charles, Maureen Cannon, the Duponts, Nappy Brown, and Robin Robinson. The deejay was getting cocky in the face of heightening anti-rock sentiment among some very powerful foes.

Freed got an early taste of the power of his foes in 1957, when a television dance show that he hosted was canceled almost before it got started. One of the first guests was the wild-child with the voice of a black angel, Frankie Lymon. The former Teenager lead singer, who would die of a heroin overdose in 1968 at the age of twenty-six, had the audacity to dance with a white girl on camera. Instant cancellation. (In his autobiography, Dick Clark cites that incident as the reason he waited a year before having black dancers on his show and even then fretted about the reaction. To his relief, there was none. Not a single complaint, he says.) Freed would finally have a successful television dance show in New York from 1958-1960 at WNEW-TV, his first and final hurrah in that medium.

The anti-rock contingent seemed to be lying in wait for any opportunity to pounce on Freed and his faithful. In Boston, where racial attitudes were not conducive to black musicians' planting suggestive lyrics in young white ears, the Board of Education banned rock-'n'-roll after a record hop at MIT resulted in a near-riot among the engineering majors and other hip techno-cats. Radio station WBMS in Boston forbid its deejays to appear at record hops because of their potential volatility when mixed with high-hormone-content teenagers, and the local musicians' association president characterized rock as "jungle rhythms," just in case anyone wondered what high-minded principles were at stake. Another rock-'n'-roll critic, this one wrapped in the church cloth, Monsignor John B. Carrol, head of the Catholic Youth Organization of the Archdiocese of Boston, proclaimed that, without a doubt, rock-'n'-roll "has left its scar on youth."

Boston was not the only seat of rock-'n'-roll revolt. The nonpartisan White Citizens Council of Birmingham, Alabama, tried to ban rock-'n'-roll from their town. When they failed in that mission, several of the members went after the next best thing. They invaded a concert by Nat King Cole, whom they somehow mistook for a rock-'n'-roller, pulled the mellow crooner off his piano stool, and were trying to beat the color out of him when police arrived.

This sort of rock backlash had an effect. In Helena, Arkansas, deejay Gene Hogan of KXL called for rockers to put anti-juvenile delinquent messages on their records. *Billboard* reporter Gary Kramer wrote in November of 1956 that "an adjustment is taking place. Many stations, of course, still do not program any rock-'n'-roll." In a survey of 179 station managers conducted by *Billboard*, seventy-nine admitted to playing more rock-'n'-roll because of listener demand. One station, WFBS in Fort Walton Beach, Florida, reported that 75 percent of the requests coming in from teens were for rhythm-and-blues tunes. But other stations were reluctant to jump on the trend. One said his station did not consider it music. Another snarled that rock-'n'-roll was "the worst influence to ever hit the music business—a disgrace." Station WJAG in Norfolk, Nebraska, reported that it rationed the music fed to its "moonstruck" teens, doling out only one Elvis disc a day. Station KHEM, in Big Springs, Texas, devoted only thirty minutes each day to rock-'n'-roll, and then each of the suspicious records was served between two pop tunes to dilute its potency.

With preachers condemning rock on Sundays and school officials railing against it at monthly board meetings, most deejays shifted into low gear. But even that was not always enough for the foes of their music. Cleveland deejay Tom Edwards, of WERE, ventured out to a church dance with the intention of giving out two thousand photographs of Elvis. The church leaders suggested he reevaluate his intentions. They forbid him even to play Elvis records or show photographs of him in a color slide show he had intended to present during the intermission.

Freed felt the anti-rock forces after a three-day concert spin in Hartford, Connecticut. Police tried to revoke the theater's license afterwards, claiming they had arrested eleven youths during the event. Freed denied that any problems had been associated with his concerts, and he went on the counter-attack. This was an anti-rock-'n'-roll conspiracy, he charged. He noted that the worst riot he had ever seen had been at a concert back in Youngstown, Ohio, in 1944. The performer onstage was that noted agitator Guy Lombardo, backed by the equally anarchic group, the Royal Canadian Orchestra.

Freed, who had no small financial interest in the continuing health and acceptance of rock-'n'-roll, continued to lead the counterattack as a guest on a television show hosted by Eric Sevareid that spring. The show featured teens talking about the music and a psychiatrist putting forth the incredible proposal that perhaps parents were the ones responsible for out-of-control children. Mitch Miller, who was no great champion of rock-'n'-roll but who had a grudging friendship with Freed, managed to straddle the issue by pronouncing that "you can't call any music immoral. If anything is wrong with rock-'n'-roll, it is that it makes a virtue out of monotony."

In his rebuttal, Freed found the good in rock, noting that eleven thousand rock-'n'-roll fans had recently worked on behalf of a Kidney Foundation project with little acclamation from the media or adult community. And then he delivered notice: "As long as there are people like me around, we're going to rock-'n'-roll until you don't want to rock-'n'-roll anymore, and then, when you don't want to rock-'n'-roll anymore, I'll give you what you want!"

As a star of radio, the concert stage, and the silver screen, Freed was also getting what he wanted. One of his perks — since he had a fear and loathing of driving — was a home office. And what a home office it was. Shortly after leading WINS out of the ratings basement and into the penthouse, he moved his family into a sixteen-room mansion in Wallach's Point, near Stamford, Connecticut. Greycliff, as Freed called the home, came complete with white wall-to-wall carpeting, a swimming pool, and a view of Long Island Sound. He had a studio built on the premises so that he would not have to drive, or be driven, into New York each day. WINS picked up the tab for the studio in his guest house, and a record company footed the bill for the wiring and an engineer. In his more festive moments, Freed would refer to various portions of the house as the Chuck Berry room or the Frankie Lymon wing. The ornate stone swimming pool, he was fond of pointing out, had been built by Atlantic records, and when Morris Levy pestered him at one point because he was not playing anything by Atlantic even though they'd built the pool for him, Freed is said to have replied, "Fill it in."

Freed and Jackie did not stay out in Connecticut all the time. They would venture into the city for shows, and Sklar remembers one evening when he accompanied them to a performance by the Treniers, a twin-brother rhythm-and-blues duo. Alan "was frenetic during the shows and gulped shots of Scotch one after another. I remember him leaning forward from our ringside table and sliding shot glasses filled to the brim across the stage floor as the Treniers finished their act and joined him in a toast," Sklar says.

After one of those nights on the town, Freed ventured into the radio station the next day and made the acquaintance of Inga, the "gal Friday" for WINS sports-announcer-turned-deejay Bill Stern. Inga was blonde, buxom, and from the Bronx, although she had the look of a Swedish milkmaid. She was twenty-two when she met Freed in 1957. He was thirty-five. He arranged for her to leave sports and come to work for him. Once again, Freed suffered from love at first sight, and once again divorce resulted.

Inga had been a fan of the Moon Dog when she first began working at the station, but she had never seen Freed until she found his photograph on a wall among those of all the station deejays. Her first impression had been surprise that he was not a Negro, as she had presumed from his hipster's slang and the music he played. "Someone told me that he was the Moon Dog, and I was shocked. He just sounded black to me," she recalls. When the opportunity came to meet him, she took it, primarily as a fan, she says. "Alan happened to be in New

York to judge a contest or something, and I walked by the elevator and he saw me, and I guess he was attracted to me," she says. "He sent someone to see if I was looking for a job, and I was and I got it."

An illicit affair began soon after she began typing for Freed, who spent less and less time in Connecticut with his wife and children. Inga found Freed to be "a very dynamic person," she says. "He loved radio. He loved what he was doing. And he was very enthusiastic," says Mrs. Freed III. "He was very exciting on the radio. He thoroughly enjoyed those four hours every night. It was heaven to him. He would have an open mike, and he would yell and clang a cowbell and beat on the telephone book—he went though quite a few telephone books."

Alan and Inga married in 1957. She says, "I was in awe of him, of course, as he was of me, which I could never quite understand. He was a very loving person, a very strong person. He told me stories of the earlier days when it started, of how it was a frightening experience for him to go onstage. He didn't know exactly what he had created, but he loved it."

After they were married, Inga led the glittery life for a while with Freed, who was always a big spender. "In those days there were so many spots. The Copa or Basin Street East were among our favorites. We were night people. He would get off the air at eleven P.M. and then we would go home and change and go out for dinner and then to a show. We had an apartment in the Coliseum Apartments on 58th, and Alan had his music publishing company downstairs," she says. They also had homes in Palm Springs, California, and Miami at one time, in addition to the home in Connecticut. At least Inga thought they owned these places.

In early 1958, Danny and the Juniors came out with "Rock-'n'-Roll Is Here to Stay," and Freed, feeling his oats and watts, acted as though it applied to him as well as his music, even amidst reports that rock-'n'-roll was moving away from its rhythm-and-blues roots towards pop music. "Pepsodent pop" was the alarm being sounded as the likes of Frankie Avalon and

Fabian, both good-looking Philadelphia boys championed by that good-looking former Philly deejay Dick Clark, were foisted on the record charts. Only slightly worse was the trend towards "ooo-eee-ooo-ah-ahhhhh" novelty-record hits, manifested by two records by another Clark pal, Ross Bagdasarian, also known as David Seville, creator of "The Chipmunks" and "The Witch Doctor."

Freed, the King, however, was cocky when he told *Billboard* that "there will be trends set within the field that no one can predict, but the power of the music is now showing up at the college level. Kids have been exposed to it for four or five years. Now they're carrying their taste right into colleges, and it looks to me as though the colleges will be completely saturated with rock-'n'-roll. . . . I've dealt with kids for sixteen years, and I believe that rock-'n'-roll has a good influence on them. And I don't think they grow out of it just because they reach eighteen or nineteen or twenty. Sure, their tastes expand. They begin to like other kinds of music, but that doesn't mean they stop liking rock-'n'-roll at all."

Then again, some folks just never got it in the first place. Even as Freed was predicting a long life for rock-'n'-roll, station KWK in St. Louis was banning it from its airwaves and promoting the decision by smashing every rock-'n'-roll record in its music library. Just "weeding out undesirable music," said the station manager. In what may rank as one of the top-ten backhanded compliments of the post-Industrial Age, rock-'n'-roll was also banned, in 1958, by the Iranian government. The decision was made by Iranian doctors who reported that many young rock-'n'-roll dancers suffered hip injuries due to the demands of the dance form. And in Springfield, Virginia, deejay Phil Burgess of WCFR auctioned off the worst rock-'n'-roll records in his collection for the benefit of the March of Dimes. Some enlightened anti-rocker purchased Elvis's "Hound Dog" and mailed it to the Kremlin.

Freed hit the road in the spring of 1958, untroubled by the latest rock-knockers wave, with his show entitled "The Big

Beat," which had broken attendance records over Christmas and New Year's at the Brooklyn Paramount. Jerry Lee Lewis and the Crickets were on the program. He also announced that spring that he would open a nightclub in Miami Beach called Alan Freed's Sugar Bowl. The club, which was really his in name only, was for teens. Freed charged on in his business endeavors even though President Eisenhower was having a tough time with a national recession. Many of the other rock-'n'-roll road-show tours decided to stay home. Dick Clark, a very canny businessman, was one who stayed put.

On May 3, Freed's tour moved into the Boston Arena, and trouble came on its heels. The trouble allegedly began when a white teen girl overcome with rock-'n'-roll emotion rushed the stage and grabbed an unnamed black singer by his unmentionables. A Boston policeman interceded, to rescue whom or what is unclear, and the rest of the cops and crowd panicked. The Associated Press reported that fifteen people, including six females, were attacked or robbed by roving gangs of teenage boys and girls after rioting broke out among six thousand at the concert. One victim, Albert Reggiani, nineteen, of Stoughton, a U.S. Navy sailor, was stabbed repeatedly in the chest. His condition was critical. Reggiani was attacked as he left the arena with two girls, who were also assaulted. The other victims included a mother of three children and her two thirteen-year-old babysitters. The fighting raged for hours, according to the AP. Police Lieutenant John T. Corkery was reported as saying that there was no racial angle involved in the rioting.

The AP said that Freed had denied the police permission to turn on the lights when the teens got loud and raucous during the show. Freed felt that the lights would only make matters worse. The cops said Freed told the audience, "I guess the police here in Boston don't want you kids to have a good time." Freed denied the statement, despite several hundred witnesses to the contrary. The police felt it was an inflammatory thing to say, even if true.

After police broke up fights outside the arena, the gangs

moved into the Roxbury and Back Bay neighborhoods, knifing, beating, and robbing, the wire service reported. An all-male gang of about twenty-five, wearing motorcycle jackets or, in an *au contraire* touch, pink coats and bandannas, attacked three men and robbed them of fifty dollars. Two teenage girls set upon a woman in the Dudley Street subway terminal, beat her, slashed her arms with a knife, and snatched her pocketbook. In Roxbury, a gang of youths beat one man and knifed another in an attempted robbery, the AP said.

Freed, according to the story he gave police, was oblivious to all the turmoil surrounding his concert. He said he'd signed autographs on a street corner for a half-hour after the show, and then he and his manager, Jack Hooke, went to the Hotel Statler, where they slept until noon Sunday. They caught a two P.M. flight to Montreal, where their next series of shows was scheduled, and they did not hear a word about problems in Boston until a reporter from the *New York Journal-American* telephoned them Sunday night during a show in the Montreal Forum, Freed said. "That's the first we knew of any trouble," he claimed.

But there was evidence that Freed did know about the trouble and tried to play it down. His manager admitted that before the show a Boston cop had pushed Freed, saying, "We don't like your kind of music here." It had become evident, over the years, that Freed's kind of show and Boston's racial attitudes did not mix. Boston, as witnessed by its bans and bad-mouthing of rock-'n'-roll over the years, had watched too many James Dean and Marlon Brando movies. Teenage anarchy was always on its municipal mind. Rumors spread about gangs of dope-smoking youths prowling the area and raping girls. "Everything that happened within a one-hundred-mile radius of the Boston Arena that night was attributed to the rock-'n'-roll show," says Inga. The inference was that the marauders were black and their prey white. It was an ugly scene, and the repercussions were greater than they had been in the past.

After the police and the prosecutors got together, they

came up with charges against Freed only. No rioters or rapists were produced. The deejay was charged with violating an anarchy statute. District Attorney Garrett Byrne said that Freed "by speech did advocate, advise, counsel, and incite the destruction of real and personal property." A Suffolk County grand jury indicted Freed for inciting a riot. The last few stops on the concert tour were canceled.

When Freed returned home, he was fired by the management at WINS. He had become too controversial, and the anti-rock forces' focus on him was hurting the station, management claimed. Freed and his supporters felt the music was a false issue. His real sin, they believed, was supporting music by blacks and black performers and introducing them to a white middle-class audience. Freed went out by resigning on the air in tears. He said good-bye and then put one last record on the turntable: "Shimmy, Shimmy Ko-Ko-Bop," by Little Anthony and the Imperials.

Freed told reporters that WINS had failed "to stand behind my policies and principles." Rick Sklar, who was an executive for WINS at the time, writes in *Rocking America* that station owner Elroy McCaw was fed up with Freed and the increasing controversy he generated. "When Freed returned to Boston, McCaw wanted no more of him. His contract was just ending, and Elroy decided not to renew," says Sklar. "Freed met all day with McCaw and tried to convince Elroy to keep him. Freed pleaded. He had a sold-out concert in Newark that weekend. The acts would perform only if Freed could play their records. Without a radio station there would be no concert. [Without a concert, Freed would be stuck with advance payment fees.] McCaw was unmoved. Freed called the arena and tentatively canceled the concert while he bargained with McCaw."

The tense scene turned even more dramatic when a concert promoter, an ex-boxer who stood to suffer considerable losses if Freed canceled his Newark appearance, barged in through a rear door near the record library with gun in hand.

He was looking for Freed. Sklar's wife, Sydelle, who was pregnant, and Freed's wife, Inga, spotted him and ducked into the library, locking the door and barricading themselves inside.

Freed and the station management, locked inside the executive offices, were unaware of his presence. The desperate promoter gave up and left. Negotiations ended in Freed's defeat about nine that evening. He had not been shot, but he had been shot down as a deejay at WINS. That night, Paul Sherman, whom Freed had championed as the crown prince to his throne as king of rock-'n'-roll, succeeded to the microphone in Freed's time slot.

"Everybody cried when he got fired," recalls Chicago deejay Dick Biondi, who like Freed was extremely popular with teens but considered dangerous by more conservative adults. "He was the first ... he gave kids something they weren't hearing before. He was like a cult leader."

Freed's firing and the Boston riot took some of the rock out of rock-'n'-roll. Concert venues dried up, sending other promoters into retreat, even Dick Clark and his Caravan of Stars. Radio station managers, who had always regarded personality jocks as prima donna pains, had even more reason to fret and to be on the alert for excesses.

It was not the best of times for personality deejays, whether in New York or Des Moines. At the first national deejay convention held in Kansas City in March of 1958, Des Moines deejay Don Bell of KRNT had spoken out against top-forty formatting as "a surrender to thoughtful programming" and a "crippling blow" to the development of disc jockeys as entertainers. He called it "a soporific to a trusting public." Bell was known as a champion of teenagers' rights. He had lobbied the Iowa legislature for student discount rates at movie theaters and recreational facilities. In his speech, he railed against top-forty management that "feeds off the progressive stations after they have exercised taste, imagination, and courageous originality. The hits-only manager is warning all talent to stay away. . . . He should be out of show business."

Although Bell was enormously popular, earning thirty thousand dollars a year, and his station controlled 55 percent of the market, those were dangerous words in an increasingly perilous climate. A month after he threw down the gauntlet, Bell was gone. His station manager told *Billboard* that "there was no sense in paying for a high-priced personality when audiences are won over simply by formula programming." Bell was picked up by a new station, KIOA, in Des Moines, and thirty days later the newcomer with the ejected deejay was rated number one.

Freed also landed at another station and on his feet, but the knockdown blow was not far off. Since ABC had signed him up to do a television sock hop before his departure from WINS, the network felt it wise to keep his deejay profile high. He was hired to do WABC radio as well. He returned to the late-night shift there, from seven-fifteen P.M. until eleven P.M., on June 2. And like most other deejays in the country with any sense at all — and that did not include all of them by any means — he kept his head down for a while, close to his shoulders, his neck unexposed.

Freed's televison show was called *The Big Beat*. One of his first guests was Buddy Holly, who mentioned his upcoming tour in an interview with Freed and talked with the deejay about all the hazardous time they had shared in planes. Holly reminded Freed of one trip on which they had landed in Cincinnati right after a helicopter had crashed. Only a few months later, in January of 1959, a plane crash would result in the deaths of Holly, J. P. "Big Bopper" Richardson, and Ritchie Valens. Surprisingly, nobody blamed Freed.

Rock-'n'-roll was hardly mentioned on the new, cleaner, and kinder Freed show, and the bawdier bands were banned. But Alan Freed as Pat Boone was like beer without alcohol and tobacco without smoke. "Freed's fans may go along with the gag for a few weeks," noted *Billboard* in its review of the show. "However, polite rock-'n'-roll isn't Freed's forte, and chances

After being fired from WINS, *Freed played it safer on* TV's The Big Beat

are *The Big Beat* won't start rocking, rating-wise, until it stops trying to sell two generations and concentrates on the one 'beat.'"

Freed's problems set deejays around the country on alert. Several jocks signed up for a State Department goodwill tour of foreign lands but agreed not to play rock-'n'-roll. Meanwhile, over in old repressive Russia, teenagers were bootlegging Elvis records by pressing them on X-ray plates.

By the fall of 1958, things had cooled down to the point that Freed, after some gun-shy hesitation, decided it was safe to venture out on the concert tour again. He had been locked out of the Brooklyn Paramount since the Boston debacle, so he took his traditional Labor Day show down the street to the Brooklyn Fox Theater. Chuck Berry, Frankie Avalon, the Kalin Twins, the Elegants, the Poni-Tails, Bo Diddley, Bobby Freeman, and the Everly Brothers signed on. The show set a new record for the Brooklyn stage, grossing over $200,000. There were no attacks by marauding leather jackets, punks in pink, or terrorists in toreador pants.

The theater owners were so gosh-darned relieved that they took out an ad in *Billboard* to thank Freed for the cleaned-up act. But it was a little too late for Freed, or any other jockey, to clean up what had long been standard practice. The stain of payola was set. And worse, an election year was coming up. The politicians were hungry for headlines, and the deejays were kind enough to set the table.

Their hijinks at the disc jockey convention in Miami Beach that spring were widely reported. Flagrant payola and attention-getting greed and corruption provided reporters and investigators with all the impetus they needed. The *Miami Herald*, later famous for tailing Gary Hart during his monkey business, sicced its fabled corps of sleuth reporters on the deejays' shenanigans, and the paper's fateful headline, "Booze, Broads and Bribes," might as well have been carved on the tombstone of the personality deejay. Even today, when the Miami convention comes up in conversation with survivors of the payola purge, nine times out of ten that headline will be recited. When Freed saw it on the morning it ran, he turned to Inga and said, "There's going to be trouble now," she recalls.

Freed's high profile as the nation's leading rock-'n'-roll radio deejay did not serve him well when assorted investigators and public figures went gunning for their own headlines in the payola purge. All of then drew a bead on him. Although payola was not forbidden by law, the Harris Subcommittee on Legislative Oversight decided to open an investigation to see if laws were warranted. Some called it a witch-hunt by publicity-seeking politicians; others called it democracy in action. As might be expected, deejays all over the country began running off at the mouth or running for the door. Radio stations, fearful of losing their federal licenses if their deejays were found to be in the wrong, began purging any likely suspects. Serious damage was done to the careers of many upright people who had done nothing illegal and nothing out of the ordinary. There were, of course, a few greedy ones out there, and their good times of glad-handing were definitely over for a while.

Righteous record producers, who had thrived by doling out monthly payola payments to low-paid jocks, began crying in the press about the high toll payola took on their business. Equally righteous deejays in Chicago and other areas began pointing fingers. Some of the same deejays were later revealed to be adept at extending their palms as well.

Although Freed's name was continuallly at the top of the list—he had made no secret of his wide financial network—the producers at WNEW-TV said they would not prejudge him. At WABC Radio, however, deejays were handed a very explicit questionnaire regarding their financial interests.

On November 14, the Harris subcommittee published a twenty-one-page memo detailing the focus of their investigation. The practices said to be under scrutiny were fairly common throughout the industry. About a week after the Harris memo was released with much the same effect as the publication of Madame Defarge's knitted list in *A Tale of Two Cities*, Freed was among those who felt the guillotine. When he refused to sign the WABC questionnaire on payola payoffs, they fired him. Freed said signing such a statement would have been "an insult to my reputation for integrity."

It apparently was not such an insult for him to sign a statement regarding his activites at WNEW television. He did sign that one, but WNEW-TV fired him, too, a week after WABC terminated him. On his final show for the station, Freed ended by staring into the camera, rubbing a record between his fingers. He went out with one final volley at the powerful establishment organization that had from the very start tried to stop the wild deejay from Cleveland and the rebellious music he championed. He said defiantly, "I know a bunch of ASCAP publishers who'll be glad I'm off the air."

Freed had figured all along that he could beat the headhunters, and he had brazenly, or foolishly, scheduled concert dates for later in the year. But without a high-profile radio job, he did not have the clout to attract major acts for long-term commitments. Freed had to cancel his tours and pay off the advance rental fees, an obligation that pushed him into bankruptcy.

Freed appeared privately before the Harris subcommittee for about two days, and, in his own words, "sang like a bird." The deejay had no desire to take his seriously abused liver into a prison cell. Afterwards, he told *New York Post* columnist Earl Wilson that Dick Clark should be the one under scrutiny, not him. Freed later claimed he had been misquoted by Wilson.

At the end of November, Freed refused to testify before a payola-probing grand jury, citing the Fifth Amendment. His broadcasting files were subpoenaed. Accompanied by Inga and his lawyer, he spent about an hour in the prosecutor's office. When an accountant from the district attorney's office went to get the files, he was refused permission by Freed's lawyers. Freed had been subpoenaed to appear because he had failed to show up previously. Freed told newsmen there that he had never received payola but had taken "consulting fees."

He later admitted to columnist Wilson that he had accepted payola but denied that he was guilty of any crimes. "A bribe is when somebody says, 'Here is a one-hundred-dollar bill. Lay on our record.' But if I, by myself, based on my nineteen years' experience, decide a record should be a hit, and I help it, am I going to turn down a gift of a bottle of whiskey or something? I've never taken a bribe. . . . Somebody said to me once, 'If somebody sent you a Cadillac, would you send it back? I said, 'It depends on the color.'"

The hounds were on Freed's heels. The United Press International reported that one record distributor claimed he had loaned Freed eleven thousand dollars then returned the interest after transferring the mortgage on which the loan was based to a record company. The distributor, Jerry Blaine, said he had lent Freed the money three years earlier, secured by a

Freed and Inga leave the prosecutor's office after he refused to testify in the payola probe

mortgage on the disc jockey's home in Stamford, Connecticut. Freed in turn made monthly payments against principal and interest for about a year, Blaine told the UPI. The mortgage was assigned to Roulette Records, Blaine said.

What the investigators and reporters and general public were about to find out was not that Alan Freed had enriched himself through payola; in fact, he was about as close to destitute as a man with four houses can get. Inga recalls spotting a headline on a newspaper at this point, as things in their life were falling part. "The front page of the newspaper said something about 'DJ Kicks Back to Promoters,' and when I opened the paper the story was about Alan," she says. "It talked about how he had earned fifty thousand dollars a year from the radio station but was kicking back forty thousand of it to pay for his promotional costs on the concerts."

Freed's financial problems were compounded by the fact that at some of his largest concerts he took home only a very small percentage of the profits, with the rest going to mobsters, according to an old friend, in whom Freed confided backstage on New Year's Eve in 1958. Freed invited the old friend and his wife to talk after the show, but they found him in tears. He had been drinking, the friend says. The tears seemed to be from frustration and fear. Freed told him that he had just gone to the mobsters who, he said, controlled the receipts. He had asked for a larger percentage, but they told him to take what he had been taking or leave it, the friend recalls.

Freed indicated to his friends that the mobsters had threatened him physically. "When he went in and made his demand, they told him to fuck off or he would wind up dead. They said 'You got a speed boat, a house, and we will take care of business,'" says the friend, recounting Freed's conversation with him.

Freed found work after leaving New York at KDAY in Los Angeles and even signed on with some investors to promote concert tours in the early 1960s in baseball parks and venues like the Hollywood Bowl. The station jumped from the twenty-second slot in a twenty-four station market to number three during Freed's show, according to *Billboard*. But shortly after Freed had settled in, he was hit with another blow.

He had come out of the Washington election-year payola investigation without having charges filed against him, but there were other politicians out there looking to snatch some headlines. Just when Freed thought it was safe, he was indicted on New York State charges by a Manhattan grand jury in May of 1960.

Although Freed gave it a game effort in Los Angeles, his legal and tax problems weighed too heavily on him, and he abruptly quit one day on the air. "I was in the outer room when he said. 'I'm sorry everybody, this is it,' and quit," remembers Inga. "I said, 'Oh my god, this is it.'"

He went on trial on the state charges in February 1962. Before the prosecution could get to him, Freed pleaded guilty to two of seven counts of commercial bribery and received a three-hundred-dollar fine and a six-month suspended sentence. He had been accused of accepting more than thirty thousand dollars in bribes from seven record companies, but he pleaded guilty to accepting two thousand dollars from one company and seven hundred from another. In January of 1963, he was arrested on a warrant charging that he had not paid the fine imposed six months earlier. He paid it, but by that time not much remained.

The payola problems continued. The Internal Revenue Service got in on the Freed feeding-frenzy when a federal grand jury indicted him in March of 1964 for income tax evasion. The IRS charged Freed had failed to report fifty-seven thousand dollars in income from 1957 to 1959 and that he owed back taxes of thirty-eight thousand dollars. Lawyers' fees devoured what little was left of the family finances.

The family was allowed to keep its small home in Palm Springs under the homesteading act. Freed took an after-midnight deejay job briefly with an FM jazz station, KNOB in Los Angeles. "It wasn't too thrilling, but it was something," says

Inga, who took a job as a secretary at the Riviera Hotel in Palm Springs to help support the family. "We had all the kids with us. Alan cooked, and I did the ironing. We had great rules."

There were rules but no money. Lance Freed recalls, "It was sad. I remember going in to tell my father that I had a toothache, and he said, 'I don't have any money to fix it.' I had to get a job when I was fifteen so I could get my teeth fixed. My dad was broke and broken-hearted as well because he could not work in a medium that he loved."

David Freed stopped to visit on a business trip and found his brother greatly changed. "I didn't recognize him," his brother says. "His vitality was gone. He'd lost his verve and the zest for life that had been his greatest characteristic. He was almost zombie-like, and he was drinking heavily. But even then he was always talking about something being on fire, somebody was going to get him a show, get him syndicated. You know, the microphone had been part of Alan since he was seventeen, and when they took it away, well, I think he just died of a broken heart, that and too much alcohol and maybe other drugs, and that body wracked up from the automobile accident. But I still think he wouldn't have had it any other way."

The year before he died, Freed spent days and days on the telephone, trying to make contacts with the many powerful people he had helped attain their power. When his telephone was shut off for failure to pay his bill, he used a neighbor's telephone.

Family members say the most crippling blow to the disc jockey was not delivered by newspaper reporters or federal investigators but by a man he had long considered his best friend, Leonard Chess of Chess Records. Inga says, "Alan never worried about money as long as he had a voice and he was willing and able to work. After he left Los Angeles, I think he felt he was being blackballed because the job offers just weren't coming in. Leonard had always said that he would take care of Alan if things got bad.

"Leonard had purchased a radio station in Chicago, and

he had told Alan he could be on it. We were planning on going to Chicago, at one point, we were already packed, when we got a telephone call from one of Leonard's lackeys saying, 'We can't mix apples and oranges, you can't be on the station.' After that, Alan could never get Leonard on the telephone. It was a low blow. That happened in about September, and Alan died in January of 1965. He was forty-three. I think he died of a broken heart more than anything else."

Freed told his son that "when this shit went down, I thought my friends would throw a lifeboat over the side for me, but they turned out to be a bunch of rats."

On New Year's Day 1965, the ostracized deejay was in the kitchen cooking a dinner for his family and some friends, clowning around like a young kid, when he doubled over in pain. He told his family he felt sick and went to the bedroom to lie down. He was bleeding profusely from a gastrointestinal ulcer when his oldest son came in to comfort him.

"There was a lot of blood everywhere, and he was very, very frightened," Lance Freed recalls. "We had had a big fight that day over something. I felt bad. I told him 'You're gonna be okay.' He said, 'Yeah, I'm really scared. Can you get me a cigarette?' I said he shouldn't have one, but he told me to just get it for him. The guys from the ambulance came and they wheeled in one of those carts, but he said to get it out. He said, 'I'm walking out of my house.' He did it."

At the hospital, the doctor told the family that Freed had only a 10 percent chance of making it through the night, but he held on for twenty days. "About ten days into it, he asked me to smuggle in a root beer float for him," says Lance. "He called them 'Boston coolers.' I said I wasn't sure that would be good for his stomach. He said, 'What's a little Hires root beer and some ice cream gonna hurt at this point?'"

The coroner's report said it was the diseased liver that did him in. The day after Freed's death, the IRS was at the door, wanting to know how Inga planned on paying off his debts, she said.

Record businessman and author Arnold Shaw offered this tribute: "By his hearty sponsorship of black artists, Freed contributed greatly to breaking down segregation in radio and TV. He also popularized if he did not introduce . . . a style of announcing that was typically black. He was exuberant and colorful; and he projected a degree of enthusiasm and excitement that brought listeners flocking to his in-person appearances. As a disc jockey, he was, in short, a rhythm-and-bluesman."

Shaw also noted that while Freed no doubt did take his share of payola, as did most deejays of that era, "He must nevertheless be regarded as a casualty of the establishment war on teenage manners, mores, and music and, more specifically, of that discrimination that has been and is still practiced against the black minority of society."

In 1978, they made a movie based on Freed's life. It was called *American Hot Wax*. Screamin' Jay Hawkins played himself, but the movie failed to capture the soul and the energy of the deejay, he says. The film had its truthful moments. However, in the end, Hawkins says, Hollywood done Freed wrong, too.

Several years ago, Alan Freed was inducted into the Rock-'n'-Roll Hall of Fame. Lance Freed accepted for the family. "He was a wonderful man, and he loved what he did. It was a shame he couldn't continue. He may never have recaptured the sort of momentum that he had when he was on top in New York, but I've got to say that he just loved radio. And when you listened to him, you could tell that he loved it," says Moon Dog's son.

FIVE

Screaming in a Straightjacket

On a school day in 1958, Superintendent W. H. Reed walked into the eight-grade classroom at Mazon Grade School in a tiny farm community in central Illinois and asked the twenty-eight students to write down where they thought they would be in twenty years.

Most of the students were farm kids who had spent the first six years of their educations in one-room schoolhouses at the edges of corn and soybean fields and cow pastures. They had a limited view of the world. There was no concert hall in Mazon, no bowling alley, no drive-in, no movie theater. But that year there was *Bandstand* on television and, by their sophomore high-school year, there would be Biondi on the radio.

Mazon parents began to worry in the fall of 1958 when their young rushed home from school every afternoon and instead of changing clothes and pitching in on the chores, they ran to the television set to tune in *American Bandstand*.

Suddenly, they started dressing differently. Their regular school clothes weren't good enough. They wanted to dress like the kids on *Bandstand.*

Soon they were dancing to radio music and records at school during the lunch hour. Then, two years after this strange behavior started, parents began to hear noises at night, muffled screams and giggles coming from their children's bedrooms. They found them under the covers, listening to transistor radios tuned to eighty-nine on the AM dial. It was that Chicago radio station, WLS, disturbing their peace and quiet from one hundred miles away.

WLS had traditionally been a country-music station, but suddenly some guy was making all sorts of rude noises, doing unmentionable things to the lyrics of "On Top of Old Smokey," and telling risque jokes— "What's the difference between a snowman and a snowwoman? Snowballs!" Fathers found their sons shaving with Gillette razors, just the way Dick Biondi had told them to do it on his commercials.

Sometimes Biondi even played music, but it wasn't the sort Dad listened to while cleaning the chickenbleep out of the henhouse. This music scrambled eggs and set the roosters to crowing. It was music from a much bigger world, music that teeny-boppers could call their own.

The high-school kids in Mazon took over the upstairs in the old dance hall downtown, even refinished and waxed the maple flooring. Then they took up a collection and paid that Chicago deejay Dick Biondi, who called himself "The Screamer," to come to Mazon and play records. All that for just playin' records?

Suddenly it was Biondi, not Father, who knew best. What would Ward Cleaver do in a situation like this? What was going on here? What had happened to the heartland's children? Parents in Mazon were not alone in their concern. Around the country mothers and fathers felt that they had been usurped by these deejay persons and their so-called music on radio and, God help us, television. Even Ed Sullivan had gone from the

American Bandstand *interfered with farm chores in Mazon, Illinois, and changed farm kids' wardrobes*

cute little puppet Topo Gigo to that sneery what's-his-name, Elvis. Rock-'n'-roll had loosened the bonds. Teenagers were thinking of the possibilities beyond the fence rows and fields of Grundy County, Illinois.

The superintendent placed the students' predictions scrawled on scraps of blue- and red-lined notebook paper inside a plastic bag and then tucked it, time-capsule fashion, in the shiny ball atop the school's new flagpole, the finishing flourish on a new baby-boom classroom addition.

The idea was to retrieve the class predictions in 1978, at the class's twentieth-year reunion. But the plan was forgotten, and the scraps of paper spent ten additional years inside the flagpole. They were finally discovered in the fall of 1988 when a faulty pulley brought custodians Dick Finch and Frank Donnelly up the ladder to fix the pole. They noticed a crack in the weathered old ball atop it and some papers sticking out the crack. They thought at first it must be a hornet's nest, but when they pulled it out, they released not angry hornets but the dreams of the class of 1958.

In the thirty intervening years, Mazon had changed from a isolated supply center for farmers into a bedroom community that supplied workers to three nearby nuclear power plants and three heavy-equipment factories. The number of farms in surrounding Grundy County had diminished from 1,112 in 1958 to 588. In their forecasts, the majority of the boys in the eighth-grade class of 1958 had planned to be farmers. Only two of them realized that dream.

Most of the girls predicted they would be housewives, and most of them were, although they also had jobs outside the home. They had predicted what was expected of them and their lives at the time, but a half-dozen of the students had added something to their notes that did not come from their parents, something that their teachers might not have expected.

In the margins, at the bottom of the scraps, or sideways up the page, they had written out their little conspiracy, a small rebellion but one shared by most of their generation. They wrote for all to see and remember: "This is the time of rock-'n'-roll!"

Neither rock-'n'-roll nor deejays disappeared in the aftermath of the payola purges. The general power of rock-'n'-roll "personality" deejays to wield influence and demand payola diminished, but the beat was too strong to be denied. Teens still listened to deejays on radio and watched their dance shows on television. But rock-'n'-roll had lost much of its badass kick as it was assimilated and sanitized for general acceptance. The Pepsodent pop kids, try as they might, just didn't have the same soulfulness as their black counterparts. But they did have their own appeal, and Bobby Darin was certainly less threatening to the teenagers of Mazon than Chuck Berry or James Brown. All of them appeared on the main rock-'n'-roll forum of the era, *American Bandstand*. There were thousands and thousands of Mazons out there watching.

"I guess hundreds of people have told me stories about *American Bandstand*," says Dick Clark. "It doesn't matter the size of the town or the place on the map, it brought the whole world together to dance. Everyone found out things they didn't know on that show. They learned dances and bought the music. It was a giant corner drugstore that everybody could go to. It was an American and Canadian phenomenon because the show did tremendously well in Toronto, too."

The show influenced a generation of teenagers by helping give them a sense of identity. Clark says, "This was the first generation in which teenagers had things that were their own. Prior to the 1950s, teenagers wore hand-me-down clothes, and they wore the fashions of the older generation. Nowadays people laugh about kids in the fifties who wore their jeans rolled up and the sleeves of their hand-me-down shirts rolled up, but they were trying to establish their own styles. The show was one of the things that helped set up their individuality."

Clark has been derided in the press and by others in the music and entertainment business for having a large ego — as if that were something unusual in Hollywood or in the music business — but he is willing to share credit for *American Band-stand*'s success and influence with the men on whom he relied to tell him what was worth playing on his television show — the radio deejays. "The guys on radio were doing all the work, and we were getting all the credit," he says. "We had one thousand radio stations backing us up."

In the aftermath of the payola investigation, radio stations and the surviving deejays generally laid low, fearful of even more strictures. For a brief time the FCC even required stations to announce that the records they were playing were freebies provided by the record companies. It was that bad. Many stations just gave up trying to appeal to teens and went to "good music" and "easy-listening" formats.

A new breed of radio deejays emerged after the payola scandal faded. Restricted by the top-forty format, they relied more on their wits and quickness than on the music for entertainment. If possible, they became even more of the show. Hyper-talk and gimmickry became the focus. These were radio stuntmen, and any stunt worth doing was done, at least once. With most radio stations playing the same music, it was left to the deejays to distinguish themselves. Underwater, up a tree, out an airplane, and with a mouthful of marbles, they tried.

Deejays around the country risked life, limb, and human dignity to draw the attention of their listeners away from other stations in their market playing "Mother-in-Law," by Ernie K-Doe, and "Traveling Man," by Ozzie and Harriet's boy Rick. The excitement had to come from somewhere. It certainly wasn't in the music. Frosty Flower at KING in Seattle looked for it at about twenty-five hundred feet. His parachute opened, to the disappointment of his competitors in the greater Seattle market.

In the spring of 1961, Dean Griffith, deejay and program director at WPGC in Washington, DC, donned a diving suit and broadcast his show from the bottom of an eight-foot tank of water. A special contact microphone was taped to his throat, and he used waterproof earphones. The stunt was staged to hype the opening of a skin-diving equipment store, 8 Fathoms Deep. Fifteen hundred people came to watch Griffith, who was only slightly more entertaining than the payola hearings.

Caught up in the rollicking fun of the Cold War years, Ernie Goldmar of KTPH in Houston lived in a fallout shelter for two weeks and made telephone reports on the air in "Operation Survival." Bomb shelter madness swept through the deejay trade in the early sixties. June Bundy, who chronicled the exploits of radio deejays for *Billboard* magazine, noted that Dave Woods of WJPS, Evansville, Indiana, Bruce Bartley of WFUN in Miami, Chuck Boyles at WHB in Kansas City, Stan Roberts at WTRY in Troy, New York, and Doug Viar of WLAY in Muscle Shoals, Alabama, were all safe from nuclear attack.

Bartley's station in Miami spun off on this theme by conducting two contests in conjunction with his shelter stay. One of these was an enticement to local teenage girls to write an essay detailing why they would like to become "Miss Radiation Shelter." The reviews were, need we say it, glowing. In his own desperate bid to do the same thing, but be different, deejay Roberts sealed himself in a shelter at Latham Corners shopping center for two weeks, but he took the little woman with him.

The deejay stunt craze was not limited to the continental United States. J. Akuhead Pupule, a deejay for KORL in Hawaii, raised five thousand dollars in cash to send the Hawaii Little League to the mainland for the Little League World Series by broadcasting from a treehouse suspended from a large banyan tree. Ken Griffin of WHYN in Springfield, Massachusetts, came up with a new twist on the marathon thing when he set out to become the first deejay to live on a thirty-one-and-a-half-ton Tower of Ice measuring one thousand cubic feet and filling a large section in the parking lot of the Tower Marts discount store. Callers vied for an automobile by guessing just how long Griffin could stay atop the giant ice cube.

Egg scrambling was another stunt of choice for these rollicking sixties jocks. Local poultry and egg industries gladly sponsored these mass egg-frying executions, and when it was just not hot enough to get the job done on city sidewalks, crews wielding acetylene torches were set upon the whites and yolks.

Ken Grant of KNUZ in Houston let teenagers throw cream pies at him during a Mount Carmel High School record hop. Grant was trying to top his previous stunt, which involved swallowing a marble during a promotion in which he and his fellow disc jockeys attempted to talk with a mouthful of shooters.

In what may have been a subconscious reaction by deejays after living in fear of losing their livelihood during the payola purges, deejay marathons were a big-ticket item in the early sixties. Sam Sherwood of KDWB in Minneapolis bowled a full forty-four hours and forty-one minutes without stopping, and doctors reported that he did it without noticeable brain damage. Don Redfield of WBSR in Pensacola, Florida, did his job—a clever stunt—for sixty-eight hours and forty-five minutes only to be outperformed by Jim Rud at KXGO in Fargo, North Dakota, who broadcast for 137 hours straight.

Some deejays conducted marathons to raise money for charities like the Heart Fund. Others did it just because they were nutty guys. And, of course, a few of them had mishaps along the way. Andy West of KUDI, in Kansas City, Missouri, broke his foot during a go-cart race with frolicsome fellow deejays. In all seriousness, allegedly, Dave Clarke of KVI in Seattle reported that his on-the-air marathon for 104 hours and three minutes had long-term effects. He said, "I had a form of amnesia at three different times during the marathon, lasting as long as three hours. During the time, I was fully conscious and still talking on the radio although I am told most of what I said did not make much sense. I also noticed that I really didn't feel good for about a year-and-a-half after the marathon."

Perhaps even more amazing in the deejay marathon stunt madness was the feat of deejay Stan Major, who staged an eight-and-one-half-day "Stay Awake Marathon" that had "absolutely no repercussions of any kind, physically or mentally, after 210 hours with no sleep." Doctors said, in fact, that he was actually in better physical condition than before the marathon started. This incredible achievement is all the more impressive when it is noted that Major, who later moved on to WJJD in Chicago, performed the feat of staying awake and increasingly healthy for 210 hours while working at a station in Peoria, Illinois.

The flatlands of the Midwest seemed to inspire some of the craziest radio shenanigans of the era. To the northeast of Peoria something strange was going on at the "Prairie Farmer" station in Chicago, WLS. In March of 1960, WLS-AM, with fifty thousand watts of punch, switched to a new format. Just when the church leaders and starched collars thought it was safe to put down their placards and protest signs, one of the most powerful radio stations in the Midwest decided to go rock-'n'-roll. The station brought in a marauding band of deejays, and the biggest gun of them all was a skinny, black-haired son of a fireman and a short-order cook from Endicott, New York. They called him "The Screamer." And although Alan Freed was one of his heroes, he wasn't about to mourn the death of all deejays just because the Moon Dog had been run out of radio.

At a time when many deejays were bailing out or decrying the end of their era. Dick Biondi had decided to stick around and make life miserable for all the station managers and program directors who demanded that their deejays wear the top-forty straightjacket. He talked like he was willing to put it on, but what he really meant was that no silly format was going to keep him off the airwaves. "At this moment the greatest deejay is the one who can live within the formula, or top-forty list, and make it sound not only happy and interesting but as if he is producing and pulling the music all by himself," Biondi said at the time, while sharpening his knives behind his back.

Biondi advocated guerilla deejay warfare. He signed on for a hitch in top-forty radio while working covertly to destroy it from within. His public proclamations that disc jockeys could live with the top-forty won him an invitation into the enemy camp. Unsuspecting WLS hired the broadcast equivalent of the

Trojan Horse to lead its new army of rock-'n'-roll deejays.

"I don't buy that the payola thing or the top-forty format killed us," he says today, as one of the golden oldies of Chicago rock-'n'-roll radio. "It made a few of us sharper. Instead of just rambling on all the time, we had to come up with something to keep the kids' interest. We had to do interesting things like teaching a kid to shave or telling them how to dye their bathwater green. We were all still in it for the ego, and it was still great."

What the radio moguls had failed to note was that this earnest young radio jock had trained under not only Alan Freed but also the legendary Hound Dog, George Lorenz, a pioneering radio freedom-fighter. Biondi's role model and class hero in his career-long struggle to break the bonds of formatted radio was another upstate-New York native, whose influence on listeners and aspiring disc jockeys along the Eastern seaboard rivaled that of the southern pioneers at WLAC in Nashville.

Born near Cheektowaga, New York, Lorenz grew up in Buffalo. Like most who were drawn to the microphone, he was graced with a glib tongue that led to his abandoning high school and visions of a law career in his senior year to perform in local nightclubs. The stage was not enough, but radio held promise. His first announcing job was on WBTA in Batavia, New York. In 1947, be began broadcasting on WXRA in Buffalo, where he would occasionally sneak on a record by one of the black performers that he had become infatuated with on the nightclub scene. He was fired after a few years because station management didn't think Buffalo was ready for the likes of "Sixty-Minute Man."

Lorenz, the son of a meatpacker, whose heritage was Bavarian rather than Hispanic as his surname might suggest, moved even further north to Niagara, New York, and radio station WJJL after that. There he did the morning coffee-break show after Ramblin' Lou's country wake-up program and an *On the Avenue* late-night show three times a week. It was on the evening show that he played more of the music that was becoming known as rhythm-and-blues. And it was in Buffalo that he picked up his nickname from the blacks who listened to his show. "It was pinned on me by the black people," he told the *Buffalo Evening News* in 1971, just a few years before his death of a heart attack. "One of the jive expressions of the time was if you were hangin' around the corner, you were doggin' around. So I'd come on and say: 'Here I am to dog around for another hour.' That's how they got to call me the 'Hound Dog.'"

The signal from Niagara reached into Canada, too, and his popularity in the Northeast resulted in a job offer from the hottest radio market in the country in 1953 — Cleveland, where Alan Freed, Bill Randle, Joe Finan, and a heavy group of deejays were tussling. The Hound Dog as hired by WSRS to do a show from nine P.M. until eleven-thirty P.M. while Freed was on WJA from eleven-fifteen P.M. until one A.M.. For a brief period, it was dueling dogs in Cleveland. "When all the hip black people heard what we were doin' on the radio, they went crazy. That's where rock-'n'-roll as everybody knows it got started," Lorenz said in 1971.

The Big Apple lured Freed away from Cleveland in 1954, and Lorenz left a year later to return to Buffalo, where his ailing mother needed his attentions. "He was offered jobs in New York, but he didn't want to leave his mother in Buffalo," says Lorenz's son, Frank. The Hound Dog went back on the air in Buffalo on radio station WKBW, which at first seemed an unlikely home for a rock-'n'-roll jock of his stature. The station's call letters stood for "Well-Known Bible Works."

"My dad knew they had a fifty-thousand-watt signal that would give him a lot of reach, so he just asked them to put him on the air from seven to midnight and let him play what he wanted to play. He told them they didn't have to pay him a salary, just pay him a commission on everything he sold. They thought he was nuts. The rest is history," Frank says.

The Hound Dog sold to the sinners at night, and he sold a lot, coming on the air on behalf of Mother Goldstein's Wine:

"It's in the sniff." Eventually, he hosted a Saturday morning *Hound Dog Hit Parade* show as well, but his big gig was the late-night show, which he did from a broadcast booth at the Club Zanzibar on William Street in Buffalo. His fans filled the club and pressed their faces against the glass of the Dog House to see the Hound in action as his engineer, Easy Ernie Bohrk, fed him the rhythm-and-blues.

Lorenz's fan club in the mid-fifties had nearly seventy thousand members, and they would pour into the Plaza Theater or Memorial Auditorium for shows he hosted—sometimes with his friend from Cleveland, Alan Freed—featuring performers such as Elvis, Chuck Berry, Fats Domino, Jerry Lee Lewis, Bill Haley and the Comets, Buddy Holly, and Little Richard. "It was a new thing, a new form of music, a new way of living," Lorenz told a Buffalo reporter. "The old people said it wouldn't last six months. That's because they couldn't understand it. They couldn't get the afterbeat."

They didn't get the Hound Dog, either. Church bulletins editorialized against Lorenz and the music he played, but he kept on playing. The Hound Dog is recognized as an innovative deejay whose antics pushed rock-'n'-roll radio to its heights. He is acknowledged as the first deejay to "rock the pot," which involved turning the volume controls up and down with the beat of the music—a practice that led station management to install "limiters" on the deejay's volume controls. He was also one of the first deejays to use instrumentals so that "the music never stopped," even as he talked and read commercials.

Lorenz was not a fast rapping-and-rhyming deejay, nor the sort that could easily adapt to the restrictions of the top-forty format. The Hound Dog knew his music and the people who performed it, and he liked to tell his listeners the history behind the songs he played. Commercials were a necessary evil. He was most inclined to play three or four records in a row. "He had this big gravelly voice, and when he talked, you thought he was speaking directly to you on the radio," says his son. "He felt very strongly about the music and was protective of the black artists in particular. He fought hard to keep their music on the radio."

In 1958, WKBS brought in a new program director to install a top-forty format, and the Hound Dog announced that he preferred to leave rather than work while wearing a leash. He has seen top-forty coming, and he had his own ideas about the sort of radio he wanted to do. He thought there might be something for the Hound Dog on the FM dial. "I remember sitting at the kitchen table with him back then and listening to him talk about what a big thing FM radio was going to be. He said it would leave AM by the wayside. He was right about that," says Frank Lorenz. "After he left WKBS, he helped pioneer the FM market by breaking the sweet music mode and playing rock-'n'-roll and rhythm-and-blues."

The Hound Dog began syndicating a show that he taped in a Buffalo studio and sold to stations around the country. In 1965, he purchased radio station WBLK-FM, the last FM-frequency station available in Buffalo and, according to its own billing, "the only full-time black-music station in New York State outside New York City." Lorenz hired black deejays and aimed his signal at the black community with church news and even a Muslim hour. Because of his long-term connections to rock-'n'-roll record companies, he was able to get records for his FM station way before they appeared on AM.

For the first few years, the high-brow FM audience treated the Hound Dog and his new station like the first black family to move into a segregated white neighborhood, but as more and more FM stations went to rock-'n'-roll and album-rock programming, Lorenz began to pull ahead financially. "He was coming on real strong, and WBLK had tried to hire him back, but he had his own station and he said, 'Now it's my turn and I'm gonna get you guys.'"

The Hound Dog never fully realized his sweet revenge. He died of a heart attack in 1972 at the age of fifty-two. Sons Frank and Fred Lorenz took over the station management. "He missed enjoying the fruits of all of his hard work at the station, and it was a sad, sad thing to lose a man with so much life and spunk and foresight," his son says. "It would be great to have him around today."

In a sense, the Hound Dog is still around. He influenced hundreds of young disc jockeys, including the one who took over for him when he left WBLK in 1958, the scrawny Italian kid Biondi. "Nobody replaced the Hound Dog, and I am serious about that," says the Screamer. "That man, along with Alan Freed, should be in the Rock-'n'-Roll Hall of Fame, and if not, there is no justice. The Hound Dog was unique. He played the stuff nobody else played, and he would jump on things first. He loved having stuff before anyone else. When he talked about the music, you knew he knew what he was talking about. You could take what he said to the bank."

Biondi took what he learned from the Hound Dog to the top. Thick-haired and hot-headed, he was rated number one in the country in 1961 and 1962, and at one time or another he was number one in about every major market. He says, "I remember going to little places like Mazon and LaSalle-Peru and LaPort, Indiana, and they would give me police protection when I signed autographs. It was such a great ego trip. People were so happy to see me. At the time I didn't realize what it was all about. I thought of myself as just another deejay, and I was having a ball."

He was one of the most admired, and probably the most fired, deejays of the sixties scene. He loved every cursed, screaming and yelling, feuding minute of it, he says. He was constantly engaged in a simultaneous lovefest with his fans and raging war with the top-forty format. War was heaven for the man with the flash-fire temper. "I stayed in there with top-forty, I adjusted to a point, but I also threw a phone at a program director and just missed his head by a half an inch," he says. "I threw an ashtray at Gene Taylor at WLS because I was fighting the format. Thank god my aim was not too great. In the one instance, if I had hit the program director with the phone, it would have improved his looks. I got into a literal physical fistfight with the sales manager at WLS because of the commercial load. I was concerned about what was going on the air. It was not an easy adjustment into top-forty."

When rock-'n'-roll radio moved into the top-forty format, Biondi became one of the most successful deejays in the country by latching onto it like a bantamweight wrestler administering a headlock. He was a shrieking, jabbering deejay who ricocheted all over radio. By one count, he was fired twenty-two times in thirty-two years, and hired and fired again. His first job was in Corning, New York. Fired. York, Pennsylvania. Fired. Buffalo. Fired. Chicago. Fired. Los Angeles. Fired. Back to Chicago. Fired. Cincinnati. Fired.

He refuses to count stations where he quit or forced management to fire him. The experts were always the ones to put the finest point on things. "A lot of those times I precipitated it because I wanted to move on. I had this reputation of being a rebel, but it was more like I would get to feeling that the audience was being screwed by too many commercials. Instead of entertaining I would end up doing what somebody else wanted. After I'd get knocked down a few times, I would say, 'Hey, screw this,'" he remembers.

"Hell, I don't regret the image a bit," he says, looking back. "There are times when I'd lie in bed at night and say, 'Oh god, why did I do that one particular thing?' but I have seen and learned and met people and experienced situations I never would have otherwise. Besides, it is no fun to look back and say 'What if?' That's bullshit. I want to be the George Burns of the disc jockey set."

Biondi was a bad boy on radio at a time when most deejays where ducking for cover. He incited listeners to throw rocks at his boss's car. He hyped records he liked by playing them for request callers who never dialed. He was high-ctane, extremely flammable and spilling all over the place. It once took two people to restrain him from turning a station sales manager's necktie into a noose. When he was burning on the air, he could consume the attentions of at least

Dick Biondi's popularity in the early sixties earned him the label of "pied piper"

half of the massive Chicago-area radio audience.

Near as Dick Biondi can remember, he was eight years old when he first started shouting into a wooden microphone in his attic playroom in Endicott, New York. "My family thought I was nuts," he recalls. At first, he says, he yearned to follow the traditional nice-Italian-boy routine: the priesthood. Then one day he saw a neighborhood girl in a swimming suit. Something told him he was not one of God's chosen ones. That divine revelation resulted in something of a change in his approach to life. Instead of hanging out near religious supply stores and eyeing the crucifixes and cassocks, he became a radio-station groupie. Someone, perhaps an inner voice, told young Biondi that even skinny Italian guys with big noses could get chicks if they had their own show.

After escaping from high school, Biondi made a half-hearted pass at higher education before hightailing it into the less demanding world of radio. He worked the split-shift at a station in Corning, New York, in 1951. Three months later, he was launched on a pattern that would mark his long, still-active career. He was fired when a new manager came in. Biondi, like thousands of fired deejays before him, put his finger to the wind and picked up Alexandria, Louisiana, where there was, if nothing else, a radio station and, it turned out, a woman willing to marry him.

Biondi was married for twenty years and has a son. But he has always preferred to keep his family life low-profile, and he still doesn't like to talk about personal matters other than his relationship with radio. "The marriage was good," he says, "but let's face it. I am the first one to admit that women in this business suffer. Most of the time, they have to live in the shadow of the disc jockeys because we are on such big ego trips. Believe me, any deejay's wife in the fifties and sixties deserves sainthood."

Shortly after he married, Biondi fell in love with rock-'n'-roll. He never tried to hide the fact that his music and his job came first. Like many others of his era, he found the music on the dark side of town. The Greystone Grill was a black club on lower Third Street in Alexandria, and Biondi found his way there when he heard about the music. Often, he was the only white man in the joint. That's where he got his training. That's where he heard the music that was at the root of rock-'n'-roll. Prior to that, he had been content to play the big bands, the Glen Millers and Duke Ellingtons. It was great stuff, but Biondi, like his teen listeners, was looking for something new.

He first realized that there were those who objected to rock-'n'-roll for reasons other than musical taste in those days in Louisiana. "I was doing an all-black show called *Jammin' Jive* at KYSO in Alexandria. And people would call up and say I was a 'nigger lover' and all that. Especially if I played something like 'Old Man River,'" he says.

By 1953, he played nothing but "race" music on *Jammin' Jive*. He was playing the hot sounds, even if he was the radio equivalent of a steno-pool girl. He says, "I was known down there as Daddy-O Substitute because I was the weekend fill-in for Daddy-O Rainey and Daddy-O Fox." He played Fats Domino, Lloyd Price, Ruth Brown, and Buddy Johnson. Then he latched onto this white cat Elvis. "Listeners would call in and ask, 'What's an Elvis?'" he recalls.

When the rock-'n'-roll explosion came, Biondi was ready. Another change in management in 1954 meant another change in location for Biondi. He headed north to small towns in Pennsylvania and upstate New York where he began preaching the gospel of rock-'n'-roll. The former top sub in Alexandria made first string in Youngstown, Pennsylvania, on the hometown team.

Things got hot when he hit Youngstown, where station management, overcome by loss of mental acuity, allowed Biondi to play whatever he could get his hands on—until his hand landed on Little Richard. Then the station manager stormed in and ripped the needle off the record. "We don't play that kind of crap around here," he told Biondi. But the station owner, plugged into what was going on around the country, overruled the manager. Soon, Biondi was riding high on the airwaves and raising heck in local concert halls. One night, he brought in Jerry Lee Lewis, the Killer, and actor Michael Landon, a.k.a. Little Joe, who was trying to stretch his fame on *Bonanza* into a teen-singing-idol career. The Killer knocked the kid out of the saddle.

Biondi says, "About four thousand kids showed up, and I put Michael Landon on first. The place went wild, absolutely crazy. Then Jerry Lee went on. He got them going again. After that set Lewis said to me, 'You better put me on first for the next set.' So I put Lewis on first, and he did fourteen songs without stopping. The crowd went nuts. He was covered with sweat. As he left the stage, he walked up to Landon, who was waiting to go on, and said, 'Okay, pretty boy, beat that.'"

During that concert stint, Biondi spent a lot of time talking with Jerry Lee, and one evening he broached the question of the Killer's religious beliefs. He had heard that Lewis had spent time in Bible college and that he often threatened to go into preaching. Finally Biondi questioned Lewis: "I said, 'Jerry, are you a real Christian?' He said, 'If I was a real Christian, instead of getting on stage and shakin' my ass all over the place, I'd be up there preachin' the word of the Lord.'"

Biondi also introduced Youngstown to Elvis in concert and did a very dangerous and foolhardy thing he'll always remember thanks to the scratch scars on his body. The deejay asked Elvis to autograph his t-shirt. When Elvis asked what Biondi was going to do with it, the jock informed him he was going to jump into the crowd and see what happened. Looking back, he says, it was a very foolish move. He should at least have arranged to have Last Rites administered before taking the leap. He says, "All those screaming girls started tearing at me like crazy. They all wanted a piece of the shirt, and no one got a piece bigger than a quarter. I wound up in the hospital emergency room with cuts and scratches."

He did the Biondi bounce in Youngstown after a few fast dances then landed in the Hound Dog's chair in Buffalo at

WKBW. He was Lorenz's protégé in spirit only, this wild-child. While the Hound Dog had a quiet growl, this kid would bark until he blew the knobs off your radio. He says, "The Screamer thing just happened. It was just my natural hyperness. When I started out, I was doing sports, and when you do sports, you tend to speak loud and fast." He was "the wild Eye-tailian, the supersonic spaghetti slurper, and the limp linguini" whose stunts included picking leaves off Elvis's lawn in Memphis and awarding them to his listeners. The Big Noise from Buffalo told the worst knock-knock jokes ever to rap on a door, and he ordered peanut-butter-and-sauerkraut pizzas and ate them on the air. He dominated in 50 percent of the highly competitive Buffalo radio market at a time when deejays were dropping like teenage girls at Elvis's feet.

Biondi was one of the deejays who led the way from the dark days of the payola investigation and top-forty format into the lighter rock-'n'-roll era. In early 1960, he was yanked for yet another guerilla attack against the management troops. His boss, who had a rather low opinion of Biondi's maniacal deejay style, returned home from a honeymoon with his young—very young—bride and came to the station the same night to twist Biondi's nose for an hour or so over some things he had heard on the drive home. He ordered the deejay to straighten up. When he left, with his back exposed, Biondi took aim and fired.

Biondi says, "When he walked out the door, I went on the air and said, 'Hey, my boss just left the studio. Can you imagine him coming in here the day after his honeymoon? He's driving down Main Street in a gray Impala. So if you see it, throw rocks at it.'" The power of deejay suggestion was not to be underestimated. One of Biondi's listeners took his prank as a command. A rock was thrown right through the windshield of the manager's car as he drove down the street. He escaped unharmed. Biondi did not. He was bounced.

He was invited to unsuspecting Chicago, to a station undergoing a radical personality transplant. WLS was a powerful station that rode a nighttime skip into infinity, or at least

Nebraska. In the spring of 1960, the station switched from the yahoos of country-western to the yah-yahs of Biondi's beat. Tennessee Ernie Ford was sent packin'. Georgia's Little Richard moved in. The home of Al Capone had just opened the door to yet another machine-gunner. He was brought into WLS with a group of new jocks that included Jim Dunbar, Mort Crowley, and Bob Hale to open an era in which Chicago radio led the revival of the rock-'n'-roll personality deejay with the likes of Biondi, Art Roberts, Dex Card, Larry Lujack, Joel Sebastian, Ron Riley, Gene Taylor, and Bob Sirott. They were an innovative, irreverent pack who played to hundreds of thousands of sixties teen cruisers chugging cheap beer and sloe gin as they drove around and around LeRoy's Drive-In, Steak 'n' Shake, and the Pizza Pan on their forced march to adulthood.

"The electricity was there, though we barely realized it

Biondi at the mike in 1988

ourselves. Other people told me that it kicked in for them immediately," Biondi says. In his first night blasting out of Chicago, Biondi set the city to talking. Not all of it was happy talk. One of the station managers had already heard enough. At the executive meeting on the morning after Biondi's first show, he announced that whatever that was on the air from nine to midnight, it had to go. He said, "Let's get rid of this nut." Biondi never has figured out why he was allowed to stick around, but he did. Like crazy glue.

Soon the teenagers were packing the corridors of WLS radio, wanting to see the Italian rapscallion. When he appeared at a benefit for a Chicago hospital in 1961, he nearly became a patient. He was forced to seek shelter from the clutches of his fans in a ticket cage. "They were ripping the clothes off me," he says. "What a high!" The ratings were right up there with Biondi's buzz. WLS figures that for their show from six to nine P.M. 44,100 adults tuned in and 57,400 teens. From nine P.M. to midnight it was 28,900 adults and 72,400 teens. Somebody out there was listening, in droves.

For all of his screaming and ranting, Biondi had a deeper appeal to the disaffected and lost souls of that tumultuous time. Like many deejays, he had his share of "moments," when the job meant more than it was supposed to mean if all the critics of rock-'n'-roll radio were right. He recalls one such incident: "One night while I was on the air at 'LS, somebody told me to look out the window at a beautiful sunset. I did and then on the air I said, 'Hey, if you haven't looked outside, take a look at the sunset, and if that doesn't make you believe in God and think things are gonna get better, nothing will.' Well, I didn't know it at the time, of course, but about that moment a lady in Michigan had just loaded a gun and was going to shoot herself and three kids because her husband had been convicted of arson—wrongly, she said—and sent to prison three weeks earlier. She wrote me a letter and said she had heard me say that about the sunset and she had gone to the window and looked out. The beauty of it made her stop and think, she wrote.

Two weeks later, the guy who really set the fire confessed and went to jail. Her husband got out, and she credited me with saving their lives." Biondi identified closely with his fans, to the point that one night he got all of the commercials out of the way in the first few minutes and then played nothing but records for an hour straight—something modern deejays are allowed to do, but it was a forbidden act back then.

In a city once divided between White Sox fans and Cubs fans, Southsiders and Northsiders, Democrats and other Democrats, new battle lines were drawn: those who loved Biondi and those who would love to see something large and sound-absorbent shoved down his throat. Even when he bashed New York, a favorite sport in the Second City, it made him enemies and influenced crazies. One night he got off work at the stroke of midnight, walked into the elevator, went down, and walked off into a pointed gun.

There was a drunk on the other side of the muzzle. He already had the building's security guard up against the wall. The gunman, so it seemed, was a New York Yankees fan who took offense at Biondi's belaboring of his team. "I'm sick and tired of hearing you insult the Yankees," snarled the drunkard. "I'm gonna blow your head off." Before he pulled the trigger, however, the police arrived, and Biondi could continue wearing hats on his head rather than on his neck.

That neck itself was often at risk. Biondi was always on the verge of another "management change," a term he uses loosely to denote a change in management's attitude about his employment status. He had not been at WLS long when he had another of his notorious Italian beefs with the station manager—and nobody was talking lunch. This time it was over a memo that restricted Christmas freebies for deejays to items worth no more than twenty-five dollars. Biondi resented the implications and the restriction. To his chortling delight, a few days after the memo appeared, a record company sent over a couple of beautiful steaks, each worth about twenty-seven dollars by Biondi's calculation. After his shift one Friday night,

Biondi went to the memo-dictator's office and plopped the meat on his desk, along with a note saying, "These were over twenty-five dollars." By Monday, his rank prank was the talk, and the smell, of the office.

Biondi's antiestablishment attitude played well with his teenage listeners, but it eventually bought him his walking papers at WLS, just three years after he arrived and after he had been named top deejay in the country two years straight while blasting from the Windy City. Legend has it that his firing was brought on by an obscene joke told on the air, but he denies that, saying that it was yet another dispute with management over the number of commercials they were scheduling on his show.

His outspoken contempt for the spots that paid the tab made him enemies, naturally, among the sales staff at the station, and one morning one of the salesmen made an impertinent comment in his direction. The Screamer's temper did not ignite until the salesman followed him into the control room. Talent and sales tangled. Management intervened. Biondi was sent to his corner and told not to report for work that night. He huffed out and decided that he had been fired though the station manager later disputed that was his intention.

Biondi did the bunny hop for the next four years, including two stops at KRLA in Los Angeles. On one landing there he holed up in a cage with a chimpanzee and a typewriter for ten days, which was infinitely more appealing than meeting with management in Biondi's mind. The idea was that the chimp would eventually type out the station call letters. Unfortunately, the chimp had the impression that it was Biondi who was supposed to do the typing.

In L.A., Biondi played the Hollywood scene, introducing the latest rock-'n'-roll sensations twice at the Hollywood Bowl. The Beatles came along just in time to remind everyone about the origins of rock-'n'-roll. They ignited a revival, and radio deejays were among the first to jump up and shout hallelujah, we been saved. The Liverpool lads had grown up listening to

American records by the rhythm-and-blues men, and their sound was a British translation of what they heard. Then the Rolling Stones jetted in behind the Beatles, just a little bit leaner and nastier in their interpretations, though the purists among the deejays wondered why anybody would pay attention to Mick Jagger when James Brown was still around. But the Brits brought rock-'n'-roll out of the doldrums, and the deejays got to come along for a mighty fine ride.

"When the Beatles came in, everybody went crazy, and we went especially nuts," Biondi recalls. "We hadn't had anything that big since Elvis. All of a sudden we had so much to talk about, and everybody was fighting to get the Beatles' records first." When a jock did somehow latch onto an early release by the Fab Four — or at least when he wanted everyone to think he had it first — he would make sure he talked over the introduction, middle, and end of the record so his rivals on the other stations could not tape it off his show and claim it as their own. "It was a great time. The entire English thing was great," Biondi says.

Always a rabid rock-'n'-roll fan masquerading as a deejay, Biondi says that Mick Jagger once paid him a most unusual compliment. He was at a party with the Stones during their first appearance in the United States, and Biondi, who is generally not inclined to scream and rant out of range of a microphone, so impressed Jagger that the rock star later told record-promotion man Sol Rabinowitz that he was surprised that the skinny Italian guy was a disc jockey because "he isn't like the loudmouth other ones we met today."

Biondi's eyes still take a strange glow when he talks about the night he introduced the Rolling Stones at the Hollywood Bowl. He says, "The concert was at night, but the flashbulbs made it look like daylight. It was incredible. And when I introduced the Beatles in L.A., they had to bring these guys in and out in an armored truck. But that is not to say that everybody liked these Brits coming over here. Late in 1963, I started playing the Beatles on KRLA, and I would get calls saying, 'Get that crap off the air and play some Beach Boys!'"

Even the most powerful deejay in the country at the time, television deejay, that is, found the Beatles too weird for words. In the fall of 1963, when a record-promo man brought Dick Clark an early copy of "She Loves You" by the new British sensations, he also handed Clark a photograph of the Beatles. "God! Are they kidding?" was Clark's response. They looked ridiculous, and their song sounded "old-fashioned, real mid-fifties, kind of hollow," Clark felt. The television deejay has never been afraid to admit that he does not have the most finely tuned ear for rock-'n'-roll, so he put it to his *Bandstand* dancers for a vote on the "Record Revue." One gave it a seventy-seven and compared the group to "the Everly Brothers and Chuck Berry mixed together." Another said "It's not all that easy to dance to. I give it a sixty-five." The third gave it a seventy, claimed, "It doesn't seem to have anything, but it's sort of catchy." Final score, seventy two.

Then Clark showed his dancers a picture of the group. They snickered and guffawed at the shaggy-dog dos of John, Paul, George, and Ringo. Clark called the record man, who had watched the show. Both agreed. The record looked like a stiff. "I left the station that afternoon without the faintest idea that the days of good old rock-'n'-roll were about to become a few scratched film clips, a list of golden oldies, and some cherished memories of growing up in the fifties," writes Clark in his memoirs.

By the time good old rock-'n'-roll was being transformed and the Beatles were moving into *Sgt. Pepper's Lonely Hearts Club Band*, Dick Biondi was back in Chicago, where the generation weaned on real rock-'n'-roll was about to demonstrate that all those preachers and parents may have been right. This music just might foment rebellion in the streets. Even the Screamer was rattled in those frightful times of the 1968 Democratic Convention, assassinations, and riots. There were bomb scares at station WCFL on a regular nightly basis.

Biondi says, "Being a rock-'n'-roll deejay, I felt sort of stuck in the middle. I was playing things by Cream, the Beatles, the Stones, all of that music of the young generation, but I really felt sorry for the policemen, who were getting human waste thrown at them. Yet when it came down to it, my audience was the rebels, and I was a rebel, so ultimately I felt I was exactly where I should be."

By 1973, Biondi was fired from WCFL, this time by a program director who didn't like his abrasive style. He says, "I had gotten this reputation as a rebel, someone who doesn't like authority. But, finally, I just couldn't handle that anymore." After being booted from WCFL, and then a station in Cincinnati after a cup of coffee in 1973, he just hopped in the car and started driving, visiting relatives along the way and taking life easy.

He ended up in Myrtle Beach, South Carolina, where he intended to play golf for several years, but out of boredom he went to a local radio station and applied for a job. The manager didn't know him, but he hired the man who had been one of the country's top deejays for ninety-seven dollars a week.

"It was beautiful," Biondi told *Chicago Tribune* writer Howard Reich. "I was playing golf, I was on the ocean, and I played what I wanted. I was sort of depleted financially, but the important thing was that I was still on the radio."

Biondi might have been content to live the rest of his life along the beach, playing records and golf, but he was lured back to Chicago by another former deejay there, Bob Sirott, who did a profile of his former colleague for a Chicago television station in 1983. The story attracted such a favorable response that Biondi was invited back to host a radio oldies show.

"Most of my generation of deejays is off the air . . . but I'm still around. And I tell you, I'm never going to stop," he says, "I'm not interested in rusting away. Do you think I mind that these songs are now called oldies or classics? That's a compliment. My music has lasted. And you know what else? The kids today know all the oldies, and they love 'em. Hey, I've made mistakes. I probably should never have left Chicago. I shouldn't have run off every time I got into a fight. But I'm here now, and I just wish that everybody could have a tenth of what I have had. I've got enough memories to keep me happy for as long as I live. I knew Mick Jagger. I knew Brian Jones, rest his soul, of the Rolling Stones. I saw Buddy Holly live onstage. I was a close friend of Bobby Darin, and Jerry Lee Lewis spent three days at my house. No matter how you stack it, I'm a lucky guy."

SIX

The Wolfman

One morning in the summer of 1951 buckets of grimy junk appeared in the Brooklyn alley directly behind the two-flat where Robert Weston "Smitty" Smith, lived with his father and stepmother. The neighbors assumed the kid and his cronies, Richie and Klepto, were up to no good. It was not an unreasonable assumption based on their history. The three aspiring hooligans were hardly into their teens, and they already belonged to a gang—the Taggers Club. They had zip guns in their pockets and larceny on their minds. Not a hubcap was safe. Klepto earned his nickname for the rapid rate at which retail inventories diminished in his presence. Richie, even at this ripe young age, was a locally renowned bowling hustler, a scrawny punk who could pick a grown man's pocket pin by pin.

Smitty was the self-proclaimed "brains" of the outfit. He may have been more self-proclamation than real brains, but nobody doubted that he was a street hustler. His father, a sometime shoe salesman and would-be magician, who at that point was writing for the *Financial World* newspaper, had split from the boy's mother not long before.

Smitty bounced back and forth between relatives and the streets. He lost his front teeth mid-bounce one day in a fight. You shudda seen da odder guy. The neighbors thought the kid was a sad case. He was known for smearing grease on his face in a pitiful attempt to make his pals think he'd just finished a steak dinner. His father tried to keep him out of serious trouble by paying an old codger named John to take Smitty and his buddies to the park to play baseball. The kid's laughingly called it "John's Club." A more effective trouble-aversion measure taken by his father was the purchase of a transoceanic radio for the boy. It was an impressive piece of 1950s high-tech equipment. Long wave, short wave. Dials galore. The radio got the kid off the streets.

A dream machine like this radio begged for a special room, a secret hideaway. So Smitty and his buddies went to work on an old coal bin in the basement. The building had converted to oil heat, but there were still chunks of bituminous in the bin, along with a lot of junk dumped by the present tenants and probably every tenant since time, or at least Brooklyn, began. A coating of soot smothered every inch, even the grain in the wood beams. After they started cleaning it out, the kids realized bums had been sleeping in the basement and the bin. They sealed all entrances except their own. Hardly bigger than a closet, the bin at least offered some shelter from the bloody knuckle scramble on 4th Avenue.

The World Series between the Brooklyn Dodgers and the New York Giants provided only a fleeting, and ultimately gut-wrenching, distraction from life in the summer of '51. The fun ended when Bobby Thomson knocked one out with two men on in the ninth to give the Giants the game and the Series, 5–4. It was one Depression, one war after the other in Brooklyn in those days. Senator Estes Kefauver was looking into crimes in

America, and the rest of the world was on the watch for Communists in China, Congress, and maybe next-door. Smitty, Richie, and Klepto were busy hanging musty old blankets from the ceiling in the basement and stringing enough antennae wire to tune in the man in the moon. They blanketed out the catcalls of the streets and dialed up to another world with their dream machine.

Sitting on orange crates in the coal bin, wrapped in a blanket to keep warm in the winter or sweating in the summer heat, Smitty especially was transfixed by the radio's reach. He spent hour upon hour in that tiny hideaway, traveling thousands of miles on late-night fantasy rides with twists of the radio dial. The deejays were his guides. He could pick up Tommy Smalls, known as "Dr. Jive"; or George "Hound Dog" Lorenz in Buffalo; "Jocko" Henderson, the rhyming rap master in Philadelphia; and, way down south in Dixie, John R., Gene Nobles, and Hoss Allen on WLAC in Nashville.

He could even cross the border where exotic carnival barkers beamed out of broadcasting's badlands in Mexico. With the aid of God, megawatt power transmitters, and the nighttime atmospheric "skip" that sent the signal around the world, these looney-tune pitchmen and preachers sold eternal salvation and potency pills on the same wavelength. Hank Williams and Ernest Tubb comprised the chorus. The "anything goes" attitude of border radio was better entertainment than that new television show about the crazy redhead and her bongo-beating Cuban bandleader husband on the new NBC network, to Smitty's way of thinking anyway

One of Smitty's favorite U.S. deejays kept moving in closer and closer without benefit of any antennae adjustments. At first the boy's radio could pick him up only occasionally out of Cleveland. Then he began picking up the madman's taped show out of Newark. And finally, the Moon Dog, as he was known, moved to New York and WINS, where Smitty hardly even needed a radio at all to hear his maniacal ranting and thumpings. By the fall of 1954, the Moon Dog was top dog in New York City, the toast of the town at 1010-AM on the radio dial.

Like the other deejays sought out by Smitty in his basement radio den, Alan Freed had a late-night show and played music different from what was heard on most music programs. This was rhythm-and-blues and, as Freed called it after the courts canned his Moon Dog act, rock-'n'-roll. Freed played music performed by Negroes, mostly: the Drifters, the Moonglows, T-Bone Walker, La Verne Baker, Chuck Berry, and, from another planet altogether, Little Richard.

Some people thought Freed was a light-skinned Negro or maybe half-Negro. It made no difference to Smitty. He ran with Negroes on the streets some. His mother had Negro women friends who visited all the time. They seemed to have something special inside, an inner strength or spirit of some kind. Smitty had always been drawn to their world, and the deejays he liked sounded like Negroes, even if they were not. They were hep cats. As a kid from a broken family, Smitty identified with their streetwise culture and the rebelliousness of the deejays, who made him feel a part of something. When he tuned in to them on the radio, it was like he wasn't alone in the coal bin of a basement in a Brooklyn tenement house at midnight.

"Alan Freed made me happy. He made me wanna party," says the grown-up Smitty. "Me and the boys cleaned out the coal bin in the cellar, and we'd sit down there every night and listen to him on the radio. I dug him so much I went out and bought an old shitty turntable and stole some records, and we'd pretend like we were him or Jocko Henderson or the other deejays we listened to." Pretending and merely listening to his heroes was not enough for Smitty, particularly as he got older and started getting around more. He began to feel like he belonged out in the world and on the radio himself. Never lacking for chutzpah, he set out to meet Freed when he heard the deejay was hosting a Rock-'n'-Roll Jubilee Show at the Brooklyn Paramount over Easter weekend in 1955. He hustled

his way backstage as a messenger. He managed to get beside
Freed backstage and introduce himself. The greasy-haired kid
from Brooklyn asked the most popular deejay in the country for
a job, and the deejay gave him the cold shoulder, sort of "Go
away, kid, don't bother me," Smitty recalls. He did end up doing
a few gofer jobs for Freed at the concert, but the country's
premiere deejay didn't have the time or inclination to notice him.
So the kid went away and didn't bother the big deejay anymore,
he says. "I don't think he ever looked me in the eye. He was a
prick to me, but I forgave him. I coulda had a problem with
Freed and what happened with him, but I didn't expect much
from him." Smitty wasn't really disappointed because he
hadn't hoped for much more than the cold shoulder from
such a hotshot deejay. He didn't come away disillusioned, only
more determined.

Smitty's next radio hero was a bit farther away in
reality, but the radio brought him into the coal bin just as
clearly. His name was John Richbourg. John R. and his soulful
southern voice sounded more black than white to Smitty's
Brooklyn-tuned ears, and he played music that was even hipper
than that played by Freed on WINS. It was pure rhythm-and-
blues where it was happening. He and the smart-alecky Gene
Nobles, another deejay on the station, were southern white men
playing Negro music and loving it, which seemed all the more
daring and defiant to Smitty.

Gotta meet this cat, Smitty told his pals. So they borrowed a car—don't ask—and lit out for Nashville. "I had to
meet him, I was that kinda kid. I loved radio and deejays. I just
said I want to go to Nashville to meet John R. and we went and
we found the station and walked into the studio and there was
this skinny guy with a big-balls voice and he waved us in,"
Smitty remembers.

When Smitty walked into the WLAC studio in the Life
and Casualty Insurance Company office building in Nashville, he found his radio Yoda, as did many other aspiring
young deejays who came before and after this swaggering

kid. John R. gave him a boost rather than a cold shoulder and stuck with his protégé as he underwent the sort of transfiguration seen previously only in Lon Chaney movies. Robert Weston "Smitty" Smith of Brooklyn became Daddy Jules who became Big Smith with the Records who became Roger Gordon who became, one full-moon night over Mexico, Wolfman Jack, the yowling-est deejay any side of the border. Oooooohwoooooooooo!

Smitty found his way out of Brooklyn and into that other world, on your radio dial.

To the later gratitude of a fledgling movie producer named George Lucas and the pimple-remedy pushers at Clearasil, Inc., John R. gave encouragement to this aspiring deejay and helped launch his career, the Wolfman says. "John R. was real nice, we kept in touch. He had like a little deejay school over the years. When you met him, he would start teaching you. I remember I was sitting there and he was talking to me and he wasn't cueing up records. He was just dropping the needle on them and his timing was perfect. To a deejay, that is wild to see somebody do that. He was doing things lopsided, but he said it was easier for him that way. He was a sweet guy. I'd get a letter from him and it would really blow me away. Even before I got on the air as a deejay, that's the way our relationship was. It was a wild situation. I was his star pupil for a while. It blew my mind. Don Williams, the country singer, even wrote a song about me and John R. I was like the Karate Kid with him as my mentor. I'd call him and ask him questions about warming my voice with exercises before a show. He taught me basic things like that."

The deejay style that Smitty would develop had little resemblance to the bourbon-smooth radio charms of his mentor. Nor would the wild Wolfman ever exhibit the courtly manner of the former actor and gentleman. John R. was a polite cough on the radio. The Wolfman was to be a loud belch. The teacher was subtle and genteel, a lean southern gentleman. The student was a street fight, balled up and rolling down the alley, defying anyone to get in its way. Smitty took notes on a number of deejays, lifted what he wanted from their varying styles, and then took off on his own mad tangent, crass, brass, and full of sass. The Wolfman comin' atcha, baby. Too cool for school.

One of the primary lessons that Smitty had drawn from listening to his favorite deejays in the coal-bin study hall was that their real appeal to him came in "moments" they created when they made a connection that made him feel as though they were talking directly to him and his feelings right that second. Whether the connection was a mutual sense of alienation and rebelliousness, a respect for the music they played, or just the sense that they were all in this alone but together didn't matter. Those moments carried him through the alienation of his parents' divorce and through his teenage years when he bounced from parent to parent, the Wolfman says. The kid could put up with the headbusting on the streets and in the schoolyards because he knew that late each night he would escape to his radio room, where he rigged up a make-believe microphone and broadcast live from radio station WBIN.

For all of his snarling, lewd, and lascivious ways, that is probably what made the Wolfman a success; his real motivation was to give his listeners something, to help them break away, forget the headbusting, and escape through the radio. There is no place that the Wolfman would rather escape to than a broadcast booth, and he likes having company in there. He says, "If I can have three or four moments at night when it makes you cry for happiness or love, something that you want to thank me for later, those are the moments. That's what these guys did for me, too. The music and the guy who set up the music put moments and realizations together. I get a lot of input from people over the phone when I'm on the air, and when you hear you've done something for them, you know you are doing a positive thing, and it makes you feel better than they do," he says.

The Wolfman gets teary-eyed and blows his nose into his table napkin when he talks about his favorite moments. "Just before I left L.A., this guy called me from a hospital and said his wife was getting ready for surgery. The guy was hurting. He was afraid his wife was gonna die. He said, 'Wolf, would you play "My Pledge of Love," by the Joe Jeffery Group?' Now that is a real obscure record, man. Me and the boys got up and we were looking all over for it, but we finally found it on a CD somewhere. I played it and asked the audience to pray for these people with a problem. The next day the guy calls me up and said, 'Wolf, my wife is fine. She wants to talk to you.' She is thanking me for saving her life, she said, 'Would you play it one more time?' I'm crying, she's crying. Then a week or so later, I got a letter with a picture showing the guy and his wife and kids all smiling. That's the reward man."

In more than thirty years on the air, the Wolfman has lived for moments like that, he says. On the deejay evolutionary ladder, from the short-haired, bop-bop-a-bee-bop Moon Dog to the snarling wheeze of the Wolfman, he is the throwback always on the comeback. The Wolfman is forever fading out and roaring back. He has been run off radio stations with his tail between his legs and forced out at gunpoint, only to reappear somewhere else, usually bigger and more rambunctious than ever on the strength of a song dedicated to him, a movie built around him, or the memories of moments in the minds of his lifetime fans. Out of the coal bin and onto your radio, televison, or movie screen, time and time again. They just can't keep the Wolfman down. "I've been busted down many times and I've seen a lot of shit go down, but I've stayed with the people over the years," he says. "John R. told me you don't work for the radio station. You work for the people out there. That's just one thing he taught me."

Being a street kid with a voice like Satchmo after three flights of stairs, Smitty had to find his way into radio through the alleys and janitors' closets, but hustlers are natural to that sort of clamber. As a teenager, he hung out at radio stations around Newark, where his family had moved. At sixteen, he landed his first job at WNJR there, mostly because he wouldn't go away. It became a pattern in his career. He cleaned toilets, fetched hamburgers, and sneaked up on the microphone whenever there was no one to bat him away. His natural salesmanship and bluster and his pure lust for the business got him jobs in the front office hustling ads and from there he sidestepped his way into the studio and onto the air. He cued up records and tested his voice on dog-food commercials and raffle pitches. He'd get thrown out of one station in a town and go find another. He met his bride, the lovely Lucy Lamb, known as Lou, in the Fred Astaire dance studio in Newport News, Virginia, where he was looking to sell some ads for radio station WYOU-AM (incredibly similar circumstances to those in which Alan Freed, one of Wolfman's heroes, met his second wife). The daughter of a North Carolina peanut and pig farmer, Lou spotted him for a hustler in a fancy hat.

"I was eighteen and working for an advertising agency. The manager of the dance studio was always trying to get me to teach dancing for him, so I had gone in to see what the heck it was he wanted," Lou recalls. "He was gonna show me the whole procedure. I had never done anything like that before, and I was scared to death. Well, Wolf was there trying to sell airtime, and we were introduced. He looked like Elvis Presley back then, I swear to gawd." The Wolfman was smitten, and when he heard the manager of the dance studio tell this young southern belle to come back for a dance party that night, he invited himself. "He drove me nuts all night," says Lou. "He was a very fast-talking Yankee. He wasn't a dancer. He would only dance the slow dances, so I knew automatically he was no big-time dancer. And he used phrases that I would never have used in those days. I was southern prim and proper. He was saying things like 'Hey, man.' It reminded me of beatnik talk, that street-corner-Brooklyn slang. And yet, you know, when I met his parents, they are very proper English types, totally different personalities. You would never know he belonged to his parents."

Now Lucy Lamb thought this Yankee was an attractive guy but just a little too slick and fast. She fended him off, but, like radio station managers from Newark to Del Rio, she quickly discovered that he was a persistent Yankee as well. "It was a problem. He would not give up. He got my phone number and started calling day and night," she says. The Wolfman finally convinced the poor little Lamb to go out for a pizza. After a few glasses of Cold Duck, they were serving up their life's stories to each other. "Once you got past all that hip shit, he was a nice guy and you had to like him," she says. They began dating, but not quite in the manner that the "fast" young Mr. Smith had in mind. "In those days he usually hung out with fast women, and I was another challenge altogether," Lou remembers. "He didn't understand at all and it has blown his mind all these years. I still challenge him, and he challenges me, too."

Lou discovered that beneath a thin layer of street grit Bob Smith was a sensitive soul. The James Dean impersonation and stories about hanging out with hoods were a mask. "He really came from a fairly well-to-do family that had hard times during the Depression but worked its way back up," she says. "When his mother and father separated, he felt neglected and tried to get by on the streets. He thought he wanted to be a hood, but he just didn't have it. I think he stole a hubcap one time, and it scared him to death. He hung out with tough guys, but he couldn't really be one of them. Don't ever show him a tear. He has a problem about hurting things. He is really very soft."

The sheep in Wolf's clothing married his Lucy Lamb in 1961, and it was off to the radio races. A daughter, Joy, was born a year later, and their son, Todd, followed two years after her just in time for a little fun in the Mexican sun. But the Wolfman and his wife spent their first year or so in Newport News. He worked as an ad salesman and part-time deejay for KYOU. The Wolfman was good at hustling a buck, and he already knew a lot about station management. But his real love was spinning records in the station's tight little studio, about the size of an old coal bin. On the air, he was Daddy Jules, playing rhythm-and-blues. "I lived for rhythm-and-blues, and I liked black people

Bob Smith, before he learned to howl

and identified with them. Their attitude was real to me. I got along with them better than white people because I understood what was going down with them," he says. "I was attracted to black music, and I tried to be somebody black people approved of. That's why I kept my identity a secret for a long time as a deejay. There is nothing worse than a square white person playing black music."

Unfortunately, a new station owner came in and decided he didn't want anybody, black, white, or undetermined, playing rhythm-and-blues. He tossed out the music and told Daddy Jules to change his tune, too. For a brief time, the hip cat became a mellow fellow called Roger Gordon, a white-bread kind of deejay just filling the time and segueing records. Marshmallow music was not his thing, however. So he and Lou hit the road for a radio station deep in country-music territory, Shreveport, Louisiana, home of the *Louisiana Hayride* on KWKH. But he hired on at competitor KCIJ, where Smitty underwent yet another transformation, becoming Big Smith with the Records and playing that soulful country sound, selling advertising, and managing the station.

Shreveport was better, but it was still a quiet burg, and there was a wild man looking to leap out of Big Smith. He was forever on the prowl for a major market, but even in his most laid-back moments, the kid from Brooklyn was not anyone's idea of a smooth-talking radio announcer. Others enunciated. He grunt-ciated. Others were silver-tongued. He had a mouth full of tipped-over garbage cans and rusted-out Chevys. The big time was not yet ready for Big Smith. So the outlaw headed for the border. The idea had always been there, since his days in the coal bin, that the border might be his kind of place. Even in Shreveport, he listened to the powerful border radio stations at night. Now that he had a handle on the business end, he was even more intrigued with the power of their signal and the outlandish performance of their preachers and pitchmen.

In their book *Border Radio*, Gene Fowler and Bill Crawford describe the radio stations that sprang up along the

U.S. border with Mexico — *la frontera* — as the perfect environment for borderline broadcasters like the Wolfman. It was the badlands of broadcasting, and he was the deejay wearing a black hat. Fowler and Crawford write, "The men and women who created border radio were frontiersmen of the ether, imaginative experimenters who came to the Southwest seeking freedom from the restrictive rules of the American media establishment. By building huge transmitters and testing new untried formats, these pioneers created a proving ground for many of the technical, legal, and programming aspects of today's broadcasting industry, and they managed to be quite entertaining as well."

Even New York newspaper columnist Walter Winchell noted that border radio was some of the best late-night listening to be had anywhere. Many of the border radio operators were free spirits fleeing the increasingly restrictive Federal Communications Commission and its hold on U.S. radio stations in the 1930s. They built their stations just across the border where the Mexican authorities were less inclined to tell them what they could do with and on their stations. The call letters issued in Mexico were also to their liking, beginning with XE. Brand-X radio. Dig it.

The border radio operators created stations with signals that could cover the entire United States and, in some cases, most of the world. At a time when most U.S. radio stations broadcast on a signal of about one thousand watts, the border bandits boomed out on as much as a million watts of power. Factor in the ozone skip effect that sends nighttime AM signals bouncing off the atmosphere like a rock skipping across a smooth pond, and you discover why the bandits were raiding not only U.S. radio markets but also those in Europe and the USSR, which eventually said *nyet* to that nonsense.

And it was nonsense, as the authors of *Border Radio* document: "Listeners to border radio stations could find a solution to almost any ailment — physical or spiritual — that could possibly be imagined." Kolorbak hair coloring to chase that gray away. Peruna Tonic to fend off colds. Crazy Water Crystals to liven up a "sluggish system." And every kind of cure for sexual problems imaginable and unimaginable. Borderline doctors and preachers followed the outlaw broadcasters to Mexico. One of the most famous was Dr. John R. Brinkley, who built his own border station, XER, to peddle "goat gland treatments," advertised as a cure for everything from hemorrhoids to cancer. One of the longest running jokes around Del Rio, Texas, was "What's the fastest thing on four legs? A goat running past the Brinkley Hospital."

The border radio preachers and psychics rivaled Brinkley and his ilk in outlandishness. Dr. Edward Owen, known as the psychic "Abra" and his Occult Astrological Institute, lured as many listeners to the border as Brinkley did. Another big draw was "radio scientist" Dr. Ralph Richards, an astrologer, who billed himself as the "Friendly Voice of the Heavens." He was eventually banned even from the border stations for bilking listeners who invested in his financial scams. Border radio was one of the first nationwide pulpits used by preachers to reach a mass audience. One of the biggest, who came late to border radio but was one of the first mass-media evangelists, was the Reverend Frederick Eikerenkoetter II, know as the Reverend Ike. He broadcast that blessings and bucks were heavenly rewards. Toss in a few tunes from country-western greats like Eddy Arnold, Ernest Tubb, Hank Thompson, and Red Foley—many of whom journeyed down to do live shows on occasion—and it is no wonder an impressionable and free-spirited hustler like Bob Smith would be lured to border radio. These were his people. The not-ready-for-prime-time players. He was born for the border, home of the freaks and the geeks and the cutting-edge crazies. But the looney tunes were not the only lure. There was big money to be made in border radio, and it didn't take the hustler from Brooklyn long to figure that out.

"I had never stopped listening to the border. I never stopped wondering what the hell was going on down there. I had everybody at the station in Shreveport listening to the border stations, and we'd get the addresses of the preachers advertising on them and then get the preachers to run their ads on our station, too. We were all enthused and interested in it, and one weekend, in about 1960, when one of the owners was gone for a Jewish holiday or something, me and another owner, Lawrence Brandon, drove down to Del Rio to see what the hell it was all about on the border," Wolfman recalls. "We had a big Cadillac convertible and it was a nice ride. When we got there, we found that the station's union members were having a meeting, so we got in a taxicab and he drove us out to the transmitter. There were no roads. It was so dark you couldn't see your hand in front of your face, and the car headlights went out into this nothingness, man, it was just sagebrush, until you came up on this one great tower and two great big buildings that looked like CBS New York out there in the middle of nowhere. We got there to the station, and they were having this union meeting, and as fate would have it, I walked into the middle of it.

"There was one guy who spoke English, Mario Alfaro, and we found out from him that they were in dire need of protection. The station had gone into receivership, and a bad guy was running it for the owner Arturo Gonzalez, who was a businessman and lawyer. The guy running it was beating people up, refusing to pay them their back pay. This guy was the government-appointed interventor, but he wasn't taking care of business."

They discovered that Gonzalez was locked in a battle with the Mexican government over mundane things like taxes, bills, and airtime allocations. The bureaucrats were threatening to take over the station. They already had a man in place, who, it turned out, was a bit of a bandit himself. The Wolfman smelled an opportunity when he learned that what the government boys really wanted was someone who could put the station back in the black so they could start taking a cut. The village of Via Cuncio languishing in the Coahuilan desert, nine miles south of Del Rio, Texas, was about to become the Wolfman's lair, like it or not.

The lawlessness and exuberant freedom of the border was a catalyst for the final stages in the metamorphosis of Smitty, the Brooklyn street punk, into Wolfman Jack, the Incredible Bulk of Radioland. Bits of Roger Gordon, Daddy Jules, and Big Smith fell off, piece by piece, and gradually the Wolfman emerged out there on the desert. This mutation was a little bit of the Moon Dog and some mad dog, with chunks of hound dogs and howling wolves tossed in. The final product was a churning urn of rasping funk that was to become a legend on radio, records, film, and television from Los Angeles to Leningrad.

The Wolfman secured his position at the border by paying an emissary fifteen hundred dollars to fix things in Mexico City with the *federales*. In the meantime, he wrangled an appointment as the U.S. representative for the station. His first official act was to kick out the bandit who had been running things. The man left, but only to go home for his guns. It was your typical heavy-handed American intervention in foreign affairs; the Grenada invasion had nothing on the Wolfman's takeover of XERF. "We had to show that we had power so we wouldn't get hit by them," he explains. "If we just sat there like lambs, we would have been inviting them to come back. So we set up and armed everybody and put out sandbags, barbed wire, strung lights all over the complex. I bought a bunch of 30-30 rifles and Smith & Wesson six guns — and even an old 60-millimeter machine gun that was just for looks man — and altogether we came up with twenty-five thousand dollars to finance this whole thing. Brandon, who was born with a silver spoon, came up with the radio station money, and I pushed it through, and his partner came back from his Jewish holiday in Shreveport and found out we had spent all of his money."

Radio station XERF took on the look of a *nuevo* Alamo, and with his loyal troops in place, the Wolfman commandeered the airwaves from seven P.M. until midnight on a 250,000-watt signal that would not be stopped by mere miles and mountain ranges. He was primed. No more restraints, no more geek station managers breathing Spearmint fumes down his neck. No more dippy Doris Day music. He did not have to pretend anymore. The Wolfman was loose and full of juice. He controlled his playlist, and he selected the mix that he had always preferred. Rhythm-and-blues, rockabilly, jazz, and rock-'n'-roll. The soulful stuff. James Brown, Johnny Otis, Count Basie, Johnny Horton. And he talked his way, "Ah ya wit me out deah? Ah ya redeeh? We gonna blow ya min' babeeh! Ah needja soul! Oooooooooowwwwwwwoooooooooohaaaaa!" It was feel good and love somebody. By day and by night he sold himself and whatever else he could get in equal volume, whatever could be offered in enough quantity to satisfy his hundreds of thousands of avid listeners. He was the outlaw bandit on the border, and they were buying whatever it was he had to sell, from chinchillas to baby chicks, record packages to potency pills. Border radio had seen a lot, but the Wolfman was a new page in its book.

The authors of *Border Radio* credit him with "Slam-dunking border radio into the sixties. . . . Amid tequila parties, shoot-outs, and high-level diplomatic negotiations, Wolfman and his cohorts pitched sex pills, diet pills, record packages, even Wolfman roach clips, guaranteed to make the intrepid insects easier to handle." The Wolfman had fun, but he took care of business, too. The advertisers and the broadcast preachers who bought time on his radio pulpit were soon mailing their payments to an address in Shreveport, where he kept his family and a hand in WCIJ, care of someone named Smith. Unlike the previous administration at the station, the Boss Wolfman kept his followers in boots and boleros and the government goons well-stocked with graft payments. Nearly fifty people lived at the station. He kept a doctor on the payroll, a real one. Wolfman was their leader and protector, and he threw a good party every now and then as well. One was a five-thousand-dollar affair, he says, with the host strutting around like "Viva Zapata," bandoleras across his chest, pistols on his hips, and bodyguards in his wake. He chewed on roasted goat legs while an occasional bullet whizzed by his head courtesy of the former radio staion regime, which had never really given up the fight. "They'd have their little wars all day and then settle down with goat tacos and tequila," Lou recalls.

The Wolfman's profits and partying got the goat of the previous station administration in exile, and the determined opposition reasserted itself one night about two weeks after the gringo with the growl had set up camp. The Wolfman and his wolfwife were enjoying each other's company in their hotel suite in Del Rio one January night in 1964. War was about to become hell. "I hadn't seen her in about two months," he says. Things had finally quieted down, and we were relaxing a little bit. I had people walking around with guns just so everyone could see we were armed. The hired guns were costing me ten dollars a day just to walk around the building, so I got rid of them and had the station help stay out there for three or four days per shift, sleeping there too, and then the next crew would come in to relieve them. I was running the station and had virtually taken it over with no problems. So I called my wife, who had had our son just a few months before, and said, 'Lou, come on down. It's a short flight. I'll get you a nice suite at the Del Rio hotel.'

"We were making love in the middle of the night and, like always, I had the radio station on. The Reverend J. Charles Jessup was on the air, and all of a sudden in the middle of preaching, this little Mexican kid opens up the microphone and says, 'Pistoleros, pistoleros!!' I could hear gunshots in the background going 'Pinnnnnnnnng, Peooooowwwwwwww!' and I said, 'Holy Shit!' and jumped about four feet in the air and said, 'I gotta do something about that.' I got my Starfire Oldsmobile, a pink one, although they called it salmon-colored, and headed over the Rio Grande. I had learned in doing business over there that you always had to carry a big wad of money in your pocket. I knew the sheriff across the border, and I gave him money to come with me and to get other people to come with us— anybody with wheels and a gun was good enough for me. One guy was driving a garbage truck, another a motorscooter. We rounded up about twenty people, including the entire second shift of the radio station, and each one had a vehicle. So we headed out and dawn was breaking just as we hit over the ridge. Here was this big radio station with one huge tower, and these guys were riding around it like Indians circling the wagon train and shooting at it. The guys inside were shooting back. So here we come, I got maybe twenty cars following me, and through the dust at first light, it must have looked like a thousand. I told everybody to honk their horns and shoot their guns. They had only maybe about twenty riders on horseback on their side, and we probably scared the shit out of them. Basically, they spun around the station one more time and took off for the hills. When we arrived, everybody had cleared out. We found one of their boys killed, but it was a close-range bullet that got him, and they figured he must have run into one of his own men's bullets and got his head blown off. My guys couldn't hit a Brink's truck they were such bad shots anyway, even with a 30-30 rifle. Three of our guys were wounded. One had a bad chest wound, but he came out okay."

The Wolfman emerged with his hands on the controls and as king of border radio with the capability of long-range vocal assault on the U.S. airwaves. He continued firing night after night as he had before the showdown, not even bothering to go on the air until six P.M. or so, until the night-skip conditions made it worth his while to crank up the generators. "That would be burning up a lot of electricity just to get to San Antonio," he notes.

In the early evening, he would step briefly back into his gentler, kinder alter ego, Big Smith with the Records, and play down-home country stuff for an hour-and-a-half, just to warm the airwaves, and then he'd do a Spanish hour to keep the Mexican government smiling. The preachers, his bread-and-butter pay-for-pray guys, had the microphone for fifteen- to thirty-minute spots. If they had the bucks, the Wolfman might let them buy up to midnight. He knew his listeners would be out there waiting when he came to howl. The preachers would be selling Jesus, and then he'd sell sin. It was hard to say who saved more souls, the preacher men or the Wolfman, but they were all hustlers, the best at their game. They all wanted their listeners to love one another, just in slightly different ways.

The Wolfman put southern California on notice that there was something funky going down on the border. James Brown, Little Richard, and the r&b boys backed him up. Double entendres were his first line of assault; triple and quadruple entendres soon followed. Subtlety was not in his repertoire. "SQUEEZE MY KNOBS. Oooooooowoooooooooooooooooooooo!" he commanded. There was hardly a jacked-up Chevy or low-riding Ford in southern California that didn't have the Wolfman howling out the windows, commanding all within earshot to "Get nekkid!" Watching submarine races, Wolfman's code phrase for making out on lovers' lane, became a national sport although he probably intruded on more tender moments than he inspired. It's tough to be romantic when your partner is snickering at the deejays's dirty little delights.

California was just the closest target of opportunity. The 250,000-watt bandito stations on the border reached into Texas and way yonder, yes, comrade, even into the Soviet Union. There had long been reports that the KGB's language specialists tuned in XERF to perfect their English, but when the Wolfman showed up and made a few nasty comments about Krushchev, the KGB started jammin'. His nasty patter was not compatible with the party line. They jammed at him, not with him.

Like his heroes back at WLAC in Nashville, the Wolfman plugged in to the record supply at Ernie's Record Mart and also at Stan's Record Shop in Shreveport, where the good stuff that couldn't be found in your typical white-bread corner record store was available in abundance: rhythm-and-blues. Stanley Lewis was a born hustler who had sold coat hangers and milk bottles during the Depression years and entered the record business through an uncle in Monroe, Louisiana, who was a jukebox man. After seeing his uncle do so well in Monroe, Lewis decided to get into the market in Shreveport. Two cousins who owned bars provided a ready market. He bought five jukeboxes and located his business in a tiny little record shop he purchased for twenty-five hundred dollars. He did not leave his day job at his father's grocery store at first, allowing his wife to run the record shop and jukebox business during the daylight hours. The record business kept his family alive. He says, "If it hadn't been for Charlie Brown's 'Troubled Blues' or John Lee Hooker's 'Boogie Children,' I would have starved to death."

As had been the case with Randy Wood, Lewis found his store's salvation by advertising record deals on the radio and sponsoring deejays to keep his profile high. One of his first deejays on KWKH was Ray Bartlett, who went by the name "Groovy Boy." He was a white man but used a "colored accent," Lewis recalls. "He was real, real popular and would hang out the window of the radio station and tell people to blow their car horns and people would drive down the street with their car horns blowin'. I bought time on his show for five dollars a spot."

Groovy's Boogie, which came on at four P.M., was the number one show in town, and everyone knew when it was on the air because of the horns honking down at the corner of Market and Texas streets and the sound of Groovy Boy hanging out a window screaming, "Helloooooooo Baybeeeeeee!" and playing the wild and raunchy rhythm-and-blues. In the early fifties, Bartlett moved on from Shreveport and the number one deejay position at KWKH went to Frank Page, who broadcast under the moniker "Gatemouth Page, the mouth of the South" and eventually renamed the four P.M. traffic-stopper show *No-Name Jive*. Page, another white, was not the babbler that Groovy had been. He was more of a cool-nik, steeped in street-jive poetry from the bad part of town: "Nothin's shakin' but the leaves on the trees, wouldn't be shakin' were it not for the breeze."

"KWKH had a sister station in Little Rock, KTHS, and we either taped or had a radio line going straight into Little Rock so we could send the shows out over KTHS, which had fifty thousand watts and went straight into the Midwest," Lewis recalls. Stan's Records began getting orders not only from the western regions but also from Chicago, Milwaukee, Nebraska, Iowa, and Minnesota. One avid listener in the small Iron Range town of Hibbing, Minnesota, near the Canadian border, was of particular note.

Stan's Record Shop pitched record package deals on the radio, bargain deals for *The Blues Special* or *Muddy Waters Special* for only $3.50. Rhythm-and-blues records were difficult to find, and the packages offered by Stan, like those broadcast courtesy of Randy's, Ernie's, and Buckley's out of Nashville, were pounced on by those young listeners who did not have access to this sort of music in the old hometown. Lewis often scanned his order list to see where the buyers were located, and he says today that the frequent requests for records from Bobby Zimmerman in the far, far reaches of northern Minnesota did not escape his notice.

In *Dylan, Barefoot in Babylon*, author Bob Spitz credits Gatemouth Page and Stan Lewis with introducing the teenage boy who would become a rock-'n'-roll poet to the music that shaped his life after he found KTHS beaming in on his radio. Spitz says, "Picture a fourteen-year-old boy in Hibbing, Minnesota, listening to this free-for-all. It would have struck him as the animalistic rumbling of Armageddon. Still, Bobby was an instant convert to Brother Gatemouth's jive-talking liturgy. He was stirred, as well, by the music's loudness, its barrelhouse rhythms, its outrageous lyrics, and its Lord-have-Mercy style of singing."

Dylan's biographer says that the records the would-be rocker ordered from Stan's "opened an inspirational floodgate" and convinced the frustrated young musician that he could play rock-'n'-roll without a lot of training and that "someday he was going to be a rock-'n'-roll star."

Not long after Lewis began advertising on the radio, the independent record promoters started showing up at his store, which he called Stan's Record Shop because there was another business in town called Stanley's and the owner threatened to sue him. Lewis never did like being called Stan. The indie men included the ubiquitious Leonard Chess, who seemed to be in several places around the county at any given moment back then. Chess and the others would give Lewis so many free records for every hundred he bought because he was able to get them played on the radio. Since rhythm-and-blues was selling so well, he got the formerly country station to play more and more of it. Lewis did the programming himself much of the time, advising his deejays about what to play just as Randy Wood had worked with Gene Nobles.

Over the years, Lewis worked with all sorts of deejays, including black jocks like Gay Pappa, whose real name, Sunrose Rutledge, was just as colorful, and B. B. Davis and C. C. Samuels, he says. When Wolfman landed in Shreveport as Bob Smith, Lewis got to know him, and their business relationship continued when Smith moved to Mexico and developed a howl. He did all right by Stan's Record Shop, Lewis says.

XERF put out five to six hundred packages of three-record sets each day through the cross-border mail at $1.95 per set. The "Lucky Forty" package for just $4.95 included albums with forty songs. And if you ordered right away, you could get a life-size glow-in-the-dark poster of the Wolfman, guaranteed to keep the bogeyman boogeying.

With the reach of his signal, the Wolfman's sales pitches were incredibly effective and lucrative, considering that he took 50 percent of the profit from anything sold on his station and got a fee for airtime as well. If it could be sold, he'd sell it by the boxcars: weight-gain and weight-loss pills, rosebushes, songbooks, dog food (a staple of da Wolfman's diet), and, jeepers-peepers, baby chicks—another item borrowed from the WLAC catalog—by the chickenhouse, sixty to eighty orders a day at $3.95 per hundred. "Now just imagine all the fun you're gonna have with these baby chicks," the Wolfman would pitch. "You lead 'em around on little leashes, you give 'em all little names, and then when they grow up—you gonna eat 'em."

Another popular item in the Wolfman catalog, at least until the U.S. government put the kabosh on it, was Florex, his uplifting antidote for a downer sex drive. "Some zing for your ling nuts," as Wolfman was fond of saying. Wolfman had listened from his Bronx basement to the pitchmen on border radio selling sexual remedies for years, so it was only natural that he would try to corner this always-eager market. He found a pill-pusher in Mexico City who could sugar coat anything, and together they concocted a harmless, medically worthless pill that the Wolfman sold as the answer to marital malaise. He hyped it as the fountain of youth in a pill, good for man and woman.

Like many of the items hyped on the station, Florex didn't go over big-time until the Wolfman had experimented a bit with his pitch, trying to find the right attack for the right audience. Fine-tuning. Eventually he decided that his best approach would be to get lost and call in a she-wolf. He says, "It didn't start out real heavy so I changed the spot around. At first I did it, then I found someone else, this black female, who did it in dialect in a sexy voice. All of a sudden, the orders went through the ceiling. Exactly why, I don't know. But right after her spot went out, we started getting four thousand orders a day, until the Federal Trade Commission sent me a letter saying I had to cease and desist. So I said screw it. I took the spot off the air, but I tell ya, man, they kept asking for it. A year, four years later, and they were still ordering the damn thing. It was amazin'."

The amazin' Wolfman had sold about everything but his true identity to the public by that point. It wasn't just coyness. Truth be told, the swaggering, hairy-chested bellows from Brooklyn was scared to death of standing in front of a bunch of people. He was balls-out on the radio, but a scaredy-cat onstage. It had taken him nearly a year to recover from his first attempt at performing in front of a live audience. In that first public exposure of the Wolfman, in 1963, he was working on the border, but his family was still living in Shreveport. Somehow, he'd let himself get talked into appearing at the Peppermint Lounge in Bossier City, just across the Red River from Shreveport. The idea of going public did not sit well with the Wolfman. "The thing was that I was portraying a real crazy dude on the radio, and to look at me in real life, wearing a skinny tie and a crew-cut and in my twenties, people wouldn't believe I was the Wolfman. I had not visualized what the character looked like, and I needed some visual trip," he remembers.

He asked Lou to concoct some sort of disguise to conceal his true identity, especially his race. "He put on dark makeup and a little goatee and a black wig that we restyled and teased. He looked half black, half Spanish," says Lou. "Actually, I was embarrassed to walk into the club with him because he looked a little more black than anything, and in Louisiana in those days it wasn't cool for a white woman to be with a black man. This was still lynching time. Somebody would getcha for that kinda thing." As it turned out, Wolfman fixed himself pretty good. He was a very nervous cat about appearing in public. To stifle his stage fright, he downed a few non-prescribed pills provided by a purported friend. He also had a few cocktails. By the time the curtain call came, "I was bombed out of my mind," he says. "I puked all over the stage. I was scared to death, and, I don't mind admitting this, I am still scared everytime I get in front of a crowd. I've never really conquered it. Especially television. It really throws me off."

The Wolfman showed the boys in Boosier City a good time, between barfing breaks backstage, but that was enough for a while, especially after he learned that a cross was burned in front of the Peppermint Lounge a few hours after his departure. He was content, after that, to be Bob Smith, station executive, in public during the day and the Wolfman, safe in the studio, come nightfall. It was working out fine. He had some control over his life that way, a place to go and let the heavy-tongued Wolfman sleep. But as his notoriety spread, listeners got more into the mystery of the Wolfman's identity. Was the Wolfman black? Mexican? Man or beast?

He recalls, "I had people calling me from *Newsweek*, *Time*, all wantin' to interview de Wolfman in person. Being a small-timer, I didn't know how to handle it. I told 'em de Wolfman don't talk to nobody. But that just made it even hotter and heavier. They started coming out to the station. I happened to be there one night when one of the reporters showed up. I answered the door, you know, as Bob Smith, and told the guy I could not allow him to see the Wolfman because it would flip him out. I finally got him to leave by telling him the Wolfman would phone him the next day in Del Rio. Then, next day, I called him and told him the Wolfman had taken off for Mexico City."

Although he had hundred of requests each week for personal appearances, the Wolfman put the word out that he wouldn't move from his lair for less than fifteen thousand dollars an hour. He figured no one would meet that price. If remaining hidden was his goal, naming an amount was a mistake. A group of college kids in Kansas City, Missouri, came up with it. The Wolfman upped the ante by telling them they would have to deliver part of it in advance, in twenty-dollar bills. They dispatched a Brink's truck. (Good wheat crop in Kansas that year.) The Wolfman was being lured from his den for the first time, but he decided to lie as low to the ground as he could. This time, he went to Hollywood.

"Yeah," he says, "they paid me fifteen thousand dollars, but I spent five thousand on two limousines, two midget magicians from San Antonio, two girls dressed up in scanty clothes, and a Hollywood makeup artist I flew down to give me the Wolfman look. He made rubber cheeks for me, gave me a head-of-hair wig, long fingernails that you cudda picked locks with, and all kinds of jewelry and stuff." The Wolfman's parade pulled into town, and he refused to get out of the limo until the college boys presented him with the rest of the money in a brown paper bag.

That done, the midgets and the girls laid out a path of perfume and rose petals and rolled out sheets for the Wolfman to strut through. "At first, I just poked my head out. It had hair standing a foot high, I had a big pair of shades on, and my face was green and black and cream-colored. As I walked, they were spraying me with perfume, and as people jumped in front of me for autographs I pushed them out of the way. I had told them I was only gonna do ten minutes onstage. I went directly to the stage with ten thousand out there. First thing I said was, 'How are all you motherfuckers out there tonight?' The college kids fell out of their chairs, man. That was the first thing I said when I hit the Kansas City stage. Then I just pranced around and told them not to forget to listen to me every night on XERF, 'We have the power that is UNLIMITED!' I was shittin' my pants the whole time, man, nervous as hell. I had a band behind me, and the girls were dancing and the midgets were straightenin' out my garb. Finally, I said, 'That's all the time I have for you assholes.' And I got back in the car and split, and that was it. They loved it, man, and y'know, that was a pretty classy college, too."

Life was good for the Wolfman at that point. He was hauling in around $150,000 and making strategic payments to the right Mexicans. He shared the wealth. He and XERF were a mini-fiefdom that supported about fifty local families. The Wolfman thought of himself as Robin Hood with his Merry Mexicans, but the evil king was sitting down on Arturo Gonzalez's ranch, plotting his return to full 250,000-watt power. Gonzalez had come to respect Wolfman's shrewd business sense, but that respect only inspired him to work harder to throw his nemesis back over the border. A gringo was a gringo was a gringo. In just two-and-a-half years, the carpetbagger with the fur on his vocal cords had paid off the back taxes on the station with the profits from his preachers, potency pills, and rock-'n'-roll show. But the heat on the street was taking a toll. The Wolfman had to watch himself everywhere he went, knowing that another charge of the night brigade was inevitable. Figuring that sooner or later Gonzalez would out-bribe him, the Wolfman decided to cash in and get out with his hide, and his bank account, intact. He struck a deal to return control of the station to Gonzalez but to stay on the air, via tape. Gonzalez was happy to have the station out of receivership and to keep the money-making Wolfman on the air. The Wolfman and another business partner had staked out a claim on another radio station—a daytime station no less—in a slightly chillier clime: Minneapolis. Minneapolis?

"I took my money and went to Minneapolis where a partner and I had bought KUXL-AM," says Wolfman, who went north mostly to mind the business end of the new station, not to howl at them. "We ran the preachers in the morning and then from noon until sign-off we ran rhythm-and-blues." But it was mostly blues, blues, and more blues for the Wolfpack: Jack, Lou Lamb, Joy, and Todd. Minneapolis was not exactly their bag, and for a night owl like the Wolfman, a six P.M. sign-off was like kissing your sister, your ugly sister.

After a little less than a year, the Wolfman cut a new deal with the Mexicans at a different station, just outside Tijuana at Rosarita Beach. California was the place he wanted to be, so he loaded up the truck and moved to Beverly Hills. From there, he took over yet another border radio station, XERB, the Big X, in 1965. He was still coming across the border on tape from XERF, and a couple of quick deals put the Wolfman on two more border stations, XEG and XELO, to boot. And boot he did. In the spirit of the times, the Wolfman grew even grittier and more outlandish. He was a rebel without a pause button. Have moicy. In two years' time, he was again a dominant force. His fingernails-across-the-chalkboard yowls were heard in the wee hours of the night on radios across the U.S. and Canada. The Wolfman was back, and the country was in the mood for his in-yer-face irreverent ways. Fred Friendly had quit as news chief of CBS because the network refused to preempt *I Love Lucy* for the Senate hearings on the escalating Vietnam War. Johnny Carson walked out on NBC and quit *The Tonight Show* but came back when they gave him gold, incense, and myrhh. Everybody talked about quitting smoking, and *The Smothers Brothers Comedy Hour* was getting away with some real smart-ass television. This was the Wolfman's kind of atmosphere.

If life at home was getting rowdy, it was pure hell in the jungles of Vietnam, but the Wolfman was able to lend some radio relaxation time there as well. In 1970, he signed up for a sixteen-year hitch with Armed Forces Radio, providing them with taped broadcasts for servicemen around the world. He was heard on 1,453 stations in the U.S. and six hundred Armed Forces Radio stations abroad. Wolfman considers it some of the most worthwhile duty he has ever done, particularly during the Vietnam War. He says: "I did Armed Forces Radio all through Vietnam, and afterwards, when they brought everybody home, they invited me to DC with eighteen thousand veterans, drunk, crying, hugging each other, guys carrying me on their shoulders in the parade. Another time after it was all over, I was doing a benefit in Radio City Music Hall. I'd just introduced Ray Charles. I was getting ready to leave, and I'm in the hallway and all of a sudden these two gigantic black dudes and one white guy out of a horror movie start coming my way, saying 'Wolfman Jack.' One of the black guys picks me up and kisses me. Then the other. They were virtually passing me around. I'm a big guy myself, but they were gargantuans. They told me that they were Vietnam vets. I spent two hours with these guys in a bar that night, and all I heard was how the Wolfman was with them when they were in tight places. That's my reward. Those are the memories I've cherished."

Meanwhile, back on the West Coast of the Mainland U.S. of A., the Wolfman's late-night mantras took his listeners for long walks on the wild side. Between the calls for revolution and the wild riffs of Jimi Hendrix and his experiences, the Wolfman came into the car through the backseat and climbed into the laps of the occupants: "How sweet are your little peaches? Lay yo hands onna radio right now an' feeeel meeee!" Life was sweet. He was where he wanted to be. He was raking in up to thirty thousand dollars a month and doing two hundred live performances a year. He moved Lou and the kids into a

$160,000 Beverly Hills pad. The mansions of Mary Pickford, Sammy Davis, Jr., Janet Leigh, Tony Curtis, and Priscilla Presley were next-door, and he knew John Lennon "poisonally." He built a $500,000 state-of-the-art thirty-two-track recording studio in Pasadena and was preparing to add a video studio behind it. He says, "I was going to make music videos, man, believe it or not, before they became big deals." But then the bad guys rode into town again. After about four years of watching the Wolfman rake in the pesos, the natives got restless. It was their turn again.

"The Mexicans went up in their price for the fee of the station," he remembers. "I was paying about fifty-five thousand dollars a month to lease it from them and billing about ninety thousand a month minus the overhead. I was paying the bills with the rest of the money as my profit. I paid all my expenses and all the staff and I was doing about a million a year and they figured, 'Shit, the station never did that much before. If we kick Wolfman out, we'll make it more legitimate and make more money, and we won't have to use fortune tellers and preachers.'" His foes put the squeeze on Wolfman by getting the Catholic-oriented government to ban the Pentecostal preachers, his bread and butter, from the Mexican airwaves. The screws were being tightened. He continues, "Well, the contract ended, and for us to renew we had to come up with a big amount, and my partner didn't have it, and we were afraid we were getting screwed. We got scared. I didn't have the money, so bingo, they took the station."

The Wolfman was out on the streets again, with a $500,000 debt chained to his fat, furry legs. Shortly after he departed, the border station welcomed his preachers back though, according to Wolfman, the new station management never enjoyed the kind of profits he engineered for it. The Wolfman found himself unwanted in the big radio markets because of his reputation for rowdy, borderline raunchy behavior. One of the founding father's of shock radio found himself unplugged, a demon ahead of his time. "I lost it all.

Bang, my station. Bang, my car. Bang, my other car. I lost everything. I was down to nothing," he says.

"We had just built this new building and recording studio and invested a lot of money, and, bang, it was gone," recalls Lou. "Oh my god, we were left owing about $500,000 when all was said and done. The lawyers said we should go for bankruptcy, but Wolf said 'No way. We'll pay the people we owe.' It took us until 1976 to pay it all off."

Although no one would have guessed it at the time, the Wolfman's saving angel appeared in the form of a young, aspiring movie producer named George Lucas, a kid from Modesto, who had listened to the Wolfman blasting from the border as a teenager. Lucas contacted the Wolfman within days of his being driven out of Mexico and into the poorhouse. He had this script, a very rough script, about small-town California life in those teenage years. He asked the Wolfman to be in the movie and to help him with the soundtrack. It didn't pay much, but how could the deejay in him refuse? It was basically going to be a movie that showed radio "moments" with the Wolfman affecting the lives of California teenagers. They worked together for months, and the Wolfman's only initial payment was one thousand dollars a day for two days of shooting his quick appearance in the movie. He compared his acting skills to those of Euell Gibbons, Rodney Allen Rippy, and Sheena, Queen of the Jungle, but he would have paid to be in this movie with its underlying ode to border radio madness. Lucas put the entire movie together for less than a quarter of a million dollars. He told the Wolfman that he hoped it would do well enough to get a couple other movie projects off the ground. In the meantime, while the final production work was put together, the Wolfman landed another job, offering a high profile at low pay.

Bob Wilson, an innovative programming wizard at KDAY in Los Angeles, hired Wolfman for a cut-rate salary to shepherd his experimental rock format — one that would eventually become the forebearer for FM radio around the country. Wolfman says, "I went from $600,000 a year to eighteen thousand, but we started the progressive format on AM stations and FMS started picking it up. I didn't like it a lot because it was just segueing records and not really the Wolfman's style." But, at that point, he didn't have a lot of alternatives.

He was so far down, it looked like up to him. Every morning, he'd pack his brown-bag lunch, hide it in a briefcase, and drive out of his heavily mortgaged Beverly Hills home like a millionaire, waving at young Jamie Lee Curtis across the street. But things were about to take a dramatic chart-busting turn the Wolfman's way. Actually, several things fell into place at once, giving him a goose like he'd never been goosed before. Perhaps an omen of better days to come was the sudden rise of a 1972 tune by the Guess Who entitled "Clap for the Wolfman." Within a year, everybody would be clapping for him, and not just because of the song.

The Wolfman got rolling when George Lucas's little movie came out in 1973 and broke box-office records, earning more than forty million dollars its first year. When it became apparent that *American Graffiti* was going to be a smash, the grateful Lucas offered Wolfman another deal he could not refuse. He gave him a percentage of the movie's profits. The Wolfman broke down and cried real tears. He says, "It was the first time in my life I ever really lucked out, man. I've worked hard all my life for everythin' else I've ever gotten. It took me totally by surprise." The exact amount the Wolfman earned from those "points" is between him and the Internal Revenue Service, he says. But when all was said and done, the lawyers were not mentioning bankruptcy any longer.

Just a few months after the movie came out, the Wolfman was asked to host a one-shot television gig called *The Midnight Special*. It featured him as host to some of the hottest rock-'n'-roll acts of the day. The "one-shot" show did so well that the producers decided to bring it back as a weekly feature with the Wolfman as the star, transforming it into a special that shone it's ever-lovin' light for nine years runnin'.

Even as that deal was going down, the Wolfman was in

negotiations on his biggest radio deal ever. After he'd been chugging along with KDAY for about a year, the Wolfman got a call from WNBC in New York. They wanted him to take on another native Brooklynite, Cousin Brucie, Bruce Morrow, a legendary deejay at WABC who had dominated local AM radio for a decade. The pay put an end to the brown-bagging from Beverly Hills — $350,000 a year. The Wolfman was rolling in it. He says, "I'll never forget those paychecks. I'd go down and pick them up, and I couldn't believe the figures. They always blew me away." Things were starting to cook for the Wolfman again. He remembers, "I went up against Cousin Brucie. Y'know deejays like to think of ourselves as gunfighters. When I went into New York, they told me they wanted WABC's ass. They paid me more money than anybody." Suddenly, the Wolfman, who had been tuckin' his tail twixt-his-legs, was strutting his stuff again, hotter than he had ever been before. When Morrow learned who his latest challenger was, he thought it ironic. In his autobiography, *Cousin Brucie! My Life in Rock-'n'-Roll Radio*, Morrow writes that when he watched Wolfman Jack in *American Graffiti*, his performance brought home the message that "like bobby socks, D.A. haircuts, and circle pins, the personality rock jock was the stuff of scrapbooks. I felt the chilling reality in my bones. I was still number one, but there were signs that my throne was being attacked by many forces."

Morrow says that when Wolfman was brought in to knock him out of the box, "They looked for a chink in my armor with a knight who'd already shown me the chink. WNBC radio was bringing the Wolfman to New York to 'bury me,' but he wasn't a match for me yet," Morrow boasts in his book. Not surprisingly, in a battle of Gotham egos, the Wolfman and Cousin Brucie portray the outcome of their fracas quite differently.

"They planted tombstones in the middle of the night in front of WABC, with an inscription that said 'Cousin Brucie's Days Are Numbered,'" recalls the Wolfman, who went on from seven P.M. to midnight Monday through Saturday to Morrow's six-fifteen P.M. to ten-thirty P.M. Miniature copies of the tombstones were sent to all of the advertising agencies in New York, and the press was lured to the bait.

The Wolfman's challenge to Cousin Brucie was a major move, and it spurred articles in *Oui* and *Cosmopolitan*, even in the *New York Times*. Reporter John Rockwell of the *Times* saw it as not only a ratings war but also an attempt to return to the radio days of deejay glory. The payola scandal of the early sixties, and the dawn of top-forty formats and FM radio had diminished the power of personality deejays. There weren't many dominant jocks left in the fading trail of Alan Freed and the Wolfman's other boyhood heroes. The Cousin Brucie-versus-the-Wolfman showdown put some punch back in New York's AM range.

In November of 1973, Rockwell wrote that the outcome of the battle might well determine whether personality deejays like those of the fifties could make a comeback. He noted that a station like WABC charged up to $268 for a sixty-second commercial during Cousin Brucie's show while lower-ranked stations got as little as $15 per second on their broadcasts. He noted too that deejays in New York could demand as much as $100,000 a year in salary along with lucrative perks.

Rockwell contrasted Wolfman and Cousin Brucie as opposites in a sort of Mr. Clean versus the Big Bad-Mouth Wolf shootout.

He also noted that in most radio of the early seventies the real power was not in the hands of the deejay, but in those of the programmers and station management. In the case of WABC, that meant Rick Sklar, director of station operations. The tight controls, Rockwell opined, reduced the deejays to mere puppets, but, in the Wolfman, the struggling WNBC had snared a deejay who transcended the local radio scene and was a nationally-recognized celebrity.

WNBC had brought in first Don Imus and then the Wolfman to see if a return to the glory days of the deejay might also restore the glory days of WNBC, which had been miserably trailing the more regimented format of Sklar and WABC.

The Wolfman, then, according to no less a chronicle than the hard-rocking *New York Times*, was a throwback to the days of deejay glory on AM radio. He had a vast appeal that reached beyond the radio station's signal, and he also appealed to hipper, more sophisticated rock-'n'-roll fans while Cousin Brucie held onto "the clean, nice kids," the reporter concluded. Despite their differences, the two high-profile deejays shared an optimism in their approach to life, and both had deep appeal to listeners, Rockwell wrote.

With such publicity, stars are made. True to his grave predictions, the Wolfman claims to have buried Cousin Brucie in the ratings. "I took over like that," he says modestly.

His opponent, no kissin' cousin, begs to differ in his account of the dueling deejays. He says, "Well, the Wolfman went on the air on WNBC, and in eight weeks he was the Pussycat Man, licking his wounds all the way back to the Left Coast."

Wolfman did leave town quickly, but, he says, for strictly voluntary reasons. The Wolfman was taking over the world at this point. He was everywhere, even in church, sort of. Always looking to catch onto a movement — except for disco, which he merely tried to survive — the Wolfman even laid his hands on Jesus Rock for a while, doing a syndicated show that featured a holier-than-howl Wolfman playing the more blessed side of rock. "My Sweet Lord" was a big tune on this show. He says, "I believe in the Lord, I do my preaching in my own way. I did a Bible show for a while, playing rock records before the real religious programming got started."

It might be hard to believe that the Lord played a real big hand in the career of someone who likes to bellow "Get nekkid!!" over 250,000-watt radio, but someone surely came to the Wolfman's rescue every time he was down and out in Beverly Hills. Failure has never stood in Wolfman's way. He's just brown-bagged it and hustled until he scrambled out of his woeful days. But success, well, the Wolfman let it go straight to his head in those glory days, and, truth be told, his nose took a good hit, too.

For a guy who'd just spent a couple years living on the edge, it was difficult not to bask in some glory, and very tough to just say no. He also found himself tugged between two coasts, and, suddenly, as impossible as it might seem, there was not enough Wolfman to go around. He says, "I couldn't get out of New York. It was like I had handcuffs on. It is one helluva city, but I had to get out of there. I was flying back and forth between the East and West coasts every week trying to do it all, and it was killing me. I finally talked Cousin Brucie into moving over to WNBC and taking over for me."

It was 1974, and the Wolfman got out of New York for more reasons than one, he says. Odes to him were performed by Todd Rundgren, Flash Cadillac, Taj Mahal, Leon Russell, and Freddie King. He toured with the Guess Who for about a year and also packaged his own concerts with the Eagles, Linda Ronstadt, Aerosmith, and Alice Cooper.

The Wolfman was a big, big dog, finally. But it all went straight to the ego, he remembers. It also lead to a common problem of that period. Everybody wanted to do something for the Wolfman, and just about everybody had a bag of cocaine in his pocket.

He admits, "If I ever had a drug problem it was then. They kept coming at me every night, somebody with some shit. Back then it was fashionable. There weren't too many people not doing it. But my wife and I almost split up over it. That was enough. She helped me get away." Lou packed her bags and invited the Wolfman to get out of town with her, but only if he left the rock-'n'-roll star baggage behind, she says.

"With the televison and the movie, it went to his head for a bit, and that's why he had a problem for about a year there," she recalls. "He never got a chance to come down. He was always on. Either flying to or from or riding to and from, with barely enough sleep because of production schedules and

TV interviews. He was also doing road-show dates, and he never had five minutes for himself. It was twenty-four hours a day.

"And if you are hot in this business, everybody wants to give you something," Lou says. "You just can't get rid of them. I just didn't like the people he was associating with. All these loser kinds of people, like groupies. They were looking for a handout. They were like leftover flower children from the sixties, y'know? Finally, in July of 1974, I said enough. No more. I'm leaving. I'm not dealing with this stuff anymore."

In *American Graffiti*, the Wolfman exhibited his alter ego, Bob Smith, to a national audience for the first time. It was just a glimpse, but it revealed the man behind the growl, a relatively quiet and thoughtful kind of guy. The peek at Smitty made the Wolfman all the more popular, but it also pretty much destroyed the private side of his life. From that point on, everybody knew what the Wolfman looked like

Figuring that his cover was already blown, the Wolfman took on more and more public appearance gigs and commercials. He did Clearasil, Jansen swimwear, Pioneer stereo, Hardee's, Arby's, and McDonald's, He toured the world to hype the movie *American Werewolf in London* and popped up on the small screen of American television on everything from *Wonder Woman* to *The Odd Couple* to *Battlestar Galactica*. The radio outlaw became a piece of Americana.

His fans expected to hear something outrageous from the Wolfman when they saw him out in public, and Bob Smith had to watch his act constantly. He pulled the Wolfman's disguise over his head as cover, and, he admits, a lot of Bob Smith got lost. "Wolfman Jack is a great act. He is much more than I could be as a person, as Bob Smith," he says in a rare bow to humility. "I've been well-trained by some of the best people in the business. It isn't just me. The Wolfman is really more than I could ever be."

The near-departure of his Lucy Lamb drove that point home in the heart of Wolfman and Bob Smith. She married Bob

Smith, an all-right guy, but Wolfman Jack kept showing up in her bed. Enough, she said. Yeah, OK, he said. Smitty packed his bags and went with her, continuing to do *The Midnight Special* until 1982 but leaving the twenty-four-hour Wolfman behind. The family moved out of a Long Island house that had begun to feel like Alcatraz to Lou and the kids. She booted out the San Diego Charger football player who had been renting the Beverly Hills house and apparently eating them out of house and home furnishings. "I don't remember the guy's name, but he was famous for eating glass. He destroyed our house. And I think he ate my chandeliers," Lou says.

The Wolfman has adopted only a slightly lower profile since *The Midnight Special* went off the air. He has continued to work the road hard, on somewhat smaller venues, including radio and televison bits with the Nashville Network—though his short-lived attempt at a country-music radio show in 1989 had him feeling like the only rock-'n'-roller at a barn dance. "They wanted me to do traditional country, but all those hurting songs screw me up. The Wolfman wants to make people feel better," he says.

He and his faithful engineer and sidekick Lonnie Napier, a technical wizard who missed a calling in international diplomacy, are on the road most of the year, terrorizing hotel buffet tables across the country as the Wolfman performs for corporate groups, concert venues, rock-'n'-roll dance parties, and other occasions.

"Just recently, he did this huge national furniture show where the owners of all the biggest furniture chains come to select their stock, and he was blown away by all these millionaires lining up for the Wolfman's autograph," Lou says. His public exposure around the country is enhanced by the Wolfman's syndicated oldies show that goes out, somewhat to his chagrin (since he would like to get it off the air and update it a bit with newer oldies), on hundred of stations around the country that just refuse to give it up.

The Wolfman too refuses to give it up, even as he moves

"Get nekkid!"

through his early fifties. He finally bowed to Lou's wish a year ago and moved his entire operation to a sixty-acre 225-year-old spread in North Carolina known as the Belvidere Plantation. It is located in the area where Lou grew up; in fact, she discovered after the purchase of the plantation that it had been in her family for a brief time. "We had enough land in Beverly Hills that I still felt like a country girl there. But really I always wanted to get back to North Carolina. I wanted to smoke a corncob pipe and smile and sit on the porch and say 'Howdy,'" she says.

It doesn't hurt her husband to get away from the glitz either. Lou says, "I still have to ask him 'Where's Bob?' from time to time. You have to call him on it occasionally. He doesn't know it, but the two people, Bob Smith and the Wolfman, are basically the same. But he thinks the Wolfman is a wild and crazy guy that everybody likes and that Bob Smith is just a boy from Brooklyn who wasn't anybody special. His first manager did a great job for him, but at one point he started insisting that I call him Wolf all the time. Not Bob, but Wolf. He even had Bob's mother calling him Wolf. After a while, I had enough. I said at home, with me, he's Bob."

When he is home, Bob Smith returns to an old habit picked up in Brooklyn. Only now, he goes down to a new state-of-the-art recording and broadcast studio on the plantation. It is a few notches up the technical ladder from the old basement coal bin he used to know, but it serves the same purpose. He spends hours in there, Lou says, tinkering with his toy, trying to come up with new formats, creating new "moments" on the radio.

He says, "It may be a five- or a ten-second thing, but it's the same feeling that Alan Freed gave me back when I was a kid when he was beating on that phone book or if he just happened to say the right word at the right time. It was like somebody shooting you with a gun. You feel it, and it stays with you. Maybe it is only two seconds long, but it stays with you, and it makes life seem so good."

Selected Bibliography

Berry, Chuck. *Chuck Berry, The Autobiography*. New York: Crown Pubs., 1987.

Brown, James, with Bruce Tucker. *James Brown, The Godfather of Soul*. New York: MacMillan Co., 1986.

Clark, Dick, and Richard Robinson. *Rock, Roll, and Remember*. New York: Thomas Y. Crowell Co., 1976.

Crawford, Bill, and Gene Fowler. *Border Radio*. Austin: Texas Monthly Press, 1987.

Eliot, Marc. *Rockonomics*. New York: Franklin Watts, 1989.

Fornatale, Peter. *Radio in the Television Age*. New York: Overlook Press, 1983.

George, Nelson. *The Death of Rhythm and Blues*. New York: Pantheon, 1988.

Gillett, Charlie. *The Sound of the City*. New York: Pantheon, 1970.

Govenar, Alan. *Meeting the Blues: The Rise of the Texas Sound*. Dallas: Taylor Publishing Co., 1988.

Guralnik, Peter. *Feel Like Going Home*. New York: Harper and Row, 1988.

———. *Lost Highway*. New York: Harper and Row, 1988.

———. *Sweet Soul Music*. New York: Harper and Row, 1986.

Hirshey, Gerri. *Nowhere to Run*. New York: Times Books, 1984.

MacDonald, J. Fred. *Don't Touch That Dial*. Chicago: Nelson-Hall, 1979.

Marcus, Greil. *Mystery Train*. New York: E. P. Dutton, 1972.

Morrow, Bruce, and Laura Baudo. *Cousin Brucie! My Life in Rock 'n' Roll Radio*. Greenville, SC: Beach Tree Books, 1987.

Palmer, Robert. *Deep Blues*. New York: Penguin Books, 1981.

Passman, Arnold. *The Deejays*. New York: MacMillan Co., 1971.

Pollock, Bruce. *When Rock Was Young*. New York: Holt, Rinehart, and Winston, 1981.

Shaw, Arnold. *Honkers and Shouters: The Golden Years of Rhythm and Blues*. New York: MacMillan Co., 1986.

———. *The Rockin' Fifties*. Jersey City: Da Capo Press, 1987.

———. *The World of Soul*. New York: Cowles Book Co., 1970.

Sklar, Rick. *Rocking America*. New York: St. Martin's Press, 1984.

Stokes, Geoffrey, Ken Tucker, and Ed Ward. *Rock of Ages: The Rolling Stone History of Rock and Roll*. New York: Summit Books, 1987.

Tobler, John. *Thirty Years of Rock*. Santa Monica: Exeter, 1985.

White, Charles. *The Life and Times of Little Richard*. New York: Crown Pubs, 1984.

Acknowledgments

I would like to thank the following people who generously offered assistance, narrative, perspective, and, in some cases, books, food and shelter: Hoss Allen, the Rev. Jackey Beavers, Dick Biondi, Barry and Maureen Birckhead and the girls, E.G. Blackman, Kent Burkhardt, Jerry "Iceman" Butler, Dick Clark, Lavada Durst, Joe Finan, Lance Freed, Inga Freed, Jack "The Rapper" Gibson, Alan Govenar, Betty Lou [Freed] Greene, Doug "Jocko" Henderson, Hugh "Baby" Jarrett, Stan Lewis, Frank Lorenz, Bill Lowery, J. Fred MacDonald, John McCormick, Lonnie Napier, Stan Raymond, Mrs. John Richbourg, Eleanor Sandford, David Satterfield, Chuck Sears, Rick Sklar, The Spahn Family, Robert D. West and Edmund P. Kaminski, Don Whitehead, Vernon Winslow, Wolfman Jack and Lucy Lamb, Randy Wood and Eric Zorn.

I owe a lot to Gene Nobles, the deejay pioneer who died as this book went to press, for sharing his unpublished memoirs with me.

For their technical assistance, I am grateful to the reference room staffs at the Nashville *Tennessean* and *Banner*, the *Boston Globe*, the Austin *American-Statesman*, the *Buffalo Evening News*, the *Chicago Tribune*, the *Atlanta Journal & Constitution*, and the Brookfield Public Library. My thanks also to my editors at the *Chicago Tribune*, Charles Leroux and Mary Umberger, for allowing me to schedule road trips around the book research, and to *Tribune* Editor James Squires for opening the *Tribune* photo library to me.

Index

291